Windows® 2

A Tutorial to Accompany Peter Norton's®

Introduction to Computers

Glencoe
McGraw-Hill

New York, New York   Columbus, Ohio   Woodland Hills, California   Peoria, Illinois

Windows® 2000
A Tutorial to Accompany
Peter Norton's® Introduction to Computers

Glencoe/McGraw-Hill

A Division of The **McGraw·Hill** *Companies*

Send all inquiries to:

Glencoe/McGraw-Hill
8787 Orion Place
Columbus, OH 43240-4027

ISBN 0-02-804407-X

Development: FSCreations, Inc.
Production: MicroPublishing

Windows 2000, Windows 98, Windows 95, Windows NT, Word, Word for Windows,
Word 6, WordPad, Notepad, Paint, MS-DOS, and *DOS* are trademarks or registered
trademarks of Microsoft Corporation.

All brand names and product names used in this tutorial are trade names, service
marks, trademarks, or registered trademarks of their respective owners.
Glencoe/McGraw-Hill is not associated with any product or vendor mentioned in this
tutorial.

Peter Norton, Peter Norton's stylized signature, and Peter Norton's crossed-arms pose
are registered trademarks of Peter Norton.

1 2 3 4 5 6 7 8 9 083 04 03 02 01 00

PREFACE

Windows 2000, one of the instructional tools that complements *Peter Norton's® Introduction to Computers,* covers the basic features of Windows 2000. Glencoe and Peter Norton have teamed up to provide this tutorial and the ancillaries to help you become a knowledgeable, empowered end user. After you complete this tutorial, you will be able to explain the concepts of this operating system.

STRUCTURE AND FORMAT OF THE WINDOWS 2000 TUTORIAL

Windows 2000 covers a range of functions and techniques and provides hands-on opportunities for you to practice and apply your skills. Each lesson in *Windows 2000* includes the following:

- **Contents and Objectives.** The Contents and Objectives provide an overview of the Windows 2000 features you will learn in the lesson.

- **Windows in the Workplace.** This element appears in the margin at the beginning of each lesson. Windows in the Workplace presents a real-world overview on how you can apply the lesson material to various tasks in the workplace.

- **Explanations of important concepts.** Each section of each lesson begins with a brief explanation of the concept or software feature covered in that lesson. The explanations help you understand "the big picture" as you learn each new Windows 2000 feature.

- **New terms.** An important part of learning about computers is learning the terminology. Each new term in the tutorial appears in boldface and italic and is defined the first time it is used. As you encounter these words, read their definitions carefully. If you encounter the same word later and have forgotten the meaning, you can look up the word in the Glossary.

- **Hands On activities.** Because most of us learn best by doing, each explanation is followed by a hands-on activity that includes step-by-step instructions, which you complete at the computer. Integrated in the steps are notes and warnings to help you learn more about Windows 2000.

- **Windows Basics.** This element appears in the margin next to Hands On activities. Windows Basics lists the general steps required to perform a particular task. Use the Windows Basics as a reference to quickly and easily review the steps to perform a task.

■ **Hints & Tips.** This element appears in the margin and provides tips for success and alternate ways to perform a given task.

■ **Illustrations.** Many figures point out features on the screen and illustrate what your screen should look like after you complete important steps.

■ **Tables.** Tables provide supplementary explanatory material along with graphic elements.

■ **Did You Know?** Read each Did You Know?, another element that appears in the margin, to learn additional facts related to the content of the lesson.

■ **Accessibility.** The Accessibility notes appear in the margin and identify areas where Windows 2000 can be customized to meet special vision, hearing, and mobility needs.

■ **On the Web.** At the end of each lesson, an On the Web section provides a brief explanatory discussion and an optional, hands-on activity that relates the lesson material to the Internet.

■ **Summary**. At the end of each lesson, a Summary reviews the major topics covered in the lesson. You can use the Summary as a study guide.

■ **New Terms to Remember.** All the new terms introduced in the lesson are identified. Verify that you can define each term.

■ **Review exercises.** At the end of each lesson are three types of objective questions: a Matching Exercise, a Completion Exercise, and Short-Answer Questions. When you complete these exercises, you can verify that you have learned all the concepts and skills that have been covered in the lesson.

■ **Application Projects.** The Application Projects provide additional hands-on practice to apply your problem-solving skills and your skills to use Windows 2000.

■ **Two appendixes, a glossary and an index.** Appendix A: Command Summary, Appendix B: Accessibility Features of Windows 2000, Glossary, and an Index appear at the back of the tutorial. Use Appendix A: Command Summary as a reference for specific commands and shortcuts. Toolbar buttons are included where appropriate. Appendix B contains information on accessibility features in Windows 2000 and instructions on connecting to the Internet. Use the Glossary to look up terms that you don't understand and the Index to find specific information.

■ **Student Data Disk.** Attached to the inside back cover of this tutorial you will find a 3.5" disk called the Student Data Disk. This disk contains Windows 2000 files for you to use as you complete the hands-on activities and the end-of-lesson activities. If you run out of storage space as you use your Student Data Disk to complete the activities in this tutorial, save additional files to a blank formatted disk.

Note: **Before** you use the Student Data Disk, make a backup copy immediately.

ABOUT PETER NORTON

Peter Norton is a pioneering software developer and an author. *Norton Utilities, AntiVirus,* and other utility programs are installed worldwide on millions of personal computers. His books have helped countless individuals understand computers from the inside out.

Glencoe teamed up with Peter Norton to help you better understand the role computers play in your life now and in the future. As you begin to work in your chosen profession, you may use this tutorial now and later as a reference book.

REVIEWERS

Many thanks are due to the following individuals who reviewed the manuscript and provided recommendations to improve the tutorial:

Carol Hernandez
Davenport College
Merrillville, Indiana

Billy Hix
Motlow College
Tullahoma, Tennessee

Joseph LaMontagne
Davenport College
Grand Rapids, Michigan

CONTENTS

CONTENTS

CONTENTS

CONTENTS

CONTENTS

CONTENTS

APPENDICES

Windows® 2000

LESSON 1

Exploring the Windows 2000 Desktop

CONTENTS

OBJECTIVES

After you complete this lesson, you will be able to do the following:

- Describe what an operating system does.
- Boot your computer system.
- Identify the elements on your Windows 2000 Desktop.
- Use your mouse to point, click, double-click, right-click, drag, and display shortcut menus.
- Activate desktop icons.
- Recognize the components of a dialog box.
- Access the Web from your desktop.

This lesson introduces the Windows 2000 operating system—software that starts and oversees every operation you perform on your computer. You will learn about the objects that appear on your computer screen, and you will use the mouse to run programs and move graphical objects. The basic techniques you master in this lesson form the foundation for more advanced skills you will develop in later lessons. You will begin by distinguishing between hardware and software and learning why computers need operating system software.

INTRODUCING OPERATING SYSTEM SOFTWARE

The computer system you work with consists of hardware and software. Usually, the *hardware* includes these components:

- A processor to manage, interpret, and manipulate the flow of data
- A keyboard to type information
- A mouse (or trackball) to point to objects and select options on the screen
- A monitor to see what you are doing
- A printer to produce hard copy output
- Disks to store information

Your computer system also needs both task-specific and general operational *software.* Software that helps you accomplish a specific task is called an *application.* You might use an application to type a letter, to manage a budget, to balance a checkbook, or to organize a mailing list. Software that allows you to operate your hardware and use applications is called *operating system software,* or an *operating system,* for short.

Sometimes the operating system manages your computer automatically. When you turn on your computer, the operating system looks up the current date and time, sets your preferred speaker volume, and displays the screen color scheme of your choice. At other times, your operating system follows your instructions, such as when you duplicate a specific file or launch a particular application. These computer instructions are called *commands.*

Not all personal computers use the same operating system software. Your computer's operating system determines not only the specific commands your system can execute but also the manner in which you give those commands and otherwise interact with your computer. This human-computer interaction is called the *user interface.* The user interface determines the look and feel of your computing experience.

Windows 2000 continues the process of combining pleasing and easy-to-use operating systems, such as Windows 98, with robust, security-conscious networking operating systems, such as Windows NT 4. Windows 98 and its predecessor, Windows 95, support a wide variety of hardware and software, and integrate *Internet* access with the basic operating system. Windows NT 4 gives corporate, network users an operating system that protects sensitive documents within a stable computing environment. To effectively combine these features, Windows 2000 utilizes a *graphical user interface* (or *GUI*), that enables you to use on-screen pictures to operate your computer.

There are two basic versions of Windows 2000—Professional and Server. Individuals who may or may not be connected to other computers in a *network* use the Professional version. A network is a system in which computers are connected to each other so that they can share information and resources. The Server version includes all of the features of the Professional version plus tools to make the network run productively and securely. These tools are part of the *directory service,* which acts as the main switchboard for managing the various computer resources on the network. In the Windows 2000 Server version, the directory service is called *Active Directory*. This tutorial can be used with either version of Windows 2000. Let's get started!

STARTING THE COMPUTER WITH WINDOWS 2000

When you turn on the computer, a complex series of events begins. First, a built-in program tests the computer. This ***Power On Self Test (POST)*** checks the memory, keyboard, display, and disk drives of the computer system. Next, files from the hard disk containing essential operating system components are loaded. Because computer systems and setups vary greatly, you may see a series of screens informing you of the progress of the startup procedure. Finally, the Windows 2000 opening screen displays. Once you turn on the power, the computer gives itself the instructions to start up or *pulls itself up by its bootstraps.* From this figure of speech, the entire process is called ***booting the system*** or performing a ***system boot.***

HANDS On

Booting Windows 2000

In this activity, you will start the computer and boot the Windows 2000 operating system. (If your computer is already on, you may need to restart your system. Check with your instructor, computer lab assistant, or network administrator for instructions.)

1. **Press the power button or flip the power switch to turn on the computer.**

2. **If the monitor connected to the system has a separate power switch, be sure to turn on that switch as well.**

3. **Observe the booting process.**

   a. **Listen for the POST sound. A single beep means the system passed all the tests; a series of beeps indicates a hardware problem. If you hear a series of beeps, check your keyboard and monitor connections, read the message on the screen, or consult your computer manual to fix the problem by yourself. You may need technical help from the manufacturer, a lab assistant, or a technician.**

   b. **Watch the screen. After a few moments, you see a memory indicator while the system checks the random access memory. Then some information appears at the top of the screen, followed by the Windows 2000 copyright screen. A progress indicator gives you a visual clue as to how much more of the operating system needs to be loaded into memory. The Log On to Windows screen appears next and requests your user name and password.**

When you ***log on*** to a computer, you inform the operating system who you are. The operating system chooses your personal settings to complete the booting process. Systems that have multiple users, such as networks, keep track of who is allowed to access the computer by assigning unique ***user names***. You may not be able to select your own user name; rather, a network administrator may assign the name to you. To provide security, each user must have a secret code or password known only to the user. In Windows 2000, each user chooses a ***password*** (up to 14 characters) that is entered along with the user name during the log-on procedure. When choosing a password, you should choose a series of letters, numbers, or special characters that would be difficult for someone else to guess. If you suspect that someone else knows your password, you should change your password immediately.

Windows
BASICS

Booting the System

1. Turn on the computer.

2. Turn on the monitor.

3. Observe the booting process.

4. Close the Getting Started with Windows 2000 window, if necessary.

4. Type your user name in the User name text box.

5. Press `Tab` and type your password.

Asterisks appear as you type your password. In this way, others who may see your log-on screen will not learn your password.

6. Click **OK**.

The system completes the boot up process. You may see the Getting Started with Windows 2000 *window,* as shown in Figure 1.1. Windows are rectangular on-screen frames in which you do your computing work. The name, Windows, comes from the visual image of these frames. The Getting Started with Windows 2000 window displays options on the left side of the screen. These options provide a means to register your operating system with Microsoft Corporation, a description of new features in Windows 2000, and a means for quickly connecting to the Internet. Rather than briefly exploring features from the Getting Started with Windows 2000 window, you will examine them in much greater detail as you progress through the hands-on activities in this tutorial.

Figure 1.1 ◀
The Getting Started with
Windows 2000 windows

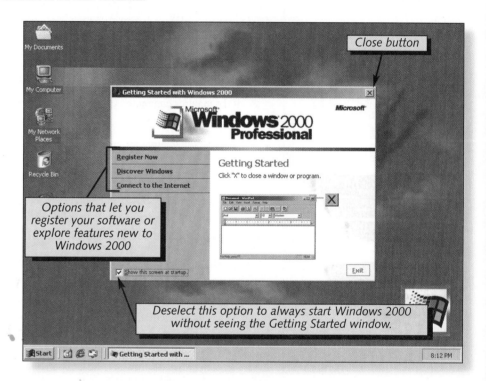

Close button

Options that let you register your software or explore features new to Windows 2000

Deselect this option to always start Windows 2000 without seeing the Getting Started window.

Hints & Tips

1. If Scandisk runs when you boot Windows 2000, the previous session was not properly shut down. Let the Scandisk run; some of the procedures that should have been performed previously will be run now.

2. Don't assume that a computer is turned off just because the screen is dark. As an energy-saving device, the computer may just be *resting*. If the screen is black, press a key on the keyboard to see if the computer *wakes up*.

7. If necessary, deselect the option to prevent the Getting Started with Windows 2000 window from appearing each time you boot your computer.

8. Click the left mouse button on the **Close button** ☒ in the upper-right corner of the window.

Now your screen should resemble Figure 1.2. This screen, called the Windows 2000 *Desktop,* is the background for your computer work. The desktop contains many of the tools for working with Windows 2000.

Your desktop details may vary, but you will still see the basic features discussed in this lesson.

Figure 1.2
The Windows 2000 Desktop

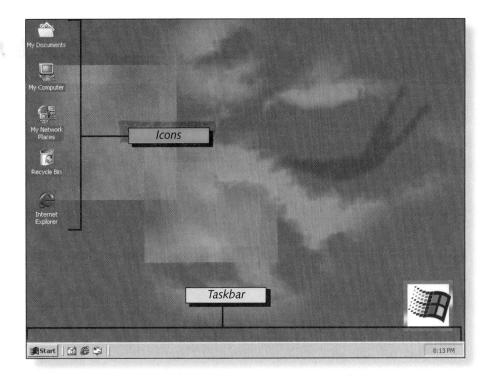

USING THE WINDOWS 2000 DESKTOP

In this section, you will learn the names and purposes of the objects on the Windows 2000 Desktop and perform useful tasks with them. You will use the desktop that you see when you install Windows 2000 onto a new computer. Since this desktop closely resembles the desktop Microsoft introduced with Windows 95, the style is called the *classic style desktop.*

Microsoft enhanced Windows 95 with many features to integrate the operating system with the Internet. Windows 2000 incorporates these updates with several optional elements and an alternative to the classic style. Users of the Internet work with an interface slightly different from the old Windows 95 Desktop—the *Web style desktop.* Besides changing the look of the desktop, the Web style changes the way the mouse works when you move or click an object on the screen. Additionally, when you set up your screen as the *Active Desktop,* information is sent to your desktop via the Internet. This information may be news articles, weather reports, stock market quotations, or sports scores. You can get this information by specifically requesting the information each time or by subscribing. *Subscribing* to a service will provide the information to you on a regular basis.

To make the desktop work the way you work, you can customize almost all of the features—you can activate the features you need and put them where they are most convenient for you. As a result, two desktops seldom look exactly the same. The desktop elements described in the next sections, however, are common to almost all screens.

Before Windows 95, Windows was really an operating *environment*. The operating *system* was DOS; Windows changed the *look and feel* of the operating system.

The Taskbar

At the bottom of the screen is the *taskbar,* as shown in Figure 1.3. On the taskbar are a number of *buttons*—a box labeled with words or pictures that you click to select or perform an action. The taskbar displays the Start button 🔲Start on the left and the Clock button ⌧1:21 PM on the right. The Start button 🔲Start lets you locate and use additional applications on your computer. The small pictures to the right of the Start button provide immediate access to some commonly used Windows 2000 features. The taskbar will also display a button with the name of any application that is currently running. You can then move from one application to another by clicking the desired button on the taskbar. You may see other buttons on your taskbar, including a button that controls the power to your laptop computer, a button that helps you add or remove hardware while the computer is running, and a button that controls your speaker's volume settings.

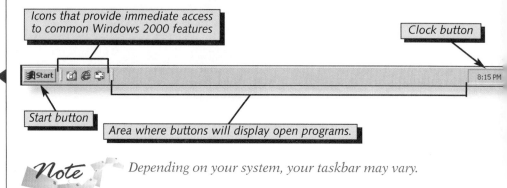

Figure 1.3
The taskbar

Icons that provide immediate access to common Windows 2000 features

Clock button

Start button

Area where buttons will display open programs.

 *Depending on your system, your taskbar may vary.*

Desktop Icons

On the left side of your screen, you should see several small, labeled pictures or *icons,* such as My Documents, My Computer, My Network Places, Recycle Bin, and Internet Explorer, as shown in Figure 1.4. Icons are graphical representations of objects, such as programs, groups of programs, disk drives, documents, or specific tasks. Because icons are memorable, attractive, and easy to use, most Windows programs use icons. The small pictures to the right of the Start button on the taskbar are also icons.

Your desktop may include other icons.

The My Computer icon represents your computer system and lets you explore and manage the system. The My Documents icon is a convenient storage area to keep letters, pictures, and other items that you create. The Internet Explorer icon lets you connect to the *World Wide Web* quickly. You use the My Network Places icon to access other computers on your network or through your modem. The Recycle Bin icon allows you to delete and recover information. Because they help you manage your computer, these icons are called *system icons.*

Figure 1.4
Windows 2000 system icons

Each desktop icon is a ***shortcut icon***, a quick way to activate the associated program or task. When you add software to your computer, other shortcut icons may appear on your desktop. You can even add your own shortcut icons—shortcuts to the work you do most often on the computer, such as writing a memo, checking an appointments calendar, or managing your household budget.

Windows

You can display icon contents within a window by ***opening*** an icon. You can ***close*** a window to remove the window from the screen or your desktop. You will open icons and close windows as you learn to use the mouse and manipulate windows more thoroughly in Lesson 2.

Hints&Tips

The Internet is full of entertaining features. Most institutions want the Internet to be used for productive, professional purposes. When in doubt, check with your instructor, computer lab assistant, or network administrator for your institution's acceptable use policy.

USING THE MOUSE

You will use the ***mouse*** extensively in Windows 2000. The mouse, the key to the graphical user interface, lets you choose and manipulate on-screen objects without having to type on the keyboard. Although the mouse is the most popular, you may also use several other pointing devices. ***Trackballs*** have buttons like the mouse, but instead of moving the mouse over the desktop, you spin a large ball. Laptops often employ either a small ***joystick*** in the middle of the keyboard or a ***touch-sensitive pad*** below the keyboard. Each of these devices, however, lets you point to items on the screen and click buttons to perform actions on those items.

Pointing

On the screen, you should see an arrow pointing toward the upper-left. This arrow is called the *mouse pointer,* or more simply, the *pointer*. Moving the mouse on a horizontal surface moves the pointer around the screen. Move the mouse to the left or right, and the pointer moves to the left or right. Move the mouse away from you, and the pointer moves up the screen; move the mouse toward you, and the pointer moves down the screen.

Not surprisingly, this technique of positioning the pointer on the screen is called *pointing.* Pointing to particular objects on the screen or giving a particular command may change the shape of the pointer. When you must wait for the computer to accomplish a task, an hourglass appears next to the arrow. Figure 1.5 shows several shapes you may notice as you point to objects on the screen.

Figure 1.5 ◀
Common pointer shapes

Normal Select	⇖
Help Select	⇖?
Working in Background	⇖⧗
Busy	⧗
Precision Select	+
Text Select	I
Handwriting	✎
Unavailable	⊘
Vertical Resize	↕
Horizontal Resize	↔
Diagonal Resize 1	↖
Diagonal Resize 2	↗
Move	✛
Alternate Select	↑
Line Select	⤵

Note For Right-Handed Mouse Users: *Keep the mouse on the right side of the keyboard. Cup the mouse in your hand so that the base of your palm or wrist rests on the desk while your index finger rests lightly on the left button. (See Figure 1.6.) Doing this lets you move and stop the mouse smoothly—the friction of your palm against the desk stops the mouse when you stop moving your hand.*

Figure 1.6
How to hold the mouse

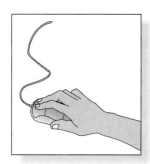

Windows 2000 lets you reassign the mouse buttons so that the right button performs the actions ordinarily performed by the left button. See Appendix B for specific information.

 For Left-Handed Mouse Users: *To follow the right-handed instructions in this tutorial, place the mouse on the left side of the keyboard and use your ring finger to click the left button.*

Clicking

Pressing and then releasing a mouse button is called ***clicking*** because of the sound the action makes. Although your mouse may have two or three buttons, you will use the left button most often. Thus, clicking refers to the left mouse button, unless an instruction specifies a different button.

What happens when you click the mouse button depends on the object to which your pointer is pointing. Clicking a button on your screen activates the command; clicking an icon changes the icon color and ***highlights*** or ***selects*** the icon. (In this tutorial, the verb *select* means to click something once with the left mouse button.) You can now perform actions specifically affecting this icon, such as copying or deleting. For this reason, Windows 2000 and other graphical user interfaces are referred to as *point and click* interfaces. Point and click software minimizes keyboarding.

Double-Clicking

To perform certain tasks, you must point to an object and click the left mouse button twice in rapid succession without moving the pointer. This technique, called ***double-clicking,*** may require some practice. Clicking two times is not the same as double-clicking. Double-clicking is a matter of timing. To assist in double-clicking, point to an object and make sure your index finger is resting on the left button. Then, just "twitch" your index finger twice to double-click. Remember to rest the base of your palm or wrist on the desk so the mouse doesn't move.

 *This tutorial assumes that your desktop uses the classic style settings. In the Web style settings, pointing the mouse selects an object and single-clicking performs an action.*

Thus far you have been using the left mouse button exclusively. Later on in this tutorial, you will see how to use the right mouse button. Some mice have a third button between the left and right buttons. The use of this button depends on the manufacturer of the mouse, the application software being used, and settings made by the user.

Hints & Tips

Practice using the mouse until you become comfortable with it. Although keyboard alternatives exist for most Windows 2000 mouse actions, you will be more efficient if you can use both keyboard actions and the mouse.

Instead of a third button, some mice have a small *wheel* between the left and right buttons. You can use this wheel primarily to view text above or below the information appearing on the screen. By rolling the wheel up, you can see the previous pages; moving the wheel down shows succeeding pages. Clicking some mouse wheels lets you move the text up or down by just moving the mouse up or down.

Drag and Drop

You can move many objects around the screen. To accomplish this task, you point to the object you want to move, press and hold the left mouse button, move the mouse to drag the object to the desired location, and then release the mouse button. This series of actions is known as ***drag and drop*** or ***dragging.***

HANDS On

Practicing Mouse Techniques

In this activity, you will use the mouse to select, open, and move objects on the desktop.

1. Point to the **My Computer icon** 🖥.

A rectangular text box, called a ***ScreenTip,*** appears on the screen showing a description of the icon.

2. Click **My Computer** 🖥 with the left mouse button to select the icon.

Notice that the selected icon highlights (changes color).

3. Point to an empty area of the desktop and click the left mouse button to deselect the icon.

The icon ***deselects,*** or returns to the original color.

4. Point to the **My Computer icon** 🖥.

5. Double-click (the left mouse button) to open the icon (display the contents).

The My Computer window appears, as shown in Figure 1.7.

6. Double-click the **Control Panel icon**.

The Control Panel window appears, as shown in Figure 1.8. It contains a series of icons that lets you customize your computing environment.

Clicking a window's Close button—the X located in its upper-right corner—removes the window from the screen.

7. Click the Control Panel window's **Close button** ✕.

The Control Panel window disappears from the desktop.

Windows BASICS

Using the Mouse

1. To select an object, point to the object and click.

2. To deselect the object, click an area away from the selected object.

3. To open an icon, double-click the icon.

4. To double-click, click the left mouse button twice rapidly without moving the pointer.

5. To drag and drop, press and hold the left mouse button over a selected object, move the mouse where desired, and release the mouse button.

Figure 1.7
The My Computer window

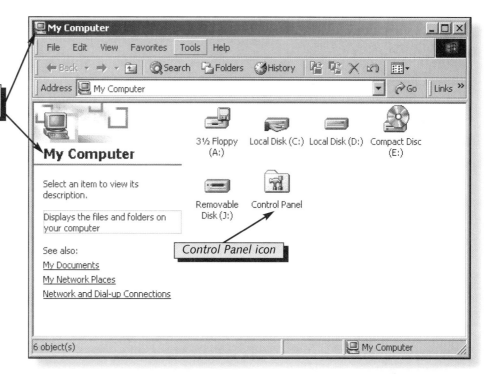

My Computer is open.

Control Panel icon

Close button

Figure 1.8
The Control Panel window

Control Panel is open.

Icons for customizing your computing environment

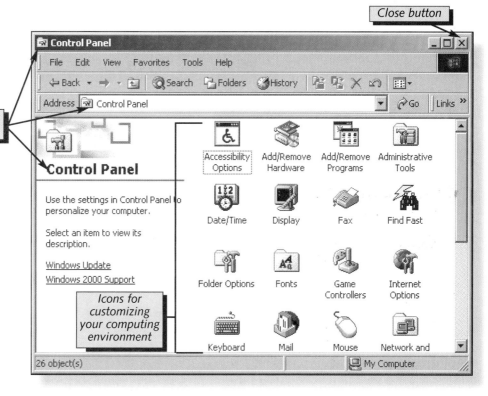

The first mouse had only one button. Functions for the right button, when present, depended on the application software in use. For example, some programs used the right button as an escape from the current action; other programs displayed a menu on top of the screen, and so on.

Next, you'll drag and drop the My Computer icon to a different location on the desktop.

8. Point to the **My Computer icon**.

9. Press and hold the left mouse button while the pointer is over the icon. Move the mouse down and away from you to drag the icon from the current position to the lower-right corner of the screen. Then, release the mouse button.

Do not drop the icon on top of another icon. Although this technique will be covered in a later lesson, you are likely to create problems if you do it at this point.

The icon should appear somewhere near the lower-right corner of the screen, as shown in Figure 1.9.

Figure 1.9
The moved My Computer icon

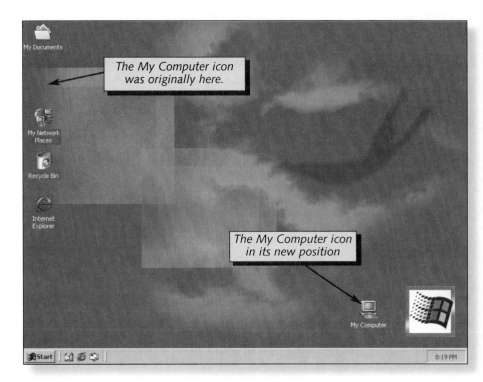

The My Computer icon was originally here.

The My Computer icon in its new position

If you couldn't drag and drop the My Computer icon, click the right mouse button on the desktop. Choose Arrange Icons and make sure no check mark appears by Auto Arrange. If a check mark appears, click Auto Arrange to remove the check mark. Then repeat steps 8 and 9.

From now on in this tutorial, step 9 will be written as "drag the My Computer icon to the lower-right corner of the screen."

10. **Drag the My Computer icon to the original location.**

Opening the Taskbar Menu

A *menu* is a list of items on the screen from which you can choose. In this activity, you will use the mouse to explore the function of the taskbar.

1. Point to an empty area on the taskbar.

2. Click the right mouse button.

A shortcut menu for the taskbar appears, as shown in Figure 1.10.

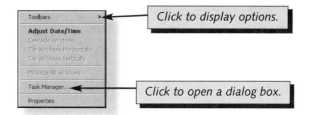

Figure 1.10 ◀
The taskbar shortcut menu

3. **In the shortcut menu, click Properties with the left mouse button.**

The Taskbar and Start Menu Properties window appears. Notice that the set of General or Advanced options is visible, as shown in Figure 1.11.

Figure 1.11
The taskbar options

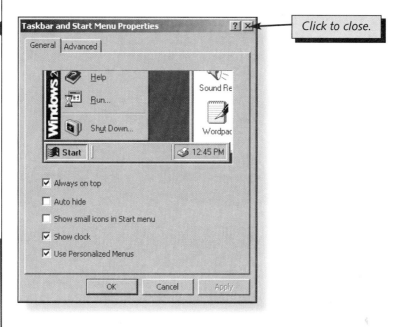

Windows BASICS

Opening the Taskbar Menu

1. Right-click an empty area on the taskbar.

2. Click Properties.

3. Click the Close button.

Warning *Do not change any of the settings in this window.*

4. **Click the Close button** ☒ **to close the Taskbar and Start Menu Properties window.**

The window is removed from the desktop.

Opening the Start Menu

In this activity, you will continue using the taskbar and mouse to display menus and select commands.

1. **Click the Start button** **on the taskbar.**

The Start menu appears, as shown in Figure 1.12. Notice the arrows next to many of the menu choices. These arrows indicate that these menu choices contain additional menus or information.

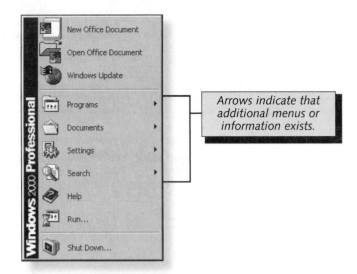

Figure 1.12
The Start menu

Arrows indicate that additional menus or information exists.

Note The Start menu and the contents of the menus on your computer may differ from those shown in the figures in this tutorial, depending on your computer system configuration.

Windows BASICS

Starting an Accessory Program

1. Click Start.

2. Point to Programs.

3. Point to Accessories.

4. Click the name of the program you want to open.

2. Point to Programs.

Another menu appears to the right of the first menu. Pointing to a menu item without clicking highlights that item; clicking selects the item.

Windows 2000 modifies your Programs menu to highlight those items you choose most frequently. If you don't see the item you want, look for and click the double arrows  that appear at the bottom of the menu. The other choices will appear.

3. Point to Accessories.

Another menu appears. As Figure 1.13 shows, you now have a series of three menus displayed.

4. Click WordPad.

The WordPad window appears on the desktop. WordPad is a word processing accessory program that comes with the Windows 2000 operating system. You will learn more about using WordPad in Lesson 6.

5. Click the Close button .

The window disappears from the desktop.

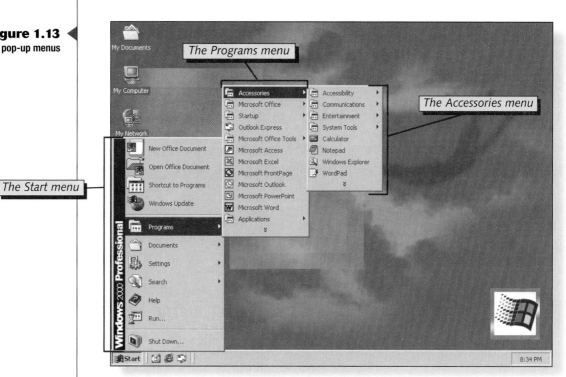

HANDS On

Windows BASICS

Clearing a Menu

1. Display a menu.

2. Click anywhere on the desktop away from the menu.

Clearing Menus

Sometimes you will want to clear menus without clicking an option. In this activity, you will learn to clear unwanted menus from the desktop.

1. Click the Start button 🔳 Start .

The Start menu appears.

2. Point to Programs.

Another menu appears to the right of the first menu.

3. Point to Accessories.

Another menu appears to the right of the Programs menu, as shown in Figure 1.13.

4. Click any location on the desktop to close the menus.

All the menus disappear from the desktop.

USING THE RIGHT MOUSE BUTTON

In Windows 2000, right mouse button use is now standardized. Clicking an item with the right mouse button displays the **shortcut menu**—a list of the most frequently used commands. Your mouse, as mentioned earlier, probably has two or three buttons. Whenever the directions in this tutorial say *click,* use the left mouse button. If you must use the right mouse button, the directions will say *right-click.* To **right-click,** point to an object, press the right mouse button, and then quickly release the mouse button.

Opening a Shortcut Menu for a System Icon

In this activity, you will use the right mouse button to display the shortcut menu for a system icon.

> **1. Point to the My Computer icon** 🖥.

The ScreenTip for the icon appears.

> **2. Right-click the My Computer icon** 🖥.

The shortcut menu for My Computer appears, as shown in Figure 1.14.

Figure 1.14 ◀
The My Computer shortcut menu

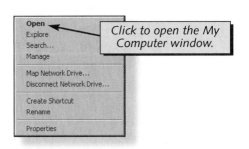

> **3. Click Open**.

The My Computer window appears.

Opening a Shortcut Menu for a Device Icon

A **device** is a piece of equipment, such as a printer or disk drive, that is part of your computer system. **Device icons** allow you to customize and use these pieces of equipment. In this activity, you will use the right mouse button to display the shortcut menu for a device icon and then choose a device icon command.

> **1. Open the My Computer window, if necessary.**
>
> **2. Point to the drive C: icon in the My Computer window.**

Drive C: is usually a hard disk drive that may be built into your computer or connected by a cable.

> **3. Right-click the drive C: icon.**

The device icon shortcut menu appears.

Opening a Shortcut Menu for an Icon

1. Right-click an icon.

2. Click the option desired and explore the settings.

3. Close the window.

4. Click **Properties**.

The Properties window for disk drive C: appears, as shown in Figure 1.15. This window provides detailed information about the C: drive of the computer you are using.

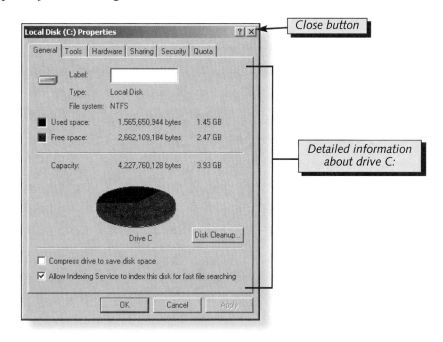

5. Click the **Close button** ⊠ for the window.

6. Click the **Close button** ⊠ for the My Computer window.

The My Computer window disappears from the desktop.

Opening and Canceling Taskbar Shortcut Menus

In this activity, you will use the right mouse button to open specific taskbar shortcut menus; then you will practice canceling these menus.

1. Right-click the **Start button** ⊞Start.

The shortcut menu for the Start button appears.

2. Click an empty area of the desktop.

The shortcut menu for the Start button disappears from the desktop.

3. Point to the **Clock** 1:21 PM on the right end of the taskbar.

Today's date briefly appears and disappears.

4. Right-click the **Clock** 1:21 PM.

The shortcut menu for the Clock appears, with different commands from the shortcut menu for the Start button.

5. Click an empty area on the desktop.

The menu disappears from the desktop.

Opening and Canceling Taskbar Shortcut Menus

1. Right-click an object (Start button, taskbar, desktop, and so on).

2. Click anywhere away from the menu to cancel the menu.

WORKING WITH A GRAPHICAL USER INTERFACE

You have already seen many features of a graphical user interface (GUI). You have used the mouse to choose commands, start programs, and view windows by pointing and clicking. As the name implies, GUIs are extremely visual. Icons represent devices, software, shortcuts, and other objects. Windows display icon contents. You use the mouse to tell the software what you want to do, such as access menus, run application software, and position objects on the screen.

All Windows programs are graphical. They share so many common elements that you may forget which program you are using. With a Windows program, the graphical environment is described as *what you see is what you get* (abbreviated as **WYSIWYG**). This means that text and graphics print exactly as they appear on screen.

Dialog Boxes

When you choose certain commands or menu options, a window appears in the middle of the screen. This window, called a ***dialog box,*** requests more information concerning your selection. Menu options that display dialog boxes are followed by ellipses (...), such as Shut Down in Figure 1.16. Figure 1.17 shows the Shut Down Windows dialog box.

Figure 1.16 ◄
Ellipses follow the Shut Down option

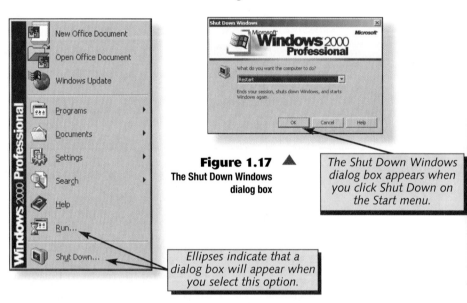

Figure 1.17 ▲
The Shut Down Windows dialog box

The Shut Down Windows dialog box appears when you click Shut Down on the Start menu.

Ellipses indicate that a dialog box will appear when you select this option.

Text Boxes

Next to some options you will see rectangular boxes into which you can type, as shown in Figure 1.18. These are called ***text boxes.*** Sometimes text boxes already contain characters. In these cases, the letters or numbers in the box are the default value. A ***default*** is a value that the software uses unless you change the value. When the characters in the box are highlighted, any characters you type replace the highlighted text.

Figure 1.18 ◄
A text box

You can type in a text box.

Command Buttons

Clickable command buttons are common dialog box features. A single click on these buttons performs the action listed on the button. Nearly every dialog box has the three essential buttons shown in Figure 1.19: *OK, Cancel,* and *Apply.*

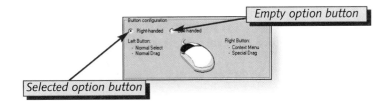

Figure 1.19 ◄
Three essential command buttons

Option Buttons

Some dialog boxes contain a group of round buttons, as shown in Figure 1.20. These are called **option buttons**. You can select only one button in a set of option buttons; that button has a solid dot. Clicking an empty option button selects the option and the previous option deselects.

Figure 1.20 ◄
Option buttons

Triangle Buttons and Drop-Down Lists

Some text boxes allow you to choose from a predetermined list of options. Occasionally the list will automatically be displayed. More often, however, these boxes have a **triangle button** to their right, as shown in Figure 1.21. Clicking this triangle button displays a **drop-down list** of options, as shown in Figure 1.22. The list remains on the screen until you click an option or click outside the list to cancel the display.

Figure 1.21 ◄
Text box with triangle button

Figure 1.22 ▶
**A triangle button with a
drop-down list**

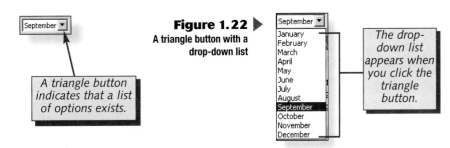

Hints & Tips

To increment the number faster, press and hold the left mouse button while the pointer is over a spinner button or press and hold ⬆ or ⬇ on the keyboard.

Spinner Buttons

A text box that contains numbers will often have **spinner buttons** to the right, as shown in Figure 1.23. Spinner buttons are composed of an up arrow and a down arrow, each in a separate box with one above the other. Clicking the up arrow increases the setting; clicking the down arrow decreases the setting.

Figure 1.23 ◄
Spinner buttons

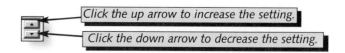

Click the up arrow to increase the setting.

Click the down arrow to decrease the setting.

Slider Controls

A *slider control* consists of a horizontal or vertical line with progressive values and an indicator. Dragging the indicator to the right or up increases the value, while dragging the indicator to the left or down decreases the value. Figure 1.24 illustrates a horizontal slider.

Figure 1.24 ◄
A horizontal slider control

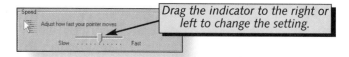

Drag the indicator to the right or left to change the setting.

Check Boxes

A square box to the left of a dialog box option, as shown in Figure 1.25, is known as a *check box.* Clicking an empty check box puts a check mark in the box to select that item. Clicking a check box that already contains a check mark deselects the item and erases the check mark. Unlike option buttons, you can select more than one check box.

Figure 1.25 ◄
A check box

☑ Automatically adjust clock for daylight saving changes

Dialog Box Tabs

Sometimes, so much information is needed for a dialog box that the information doesn't all fit in one window. In these cases, and when separating options on several screens is more logical, two or more *tabs* will appear at the top of the dialog box. Clicking a tab displays one of the screens in the dialog box. The Date/Time Properties dialog box in Figure 1.26 shows the screen that appears when the Time Zone tab is clicked.

Figure 1.26 ◄
Date/Time Properties dialog box

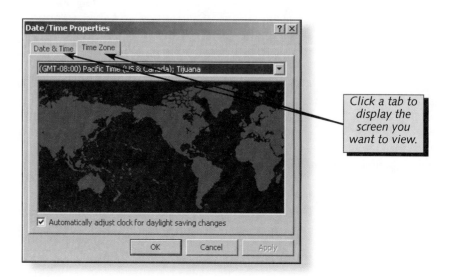

Click a tab to display the screen you want to view.

Changing the Settings on Your Computer

The ***Control Panel*** is a window full of system icons that lets you change the settings on your computer. In this activity, you will use the Control Panel to open a dialog box to change the time displayed by the clock on your taskbar.

Do not make any changes other than those described here, or you may inappropriately change the settings on the computer you are using.

1. Double-click the My Computer icon 💻.

The My Computer window appears on the desktop.

2. Double-click the Control Panel icon.

The Control Panel window appears.

3. Double-click the Date/Time icon.

The Date/Time Properties dialog box appears.

4. Click the Date & Time tab, if necessary.

5. Click the Month triangle button ▾ **in the set of Date options.**

A list of months drops down.

6. Click October.

7. Click 30 in the box of days for the selected month.

The Current Day setting highlights.

8. Select the Current Hour number in the set of Time options.

9. Type 11

10. Select the Current Minutes number, and use either the mouse or keyboard to change the setting to 59.

11. Select the Current Seconds number, and use either the mouse or keyboard to change the setting to 45.

12. If necessary, change the AM/PM indicator to PM.

Your screen should look similar to Figure 1.27.

Figure 1.27
The Date & Time tab with new settings

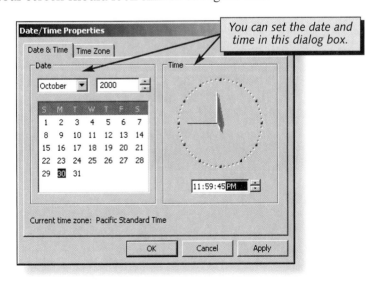

13. Click Apply.

The new settings are applied to the system's internal clock. Watch the clock in the dialog box after you've applied the changes. You see the time switch to the selected time and the second hand begin moving. After the time changes to 12:00 AM, notice that the Current Day setting changes to 31.

Resetting the System's Internal Clock

In this activity, you will reset the current date and time settings to reflect today's date and the current time.

1. Open the Date/Time Properties dialog box on the desktop, if necessary.

2. Select the appropriate month, day, hour, and minutes settings to reflect today's date and the current time.

3. Change the AM/PM indicator, if necessary.

4. Click Apply.

The changes are applied to the system's internal clock.

5. Click OK.

The changes are stored and the dialog box disappears from the desktop.

6. Click the Close button ☒ for the Control Panel window.

The window disappears from the desktop.

LOGGING OFF WINDOWS 2000

Just as organized people clear their desks before leaving the office for the day, you should develop the habit of closing all open applications and using the proper procedure to log off Windows 2000 when you are finished working with the computer. In fact, turning off the computer while applications are running is dangerous. Some of the work you have been doing may not have been saved onto disk and will be irretrievably lost. In addition, you will not have given the operating system the opportunity to erase information temporarily stored on disk. Follow these steps to log off the Windows 2000 operating system. You will be able to start and quit Windows at any point in the lessons that follow.

The following Hands On activity includes directions to log off the computer. Check with your instructor or computer lab assistant, however, for the "log off" procedures in your lab or school environment—if you are ready to quit working at the computer.

Shutting Down Your Computer

1. Click Start.

2. Click Shut Down.

3. Click Log Off.

4. Click OK.

5. After a message appears, turn off your computer.

Logging Off Your Computer

In this activity, you will log off your computer.

1. Click the Start button .

The Start menu appears.

2. Click Shut Down.

The entire screen darkens slightly and the Shut Down Windows dialog box appears, as shown in Figure 1.17 on page 20.

> *Note* *If you want to continue with the On the Web section that follows, or if you want to proceed directly to the exercises for this lesson, click Cancel. If you are finished with your computer session, go to step 3.*

3. Click the triangle button  **and click Log off from the drop-down list.**

4. Click OK.

After a few moments, a new Log On to Windows screen appears.

> *Note* *If necessary, and if you have permission, you may turn off the computer by selecting Shut Down from the drop-down list. When prompted, turn off the computer's power switch. If your monitor does not turn off automatically, turn the monitor off as well.*

ON*the*WEB

INTRODUCING THE INTERNET

As you progress through these lessons, you will have the opportunity to explore features of the Windows 2000 operating system that directly and indirectly involve the Internet. In this introduction to the Internet, you will see a few Web sites. Moving from one Web site to another is called *surfing the Web.*

To view Web pages, you need a program called a *Web browser,* or *browser* for short. Included with Windows 2000 is Internet Explorer—Microsoft's software package that lets you access the major components of the Internet. In later lessons, you will use Internet Explorer more extensively. In this activity, you will learn how to connect to the Internet using your Web browser.

1. Click the Internet Explorer icon 🅔 **on the taskbar.**

If the icon is not on your taskbar, click the Desktop icon or click the Start menu, point to Programs, and then click Internet Explorer.

 If your computer is not connected to the Internet via an Internet service provider or through your network, you will receive a message indicating that no connection could be established. See your instructor, computer lab assistant, or network administrator for instructions.

Be patient! It may take several minutes for you to connect to the Internet, but once you are connected, you will see an initial Web page.

2. Click the Favorites menu.

3. Click Web Events.

You will see a screen of information similar to that shown in Figure 1.28.

4. Click the Maximize button ▢ **, if necessary.**

5. Move your pointer over the Web page, noting places where the pointer changes to the shape of a hand.

Your pointer changes to the shape of a hand when you pass over certain text or graphics areas. These areas are called *links*. When you click a link, your browser jumps to another screen of information.

6. Click a link that interests you.

Depending on the speed of your connection and the amount of traffic on the Internet, you will soon see a page full of information on the new site.

7. Click the Back button ⬅ Back ▾ **on the toolbar.**

ON*the*WEB

Figure 1.28 ◀
Microsoft WindowsMedia.com
Internet audio-video guide

Your browser redisplays the previous screen. Use the Back ⟸Back ▾ and Forward ⇒▾ buttons to revisit pages you have viewed during the current Internet session.

8. **Continue to view pages and move back and forth as you familiarize yourself with Internet Explorer.**

9. **Click the Close button ☒.**

You will return to your desktop.

 Your computer may not automatically disconnect from the Internet when you close Internet Explorer. If you see a connecting icon 🖳 next to your clock on the taskbar, right-click the icon. Click the Disconnect option from the menu that appears. Check with your instructor or computer lab assistant if you need additional instructions to disconnect from the Internet.

10. **You may proceed directly to the exercises for this lesson. If, however, you are finished with your computer session, log off the computer you are using.**

 Follow the "log off" procedures for your lab or school environment.

Lesson Summary & Exercises

SUMMARY

After you complete this lesson, you should know how to do the following:

Introducing Operating System Software

■ Understand the components of a computer system and the function of the operating system.

Starting the Computer with Windows 2000

■ Turn on the computer and load the Windows 2000 operating system.

Using the Windows 2000 Desktop

■ Identify the main components of the Windows 2000 screen, including the taskbar and desktop icons.

Using the Mouse

■ Use the mouse to point to objects and menu items on the screen.

■ Click to select objects or menu items on the screen.

■ Double-click to perform an action on a selected icon or screen object.

■ Drag and drop objects on the desktop. Press and hold the left mouse button while pointing to an object. Move the mouse to move the object on the screen. Release the mouse button when the object is in the desired location.

Using the Right Mouse Button

■ Right-click to display the shortcut menu appropriate to the action you are performing.

Working with a Graphical User Interface

■ Type information into a text box within a dialog box. Highlighted text in the text box is the default value. Typing new text replaces the highlighted text in the box.

■ Click command buttons in a dialog box. Click OK after you have concluded your selections. Click Cancel to quit the dialog box without making any changes.

■ Click option buttons to make a choice between several possible actions. Only one button can be in effect at a time.

■ Click a triangle button to see the options in a drop-down list.

■ Increase or decrease settings in a box by using spinner buttons.

■ Drag indicators along slider control lines to change values.

- Make selections by using check boxes. Check boxes have a check mark in them when the option is selected and are empty when not selected.

- Click tabs to display different screens within one dialog box.

Logging Off Windows 2000

- End your computer session by using the Shut Down option that appears on the Start menu. Using the Shut Down option ensures that data is saved and temporary files are erased before another user accesses the computer or you turn off the computer.

On the Web: Introducing the Internet

- Click the Internet Explorer icon  on the taskbar to display a Web site. Click the links to surf the Web.

NEW TERMS TO REMEMBER

After you complete this lesson, you should know the meaning of these terms:

Active Desktop	hardware	software
Active Directory	highlight	spinner buttons
application	icon	subscribe
booting the system	Internet	surfing the Web
browser	joystick	system boot
button	links	system icon
check box	log on	tab
classic style desktop	menu	taskbar
clicking	mouse	text box
close	mouse pointer	touch-sensitive pad
commands	network	trackball
Control Panel	open	triangle button
default	operating system	user interface
deselect	operating system software	user name
desktop	option button	Web browser
device	password	Web style desktop
device icon	pointer	wheel
dialog box	pointing	window
directory service	Power On Self Test (POST)	World Wide Web
double-click	right-click	(the Web or
dragging	ScreenTip	WWW)
drag and drop	select	WYSIWYG
drop-down list	shortcut icon	
graphical user interface	shortcut menu	
(GUI)	slider control	

Lesson Summary & Exercises

MATCHING EXERCISE

Match each of the terms with the definitions on the right:

Terms

1. clicking
2. dialog box
3. drag and drop
4. graphical user interface
5. icons
6. mouse pointer
7. pointing
8. taskbar
9. window
10. WYSIWYG

Definitions

a. On-screen arrow pointing to the upper-left corner of the screen that can be moved with the mouse

b. Mouse action or technique used to position the pointer in a specific location

c. Rectangular object that displays an application program, a document, and other features and that can be sized and positioned anywhere on screen

d. Element at the bottom of the screen that contains the Start button, the Clock, and a button for an open application

e. Mouse action or technique in which an object is moved from one location to another

f. Operating system in which commands and options are represented by pictures or icons that can be selected with a mouse

g. Characteristic of a graphical user interface (GUI) in which the appearance of a document or an image on screen very closely resembles its appearance when printed on paper

h. Rectangular object that displays one or more options a user can select to provide a program with the additional information necessary to carry out a command

i. Mouse action or technique in which a button is pressed (and released) once very quickly

j. Small pictures or on-screen objects that represent commands or programs, which carry out an operation when selected with the mouse

1. i
2. h
3. e
4. f
5. j
6. b
7. b
8. d
9. c
10. g

Lesson Summary & Exercises

COMPLETION EXERCISE

Fill in the missing word or phrase for each of the following:

1. _Check boxes_ in dialog boxes contain a check mark when the option is chosen.

2. _Double clicking_ is a technique in which a mouse button is pressed and released twice very rapidly, such as to open a window.

3. In some dialog boxes you can type information in a(n) _text box_ to supply a program with the additional information necessary to complete a command operation.

4. In some dialog boxes you can select from a set of options that appear on a(n) _____.

5. For some elements on screen in the Windows 2000 environment, you can click the _right_ mouse button to display a shortcut menu.

6. The _operating system_ consists of the hardware, applications software, and the user.

7. To help you remember and choose them, lists of commands and options appear on _____.

8. _____ appear as small images on the desktop or in windows and dialog boxes.

9. A(n) _____ setting is one that the computer, or an applications program, uses automatically until the user specifies another.

10. _____ is an acronym for *what you see is what you get*.

SHORT-ANSWER QUESTIONS

Write a brief answer to each of the following questions:

1. Describe an example of a user's direct interaction with an operating system and an example of a user's indirect interaction with an operating system.

2. Briefly describe what occurs during a computer's Power On Self Test (POST).

3. List three ways in which you can use the taskbar.

4. What is selection? How do you do it and why is it important to Windows 2000?

5. List and briefly describe the different types of options that can be available in dialog boxes.

6. What is a device? What are some of the device icons that you might see on your computer screen?

7. As you explore Windows 2000, you might open dialog boxes with settings you do not understand. OK, Cancel, and Apply are three buttons you will see on most dialog boxes. What is the function of each? Which button is safest to click with an unfamiliar dialog box, and why?

8. In this lesson you learned the basic mouse actions. What is the difference between pointing, clicking, right-clicking, double-clicking, and dragging and dropping?

9. What is meant by a user interface? A graphical user interface?

10. What steps should you follow to end a computing session?

Lesson Summary & Exercises

APPLICATION PROJECTS

Perform the following actions to complete these projects:

1. Practice some mouse techniques by doing the following:

   Right-click the My Computer icon. Then select Open. Click the My Computer window's Close button. Drag the My Computer icon to the lower-left corner of the desktop. Double-click the My Computer icon and then double-click the Control Panel icon. Close the Control Panel window. Drag the My Computer icon back to the original location.

2. Right-click the Clock button on the taskbar, and then click Adjust Date/Time. Click the Time Zone tab in the Date/Time Properties dialog box, if necessary. Display the drop-down list of time zone options and click the option (GMT-10:00) Hawaii. Click the Date & Time tab and note the change to the time setting. Click the Date/Time Properties dialog box's Cancel button.

3. Windows 2000 often provides more than one way to accomplish the same task. Follow these steps to practice three different ways to open the Control Panel icon. Determine which method you prefer and state why.

   First way:

      a. Double-click the My Computer icon.

      b. Point to the Control Panel icon.

      c. Right-click to display the shortcut menu for the icon.

      d. Click Open.

      e. Close the window.

   Second way:

      a. Double-click the My Computer icon.

      b. Select the Control Panel icon.

      c. Click Open from the File menu.

      d. Close the window.

   Third way:

      a. Double-click the My Computer icon.

      b. Double-click the Control Panel icon.

      c. Close the window.

4. Beginning at the desktop with all windows closed and menus hidden, make your own step-by-step instructions to do each of the following:

    a. Open the C: drive window.

    b. Display the Date/Time shortcut menu.

    c. Identify Start menu items that lead to a dialog box.

5. Many dialog boxes have the same three buttons: OK, Apply, and Cancel. Follow these steps to observe the difference between these three commands:

Change Date and Apply:

    a. Open the Date/Time Properties dialog box.

    b. Set the date for January 1, 2055.

    c. Click the Apply button. Does the dialog box close?

    d. Point to the Clock button on the taskbar. What date is displayed?

Change Date and Cancel:

    a. Open the Date/Time Properties dialog box.

    b. Set the date for September 12, 2001.

    c. Click the Cancel button. Does the dialog box close?

    d. Point to the Clock button on the taskbar. What date is displayed?

Change Date and OK:

    a. Open the Date/Time Properties dialog box.

    b. Set the date for today's current date.

    c. Click the OK button. Does the dialog box close?

    d. Point to the Clock button on the taskbar. What date is displayed?

6. You must be able to connect to the Internet to complete this On the Web project. Click the Internet Explorer icon  on the taskbar. When connected to a Web site, find and click a link. Write a brief description of the Web site to which the link leads you. Click another link on the screen. Write a brief description of this site. Continue the process until you have visited five sites (not including the first site). Report your findings to the class. Compare your exploration with those of other members of the class.

Working with Windows

CONTENTS

OBJECTIVES

After you complete this lesson, you will be able to do the following:

- Recognize the common window elements, such as the title bar, menu bar, toolbars, and scroll bars.
- Size, minimize, maximize, and restore windows.
- Display multiple windows on the desktop simultaneously.
- Find Help on Windows 2000 topics.
- Search the Internet for online support.

A dictionary might define the word *window* as "an opening, set in a frame, for looking outside of a structure or letting in light and air." While you usually think that windows are in a house or a car, computer windows are frames on the screen through which you view documents, programs, and information. Unlike the windows in your home or car, you can close windows on the computer so that they are completely invisible. You, the user, determine the size and position of windows.

In this lesson, you will learn all about windows—how to open, close, size, and position them, and how to move through the information contained in windows. When you have mastered the techniques for working with windows, you will be well on your way to mastering Windows 2000.

COMMON WINDOW ELEMENTS

All the work you do in Windows 2000 takes place inside windows. Most Windows 2000 objects are in icon form, represented by their small on-screen picture. To work on a specific letter, a budget, an application, a control panel, or other Windows 2000 object, you must open the icon to see the respective window. Then, as you use the object, you change the appearance, the size, and the location of the window for efficient work.

To give an object as much workspace as possible, you **maximize** or expand the window to fill the entire screen. To keep an object available but hidden, you **minimize** the window to a taskbar button. To confine an object to only a portion of the desktop, you **size** or change the dimensions of that window. You can see the contents of the sized window, but the window takes up less than the full screen.

Windows can overlap each other, partially hiding windows behind them. You can move windows around on the desktop and even change the size of the window. In the exercises in this lesson, you will develop the skills required to manipulate windows.

Components and Types of Windows

Figure 2.1 identifies the major components of each window.

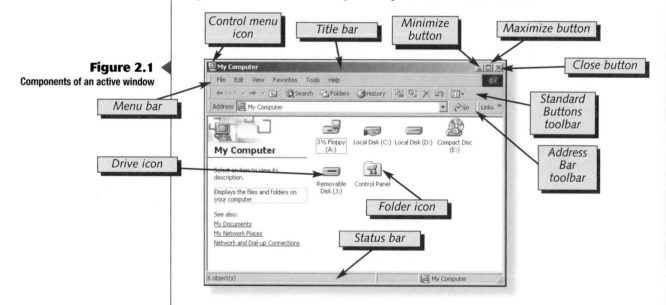

Figure 2.1 ◀
Components of an active window

The Title Bar

Across the top of the window is the *title bar.* The name of the object appears in the title bar. When the title bar has a color such as blue or pink, the window is *active*—ready to accept your input from the mouse or keyboard. Only one window can be active at any given time. Any other windows on the desktop will have clear or gray title bars, indicating that they are *inactive*—temporarily out of use.

On the left side of the title bar is the **control menu icon.** Clicking this button displays a menu that, among other options, lets you minimize, maximize, or close the window. On the right side of the title bar are buttons you use to minimize, maximize, or close the window by clicking. A maximized window has a **Restore** rather than a Maximize button ☐. The Restore button ⬚ shrinks the maximized window to its previous size and location.

The Menu Bar

Below the title bar is the **menu bar.** It contains the names of menus you can use within this window. Although menu names vary, the first menu name is almost always File and the last, Help. Clicking a menu name displays menu options below the name, such as the File menu in Figure 2.2.

Figure 2.2
The File menu

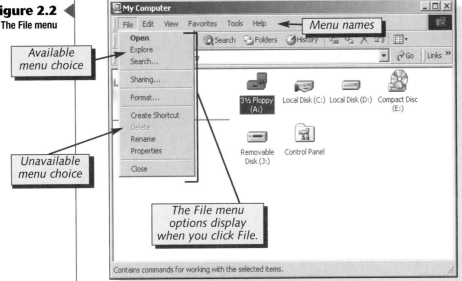

Available menu choice

Unavailable menu choice

The File menu options display when you click File.

 *Your File menu might have other options visible, depending on the selected drive and options installed. For example, sharing will appear as a File menu option if your computer has enabled print/folder sharing.*

Menu options are context-sensitive, and not all may be available at any given time. Available menu items are dark, such as Open or Close in Figure 2.2; unavailable menu options are dimmed, such as Delete in the same figure. Moving the mouse toward you moves the highlight down the list of menu options. When the highlight covers the option you want, you can choose the option by clicking. To leave a menu without choosing an option, either click the menu name or move outside the menu and click.

You can also use the keyboard to make menu selections.

■ To select a menu name, hold down [Alt] on the keyboard and press the letter underlined in the name, such as [Alt]+ **f** to display the File menu.

- To select a menu option, use ⬇ or ⬆ to highlight the desired option and then press Enter⬅. Alternatively, you can type the underlined letter of the desired option, such as **o** for Open.

- To close a menu without choosing an option, press Esc. Press Esc a second time to remove the highlight from the menu name.

Some options have keyboard shortcut keys printed beside them. The shortcut keys displayed on the menu serve as a reminder that you can select the option without going to the menu. For example, you might see F3 beside the Save As option on some File menus. This means that a third way exists to select the option. Using the first method, you can click the File menu and click Save As; using the second method, you can hold down Alt, type f, and select Save As; the third way is to just press F3.

Toolbars

Below the menu bar are the **toolbars,** rows of icons representing frequently used commands. By default, you should see two rows of toolbars on most of the windows used in this lesson: the Standard Buttons and the Address Bar. You will learn more about the functions of the buttons on these toolbars in later lessons.

Note   *Although toolbars are common to most programs, not all programs use them. If you don't see a row of toolbars, you may check the software's View menu to see if the toolbar option is turned off.*

Windows 2000 has several features that let you enlarge all or part of the screen for easier viewing. See Appendix B for specific information.

POSITIONING AND SIZING A WINDOW

You can position a window on the screen and change the size using the mouse.

Positioning a Window

To move a window to a new location, drag the title bar and move to the desired location. The computer you are using may be set to show an outline of the window while it is being dragged. When you release the button, the contents of the window will appear in place of the outline.

Did you know?

The first hard disk drive manufactured for the IBM PC was 5 MB. Today, you need over 120 MB of hard disk space just to install the operating system!

Moving a Window

In this activity, you will move a window.

1. **If necessary, log on the computer to boot the Windows 2000 operating system. If the monitor has a separate power switch, turn it on.**

Moving a Window

1. Point to the title bar.

2. Drag the window to the desired location.

Figure 2.3
The moved window

Close the Getting Started with Windows 2000 window if necessary.

2. Double-click the My Computer icon 🖳.

The My Computer window opens.

3. Point to the title bar.

4. Drag the My Computer window down to the lower-right corner of the screen, as shown in Figure 2.3.

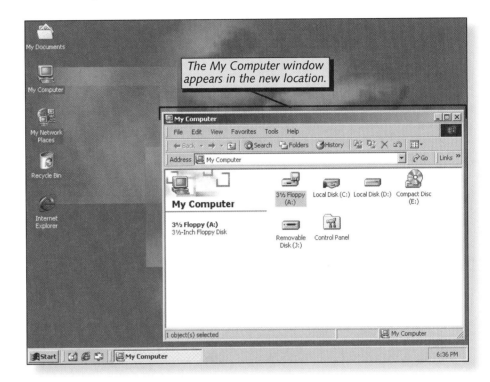

Sizing a Window

When you point to the edge of a window, the pointer changes shape to indicate the direction in which the window edge can move. A pointer on the left or right edge of a window becomes a horizontal double-headed arrow; pointing to the top or bottom edge of the window changes the pointer to a vertical double-headed arrow. Pointing to one of these locations allows you to drag that window edge to change the size of the window. For example, dragging the left edge of the window to the right makes a narrower window; dragging the bottom edge down makes a longer window.

If you point to one of the four corners of the window, the pointer becomes a diagonal double-headed arrow. Dragging a corner of the window stretches or shrinks two sides simultaneously. You can move a window by clicking the control menu icon and selecting the Move command. A four-way arrow appears, and you can then move the window. Figure 2.4 shows the various pointers you can use to size and move windows.

When you size a window, drag the corner to maintain the relative dimensions (height and width) of the window. If you drag the top or sides you will be stretching or shrinking only one dimension at a time.

Figure 2.4
Pointers for sizing and
moving windows

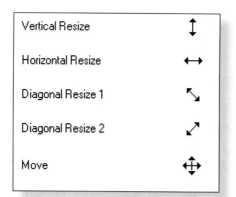

Vertical Resize	↕
Horizontal Resize	↔
Diagonal Resize 1	↖↘
Diagonal Resize 2	↙↗
Move	✛

Opening a Window Using the Keyboard

1. Press and hold [Alt] and press the underlined letter of the menu you want to open.

2. Release the [Alt] key.

3. Press the underlined letter of a menu option.

Opening a Window from the Keyboard

In this activity, you will use the keyboard to open another window.

1. Click Control Panel in the My Computer window.

The Control Panel icon highlights.

2. Press and hold [Alt] and press f. Release the [Alt] key.

The File menu appears, as shown in Figure 2.2 on page 37.

3. Press o.

The Control Panel window opens. Depending on your desktop settings, your Control Panel may have replaced the My Computer window. Otherwise, your My Computer window will still be open, but hidden behind the Control Panel window. If the My Computer window *does not* appear as a button on the taskbar, go to step 4. If both buttons appear on the taskbar, skip to the next section called *Changing the Size of a Window*.

4. Click the Back button ⟵Back ▾ on the toolbar.

You return to the My Computer window. The Forward ⇒▾ and Back ⟵Back ▾ buttons let you revisit windows you have recently opened. For example, if you were to press the Forward button ⇒▾, you would return to the Control Panel window.

5. Click the Tools menu.

6. Select Folder Options.

7. Click the General tab, if necessary.

8. Click Open Each Folder in its Own Window.

9. Click **OK**.

10. Double-click **Control Panel**.

This time the Control Panel window opens *without* replacing the My Computer window. The taskbar shows a button for My Computer and for Control Panel.

HANDS On

Changing the Size of a Window

In this activity, you will use standard Windows features to change the size of open windows.

1. Click the **Maximize button** ▢ on the Control Panel window.

The selected window enlarges to cover the full screen. The Maximize button changes to a Restore button.

2. Click the **Minimize button** ▬.

The Control Panel window closes and the button on the taskbar appears raised, as shown in Figure 2.5.

Figure 2.5 ◀
The Control Panel's taskbar button

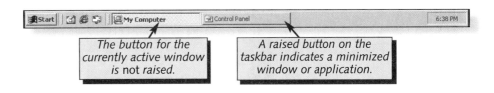

The button for the currently active window is *not* raised.

A raised button on the taskbar indicates a minimized window or application.

Windows BASICS

Changing the Size of a Window

- Click the Maximize button, the Minimize button, or the Restore button.

- Drag the border of the frame to the desired size.

- Drag the corner of the frame to the desired size.

3. Point to the right edge of the My Computer window.

The pointer changes to a horizontal, double-headed arrow.

4. Drag the window so that the size is approximately the size shown in Figure 2.6.

5. Click the **Maximize button** ▢ on the My Computer window.

The window enlarges to cover the full screen. Notice that a Restore button has replaced the Maximize button.

6. Click the **Restore button** ▣ on the My Computer window.

The window reduces to the previous size.

7. Point to the top border of the My Computer window.

Notice that the pointer changes to a vertical, double-headed arrow.

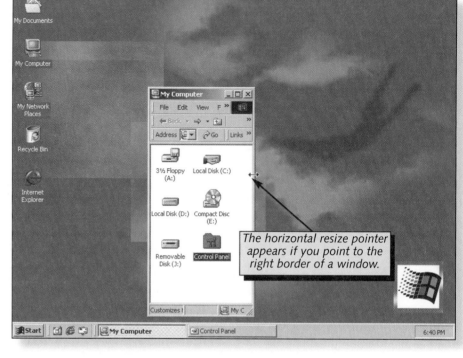

Figure 2.6
Resizing the My Computer window

The horizontal resize pointer appears if you point to the right border of a window.

The original DOS operating system could handle 640 KB of memory (RAM). Since the first PCs were sold with only 16KB or 64KB, that didn't seem like much of a limitation. Today, you *need* 64MB just to run Windows 2000.

8. Drag the top border outline up to near the top of the screen.

The window expands vertically.

9. Point to the right border of the window.

Notice that the pointer changes to a horizontal, double-headed arrow.

10. Drag the right border near to the right edge of the screen.

The window expands horizontally to resemble Figure 2.7.

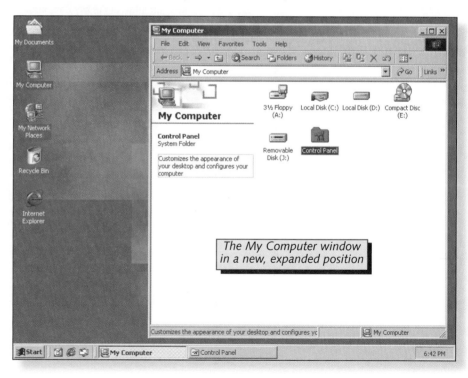

The My Computer window in a new, expanded position

Figure 2.7
The My Computer window with new dimensions

ARRANGING MULTIPLE WINDOWS WITH THE TASKBAR MENU

Occasionally, several application windows will be open. Although you can position and size individual windows using the techniques you have just learned, you will want to use the arrangement commands built into Windows 2000: cascade, tile horizontal, and tile vertical. These commands will allow you to arrange multiple windows more quickly.

Cascading Windows

Cascading open windows sizes them proportionately and stacks them, one upon another, so that only the top window is fully visible, as shown in Figure 2.8.

Figure 2.8
Three open windows in a cascade arrangement

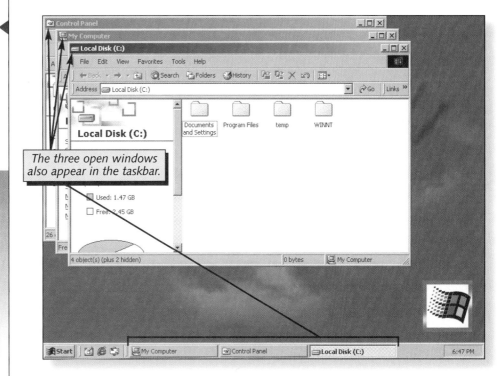

The three open windows also appear in the taskbar.

Before running a program from the Start menu, be sure the program isn't already open, but minimized on the taskbar. Running the program a second time may cause a second copy to be opened.

When you cascade windows, the window that is active when you select the Cascade command appears on top of the stack, but all of the windows are inactive. To activate a different window, you click any visible portion of that window (for example, the title bar). Activating a partially hidden window brings that window to the top of the stack.

HANDS On

Cascading Multiple Windows

In this activity, you will open three windows and display them in a cascade arrangement.

1. **Open the My Computer window, if necessary, and ensure that the Control Panel button appears on the taskbar.**

BASICS

Cascading Windows

1. Open two or more windows.

2. Right-click the taskbar and click Cascade Windows.

 *If the Control Panel button does not appear on the taskbar, double-click the icon in the My Computer window, click the Maximize button ☐ for the Control Panel window, and then click the Minimize button ▁.*

2. Double-click the C: drive icon.

The window will appear on the desktop. Your window objects will probably be different from the ones in Figure 2.8.

3. Click the Control Panel button on the taskbar.

The Control Panel window opens on the desktop in full-screen size, hiding the other two windows.

4. Right-click an empty area on the taskbar.

The shortcut menu for the taskbar appears, as shown in Figure 2.9.

Figure 2.9 ◄
The Taskbar shortcut menu

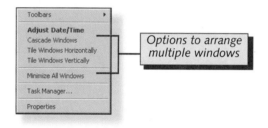

 If your shortcut menu does not look like the one in Figure 2.9, you have probably clicked a button or icon on the taskbar. In such a case, click an empty area of the taskbar to clear the menu, and then right-click that empty area.

5. Select Cascade Windows.

The open windows are sized equally and cascade on the desktop (similar to those shown in Figure 2.8 on page 43).

Tiling Windows

Tiling open windows sizes them equally and arranges them, either horizontally or vertically, so that they occupy equal portions of the desktop. Figure 2.10 shows open windows tiled in a horizontal arrangement.

To tile windows, point to an empty part of the taskbar, and then right-click to display the taskbar shortcut menu shown in Figure 2.9. Then select Tile Windows Horizontally or Tile Windows Vertically. To select (activate) a tiled window, you would click anywhere on that window. When you tile windows, the active window remains active.

Tiling Multiple Windows Horizontally

In this activity, you will tile the open windows horizontally on the desktop.

1. Right-click an empty area on the taskbar.

The shortcut menu for the taskbar appears.

2. Select Tile Windows Horizontally.

The three open windows are sized equally and arranged horizontally so they each occupy approximately one-third of the desktop area, as shown in Figure 2.10.

Windows BASICS

Tiling Windows

1. Open two or more windows.

2. Right-click the taskbar and click Tile Windows Horizontally or Tile Windows Vertically.

Figure 2.10 ◀
Three open windows tiled horizontally

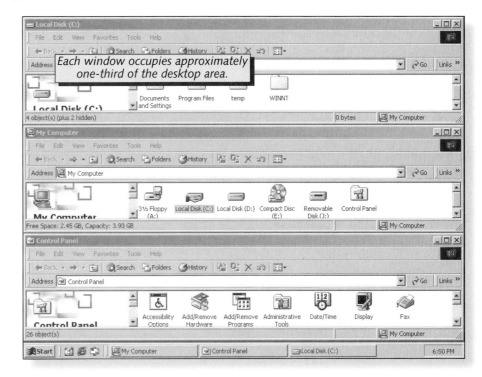

Each window occupies approximately one-third of the desktop area.

Tiling Multiple Windows Vertically

In this activity, you will tile the open windows vertically on the desktop.

1. Right-click an empty area on the taskbar.

The shortcut menu for the taskbar appears.

2. Select Tile Windows Vertically.

The open windows are sized equally and arranged vertically so they each occupy approximately one-third of the desktop area (similar to those shown in Figure 2.11).

Figure 2.11
Three open windows
tiled vertically

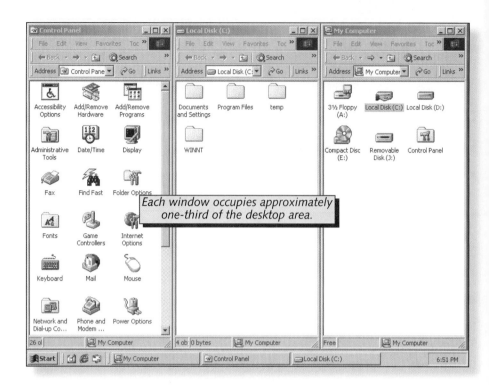

Each window occupies approximately one-third of the desktop area.

The ⊞ key can be used alone or in combination with other keys. Pressing ⊞ + D will minimize all open windows. Pressing ⊞ + D again will restore the minimized windows to their previous positions.

Note — *The order of the tiled windows may be different on your screen.*

After you have arranged application windows in order with either the Cascade command or one of the Tile commands, you can still size or position any window. Remember that if you maximize any window to full size and then later select the Restore button 🗗, the open windows will return to the same arrangement that existed before you enlarged the window. For example, if you maximize the Control Panel window among windows in a cascade arrangement and then later select its Restore button 🗗, the open windows will again cascade on the desktop with the Control Panel window on top of the stack.

HANDS On

Windows BASICS

Minimize all Open Windows

1. Open two or more windows.

2. Right-click the taskbar and click Minimize All Windows.

Minimizing All Open Windows

Sometimes you want to minimize all desktop windows in order to have a clean workspace. In this activity, you will minimize all open windows in a single operation.

1. Right-click an empty area on the taskbar.

The shortcut menu for the taskbar appears.

2. Select Minimize All Windows.

All open windows are minimized, and their corresponding buttons appear on the taskbar.

Note *If you want to see a clean desktop temporarily, click the Show Desktop button 🗗 on your taskbar. To return to your previous window arrangement, click the Show Desktop button 🗗 twice.*

ARRANGING ICONS

You can also move and position icons on the desktop. To position an icon, drag the icon to the desired location. (Be careful not to click or double-click the icon unless you intend to work with the program.) Program icons tend to stay where you put them. If you have a lot of icons on the desktop, they might be scattered around—they might become hidden behind other icons or windows. To display the icons in neat rows, use the Arrange Icons command on the shortcut menu that appears when you right-click an empty area on the desktop.

Arranging Desktop Icons

In this activity, you will practice arranging the desktop icons.

1. **Minimize all open windows.**

2. **Drag the My Computer icon 🖳 to the bottom right corner of the desktop.**

Note *If the My Computer icon 🖳 won't hold the position, the Auto Arrange command is on. Turn off Auto Arrange by pointing to an empty area of the desktop, right-clicking, clicking the Arrange Icons command, and then clicking Auto Arrange. Now, repeat step 2.*

3. **Drag the Recycle Bin icon 🗑 to the center of the desktop.**

4. **Move any other icons on your desktop to other places on the screen.**

5. **Right-click an empty area of the desktop.**

The shortcut menu for the desktop appears.

6. **Point to Arrange Icons and then click Auto Arrange from the submenu.**

The desktop's system icons align vertically along the left edge of the desktop (screen). The shortcut menu also lets you arrange desktop icons by name, type, size, or date.

Now you will rearrange the desktop icons as they were previously.

7. **Right-click an empty area of the desktop.**

8. **Point to Arrange Icons and then click by Name.**

HANDS

Arranging Window Icons

Arranging Window Icons

1. Open the window whose icons are to be arranged.

2. Click the View menu.

3. Click Arrange Icons and select Auto Arrange.

In this activity, you will practice arranging icons within an open window.

1. **Minimize all open windows.**

2. **In the taskbar, click the Control Panel button.**

The Control Panel window opens on the desktop.

3. **Resize the window to occupy 25 percent of the desktop.**

The icons rearrange themselves to fit the window.

4. **Click the View menu.**

The View menu appears.

5. **Click Arrange Icons.**

Another menu appears. Your menus will resemble Figure 2.12.

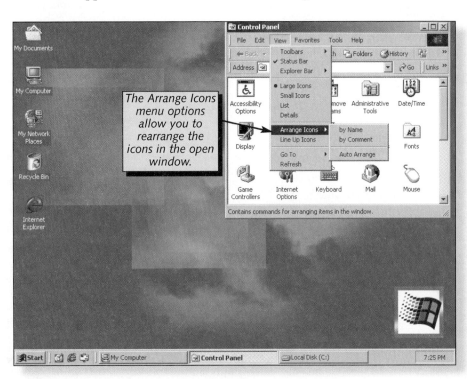

Figure 2.12
Locating the Arrange Icon
menu options

6. **Click by Comment.**

The icons for the Control Panel window rearrange themselves, as shown in Figure 2.13. The by Comment option arranges icons alphabetically according to the descriptions that appear for them on the status bar.

Figure 2.13
The Control Panel window's
rearranged icons

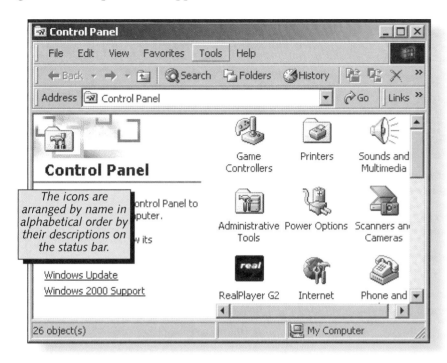

7. **Point to the upper-left corner of the Control Panel window.**

The pointer changes to a diagonal, double-headed arrow.

8. **Drag this corner of the window down and to the left to size the window as shown in Figure 2.14.**

 *Depending on the setup of your computer, your screen may differ.*

Figure 2.14
The sized Control Panel window

Many DOS users have made fun of Mac users with their friendly looking icons, WYSIWYG windows, and mouse clicks. These same users now have a very similar GUI in Windows 2000.

Notice that because you rearranged the icons by Comment, the icons stay in this order whenever you resize the window.

HANDS On

Changing the Size of a Window's Icons

Windows 2000 allows you to view icons in two different sizes. *Large icons* are easy to distinguish, but they take up more room. *Small icons* are about a quarter of the size of large ones, so you can see many more icons in a window. In this activity, you will modify the size of icons displayed in an open window.

1. In the Control Panel, click the **View menu**.

The View menu appears.

2. Click **Small Icons**.

The icons change to a smaller display size.

3. Click the **View menu**.

4. Point to **Arrange Icons** and then select **by Name**.

The icons rearrange to conform to the shape of the window. Notice that they are also arranged alphabetically by name.

5. Click the **View menu**.

6. Click **Large Icons**.

The icons appear in a larger display size.

Windows
BASICS

Changing the Size of an Icon

1. In an open window, click the View menu.

2. Select Large Icons, Small Icons, or Arrange Icons.

USING SCROLL BARS

A *scroll bar* appears along the right and/or bottom side of a window when there is not enough room to display all of the contents of the window. If the unseen information is above or below that viewed in the window, you see a *vertical scroll bar*; if the information is to the left or right, you see a *horizontal scroll bar*. Both types of scroll bars are illustrated in Figure 2.15.

Did you know?

Although rarely used by today's applications, the `Scroll Lock` key affects how the information scrolls on the screen in a few programs. Windows 2000 has no assigned meaning for `Scroll Lock`.

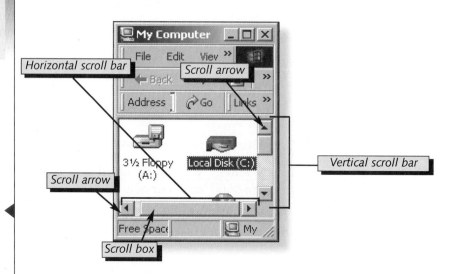

Figure 2.15
An open window's scroll bars, arrows, and boxes

Within the scroll bar is a rectangle known as the ***scroll box.*** This box indicates the relative position of the screen information within its window. If the scroll box is at the top or left of the scroll bar, you are viewing the top or left part of the information. If the scroll box is at the bottom or right of the scroll bar, you are viewing the bottom or right of the information. Clicking the scroll bar shifts the display to view another screen of information. Clicking below the scroll box on a vertical scroll bar displays the next screen of information. Clicking above the scroll box displays the previous screen. You can also drag the scroll box to move quickly to the desired position within a document or list of information.

Scroll arrows at either end of the scroll bar allow slow window navigation. Clicking a scroll arrow moves one line up or down on a vertical scroll bar or right or left on a horizontal scroll bar. Pressing and holding a scroll arrow permits line by line scrolling in the direction the arrow points.

Scrolling

- Click the scroll bar to view information not currently visible.

- Click below or after the scroll box to view more information.

- Click above or before the scroll box to view the previous screen.

- Click a scroll arrow to move one line up or down vertically or right or left horizontally.

Scrolling Vertically

In this activity, you will practice using scroll bars to scroll the contents of a window.

1. **Display the My Computer window, if necessary, and size the window similar to Figure 2.15.**

2. **If necessary, click Auto Arrange from the Arrange Icons submenu of the View menu to toggle this option off.**

3. **Point to the vertical scroll bar, anywhere below the scroll box and click.**

The column of icons appears to scroll upward as the scroll box moves downward.

4. **Click to move the scroll box to the bottom of the vertical scroll bar.**

The column of icons scrolls. Notice that the last icon is visible at the bottom of the window.

5. **Point to the scroll arrow at the top of the scroll bar.**

6. **Click to move the scroll box to the top of the vertical scroll bar.**

Scrolling Horizontally

In this activity, you will change the display size of icons and practice using the horizontal scroll bar of a window.

1. **With the My Computer window still open, click the View menu.**

2. **Click List.**

The icons change to a smaller size, in two or more columns.

3. Click the horizontal scroll bar to the right of the scroll box.

The contents of the window scroll to the left as the scroll box moves to the right.

4. Point to the scroll arrow to the left of the scroll bar.

5. Click until the scroll box moves to the left end of the horizontal scroll bar.

The contents of the window scroll to the right as the box moves to the left.

CLOSING ALL OPEN WINDOWS

Get into the habit of closing all open windows that you are not currently using.

Closing Open Windows

In this activity, you will restore and close the currently active windows.

1. Click the **C: drive button** on the taskbar.

The window opens to the previous size and position.

2. Restore each minimized window.

The three windows you last tiled vertically open in the same arrangement on the desktop.

3. Click the **Close button** ⊠ on the Control Panel window.

The Control Panel window is closed and disappears from the desktop.

4. Click the **Close button** ⊠ on the (C:) window.

The (C:) window is closed and disappears from the desktop.

5. Click the **Close button** ⊠ on the My Computer window.

The My Computer window is closed and disappears from the desktop.

GETTING HELP ON SCREEN

Now that you can scroll to view window information, you are ready to use the powerful *on-screen Help* system built into Windows 2000. If you don't know how to do something or forget a command, you can search for your answers in the Help system.

One of the Start menu choices is Help. This command displays the Windows Help window, as shown in Figure 2.16.

The Help window is divided into two panes. A *pane* is a portion of a window. You use the left pane of the Help window to locate the topic on which you want help. The right pane of the Help window displays the actual information.

Figure 2.16
The Help window

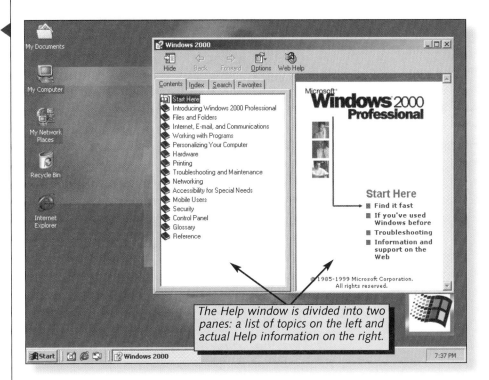

The Help window is divided into two panes: a list of topics on the left and actual Help information on the right.

The Help Window Tabs

Near the top left of the Help window are four tabs: Contents, Index, Search, and Favorites. These tabs represent pages. The front tab is the page that is currently open, and the contents are displayed below the tab. In Figure 2.16, the **Contents tab** is open, and you see Help topics in the window. If you click one of the topics, you either display help on that subject or a list of books contained within that book. You can click the desired book to display the contents. Sometimes, more topics are available than fit on the screen. The vertical scroll bar lets you find these topics.

Clicking the **Index tab** allows you to see an alphabetical listing of Help topics. You can navigate quickly to the desired topic by typing in the text box at the top of the Index window. When you type a letter, the display scrolls to the first topic beginning with that letter. As you continue typing, you will get closer to the topic you want. You can also use the scroll bar to find the desired topic. When you've highlighted the topic you want, click the Display button to show the information on that subject. The **Search tab** lets you search for words in the description of the Help information, rather than searching by topic. The **Favorites tab** lets you save particularly useful Help topics for later review.

Figure 2.17 shows the Windows 2000 Help window that appears when you select the *Start a Program* topic. You can use the vertical scroll bar to scan through the Help text. You may see underlined words and phrases in the Help text. Your pointer changes shape when you are pointing to underlined text. Some of these terms are ***glossary terms*** or keywords. Clicking these words displays a definition of the word or phrase, as shown in Figure 2.17. Clicking other underlined words or phrases may take you to related Help windows or dialog boxes.

Mastering a good help system is essential to learning computer software. Making use of your help resources should be your first attempt to solve a problem or answer a question. When you get stuck, however, talk to your local human support system.

Figure 2.17 ◀
Glossary term

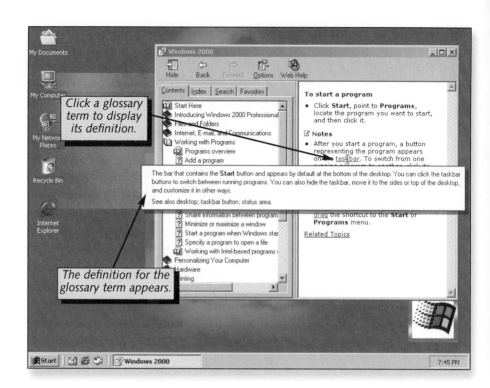

Getting Assistance with Windows 2000 Help

In this activity, you will practice using the Windows 2000 Help system to discover how to start a program.

1. Click the Start button .

The Start menu appears.

2. Click Help.

The Help files load and the Windows Help window appears, as shown in Figure 2.16 on page 53.

3. If necessary, click the Contents tab to display the list of topics.

4. Click the book icon labeled Working with Programs.

Many documents within the topic are displayed, as shown in Figure 2.18.

5. Click the document icon labeled Start a program.

The pane on the right displays the procedure for starting an application program, notes, and a link to another topic. (See Figure 2.17.)

Note Depending on the width of the left pane, only part of the book's title may be visible.

Using Help

1. Click Start.

2. Click Help.

3. Click the tab you want to use and explore for help.

Figure 2.18
Documents within
Working with Programs

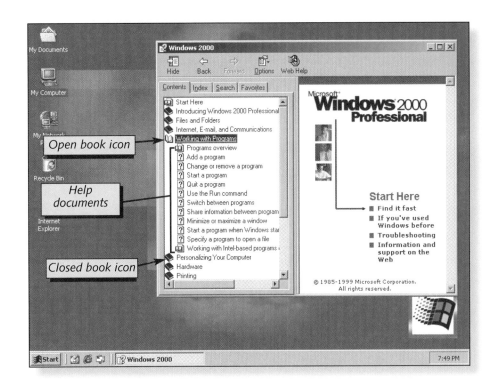

HANDS On

Using the Windows Help Index

In this activity, you will use the Windows Help index to learn about printing.

1. Open the Windows Help window, if necessary, and click the Index tab.

The Windows Help set of index topics appears, as shown in Figure 2.19.

Figure 2.19
The Windows Help Index tab

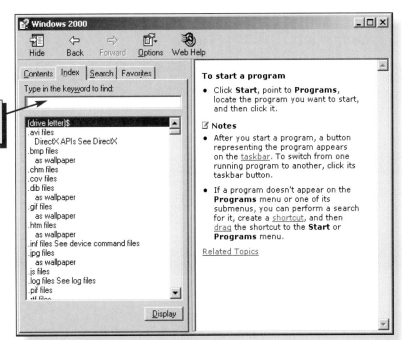

Notice that a blinking insertion bar appears in the text box.

2. Type printing **in the text box.**

As you type letters, the list of Help topics scrolls down. A set of printing topics appears.

3. Click the subtopic common tasks.

4. Click the Display button.

A Help window appears in the right pane with information on printing documents.

Using the Search Tab

In this activity, you will practice using the Windows Help Search feature to learn how to cascade open windows.

1. Open the Windows Help window, if necessary.

2. Click the Search tab.

The Help Search window appears, as shown in Figure 2.20.

Figure 2.20
The Windows Help Search feature

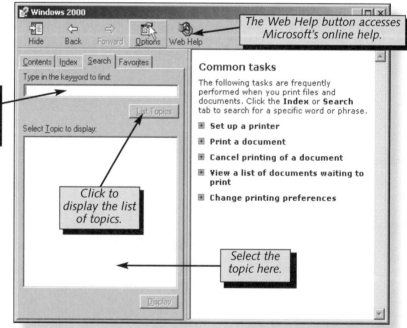

Getting Online Help

1. Open Windows Help.

2. Click the Web Help button.

3. Click <u>Windows 2000 home page</u>.

3. Type cascade **in the text box.**

4. Click the **List Topics button**.

Two topics appear in the Topic screen.

5. Click the topic **Arrange all open windows**.

6. Click **Display**.

The Help document appears in the right pane with information on the selected topic.

Local versus Remote Help

You have now seen the built-in help manual that is part of the Windows 2000 operating system. This help manual is located on your hard disk drive. You can call the help features on your own computer *local* help. Windows 2000 has another feature that lets you access help on the Internet. This feature can be called *remote* or online help.

 *You may explore the online Help feature by continuing with the On the Web section that follows, or you may proceed directly to the exercises for this lesson. If you are finished with your computer session, log off the computer you are using.*

 Follow the "log off" procedures for your lab or school environment.

ON*the*WEB

GETTING ONLINE HELP

Windows 2000 has a Help feature that lets you search for assistance when you can't find the information you need within Windows 2000. Microsoft maintains an Internet site specifically for this purpose.

1. Open the Windows Help window, if necessary.

2. Click the Web Help icon  **near the top of the screen.**

In the text that appears in the right pane, there is a link, or jump, to online help.

3. Click the link Windows 2000 home page.

Note *If you receive a message indicating no Internet connection could be established, consult your instructor or computer lab assistant.*

After a short while, your Internet connection is made and you should see the Windows 2000 home page, as shown in Figure 2.21.

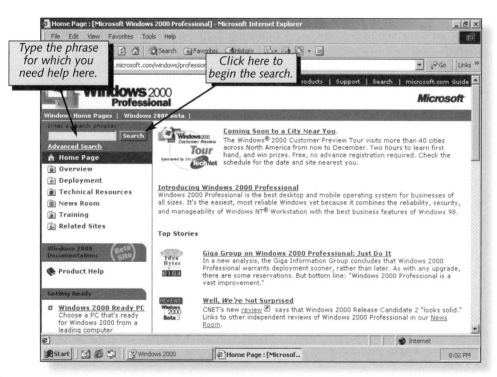

◀ **Figure 2.21**
The Windows 2000 home page

4. Click the Maximize button ☐ **, if necessary.**

5. Type printing **in the Enter a search phrase: text box on the left side of the screen.**

6. Click Search.

ON*the*WEB

Warning

You may see Security Alert and/or Security Warning windows informing you that you are about to send information over the Internet. If you do not trust the organization to which you are connected, click No. Otherwise, click Yes and continue.

Figure 2.22 shows a series of helpful articles that might appear from your search. As new solutions and problems occur, Microsoft frequently updates this list, so don't be surprised if your list is quite different.

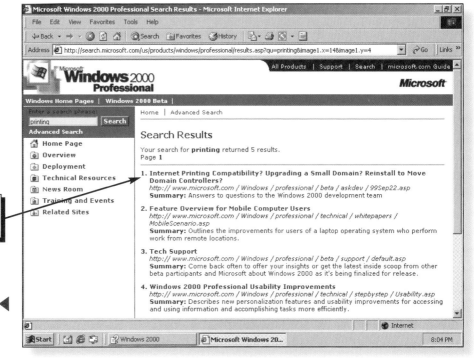

Click an article's title to read the article.

Figure 2.22 ◀
The result of a Web search for help on printing with Windows 2000

7. Click **Close** ☒.

Warning

Your computer may not automatically disconnect from the Internet when you quit the Online Help screen. If you see a connecting icon 🖥 next to your clock on the taskbar, right-click it. Choose the Disconnect option from the short-cut menu. Check with your instructor or computer lab assistant if you need additional instructions to disconnect from the Internet.

8. Click **Close** ☒ on the Windows Help window.
9. You may proceed directly to the exercises for this lesson. If, however, you are finished with your computing session, log off the computer you are using.

Warning

Follow the "log off" procedures for your lab or school environment.

Lesson Summary & Exercises

SUMMARY

After you complete this lesson, you should know how to do the following:

Common Window Elements

■ Identify common window elements, such as the title bar, the menu bar, drive icons, and buttons.

Positioning and Sizing a Window

■ Move a window to a new position on the desktop by clicking the title bar and dragging to a new location.

■ Change the size and shape of a window by dragging the window borders.

Arranging Multiple Windows with the Taskbar Menu

■ Use the Cascade Windows option to display the title bars of all open windows simultaneously.

■ Use the Tile Windows options to display the contents of all open windows simultaneously.

Arranging Icons

■ Drag icons to new locations within a window or on the desktop.

■ Neatly organize the icons within a window or on the desktop by right-clicking and selecting the Arrange Icons option.

Using Scroll Bars

■ Use the scroll bars to bring contents that are out of view in a window into view.

Closing All Open Windows

■ Click the taskbar button to restore minimized windows, and then click the Close button for each open window.

Getting Help on Screen

■ Find Help on any Windows 2000 topic by clicking the Start button and selecting the Help option.

■ Display definitions of Windows 2000 terms by clicking them in a Help window.

On the Web: Getting Online Help

■ Click Web Help on the Windows Help window to get answers to questions on the Internet that you can't get from your local help system.

Lesson Summary & Exercises

NEW TERMS TO REMEMBER

After you complete this lesson, you should know the meaning of these terms:

active window	large icon	scroll box
cascade	maximize	Search tab
Contents tab	menu bar	size
control menu icon	minimize	small icon
Favorites tab	on-screen Help	tile
glossary term	pane	title bar
horizontal scroll bar	restore	toggle
inactive window	scroll arrows	toolbars
Index tab	scroll bar	vertical scroll bar

MATCHING EXERCISE

Match each of the terms with the definitions on the right:

Terms

1. cascade
2. control menu icon
3. document window
4. Maximize button
5. menu bar
6. Minimize button
7. active window
8. scroll bar
9. tile
10. title bar

Definitions

a. Standard window element on the right end of title bars that reduces a window to a button on the taskbar

b. Windows 2000 command that arranges all open windows on the desktop so that each is in view and occupies the same amount of screen area

c. The window that you are currently using; the one with the colored title bar

d. Standard element in application windows, generally located near the top of the window and below the title bar, that contains pull-down menu names

e. Standard window element that allows the contents of a window to be brought into view, either vertically or horizontally

f. Standard window element that is at the top of every window and that contains a set of icons or buttons for controlling the size and placement of a window

g. Standard window element on the right end of title bars that enlarges a window to full-screen size

h. Specific type of window that displays information within an application window

i. Standard Windows icon that appears on the left end of title bars and that displays a menu for controlling the size and placement of the window as well as closing the window or switching to another application window

j. Windows command that arranges all open windows on the desktop so that they overlap, with the active window in front

Lesson Summary & Exercises

COMPLETION EXERCISE

Fill in the missing word or phrase for each of the following:

1. All of the work that you do in Windows 2000 takes place inside a(n) _____.

2. To view information that exists below the last visible line at the bottom of a document window, you can use the _____.

3. A(n) _____ is a screen element that you can drag to bring information into view in a window or list, and represents the approximate location of the visible information in the document or list.

4. Click the _____ to enlarge a window to fill the desktop.

5. The _____ command arranges open windows in a stack with small portions of open windows visible.

6. In Windows 2000 Help windows, you can click _____ to display definitions.

7. A menu option that alternately turns on and off each time you click it is called a(n) _____.

8. A submenu appears when you click a name on the _____ in an application window.

9. If you want to keep an application window available but out of the way while working with another application or feature, you can reduce the window to a taskbar button by clicking the _____.

10. The _____ on the title bar of a full-screen window returns the window to the previous size before you maximized the window.

SHORT-ANSWER QUESTIONS

Write a brief answer to each of the following questions:

1. List at least five objects or elements that are common to both application and document windows.

2. Differentiate between maximizing, minimizing, and restoring a window.

3. List and describe briefly the three types of pointers that let you change the size of a window.

4. Describe briefly the advantages and disadvantages of the Cascade Windows and Tile Windows commands for arranging information on the desktop.

5. List and describe briefly the purpose of the four elements on a scroll bar that you can use for scrolling information.

6. What is the purpose of on-screen Help?

7. What is the purpose of Web Help?

8. Why don't all windows have a Restore button?

9. When multiple windows are open, how do you identify the active window?

10. What is a toggle command?

APPLICATION PROJECTS

Perform the following actions to complete these projects:

1. Open the My Computer window, the Control Panel window, and the **Printers** folder window so all three windows are on the desktop. Right-click the taskbar. On the shortcut menu, click Cascade Windows. Activate each window separately by clicking any visible part of an inactive window. Display the shortcut menu for the taskbar twice more to select Tile Windows Horizontally and then Tile Windows Vertically. Practice activating windows in each arrangement, and then close all of the open windows.

2. Click Start and then click Help to load the Windows 2000 Help system. Open the Contents tab and click the topic *Introducing Windows 2000 Professional.* Then click the subtopic *How to Use Help.* Click the *Help Overview* Help document. Does the text that appears contain a glossary term? If so, what is the term? Display and read its definition. Close the Help window.

3. Click Start and then click Help to load the Windows 2000 Help system. Open the Search tab and see whether you can locate the following terms: *embed, taskbar,* and *pane.* How many could you find? If you find any, display and read the information that contains these terms. Close the Help window.

4. Open the My Computer window. Use the dragging technique to size the window so that it occupies about half the horizontal desktop area. Maximize the window and then restore the window. Close the My Computer window.

5. Open the Recycle Bin window. Use the dragging technique to reposition the window in the lower-right corner of the desktop. Next, use the control menu icon to close the Recycle Bin window.

6. You must be able to connect to the Internet to complete this On the Web project. Use Web Help to find information on the "Internet." Record the names of three articles that are displayed as a result of this search.

Investigating Your Computer

CONTENTS

_Opening the My Computer
Window

_Examining System Properties

_Using the Printers Folder

_On the Web: Updating Device
Drivers

OBJECTIVES

After you complete this lesson, you will be able to do
the following:

- Recognize the types and drive letters of the
  storage devices attached to your computer.
- Distinguish among system, program, and
  document files.
- Search through the contents of disk drives.
- Use the Control Panel to examine the hardware resources of your computer.
- Expand and collapse the display of hardware devices and their properties.
- View the settings and capabilities of your
  printer.
- Get the latest software from the Internet to
  keep your devices working at peak
  efficiency.

To work on the same project from one day to the next, your computer stores or saves information from one computing session to another. Files contain the data that you, the operating system, and the application software need to perform any task. Modern computing systems have thousands of files. The Windows 2000 operating system alone consists of hundreds of files. With so many files, you must organize them for efficient use. This lesson discusses file organization and provides instructions to locate and display the files stored on your computer. You will investigate your computer system to learn how the system organizes and displays information.

WORKING INSIDE THE MY COMPUTER WINDOW

Each named, ordered collection of information stored on a disk is called a *file.* The My Computer icon lets you find information about the devices and files that compose your computer system. You will open this window to examine your disk storage system and your printer and hardware settings. Opening this icon displays a window like the one shown in Figure 3.1. Since this information is computer-specific, your window may contain different icons than those displayed in Figure 3.1. Lesson 3 concentrates on the items found on most computer systems.

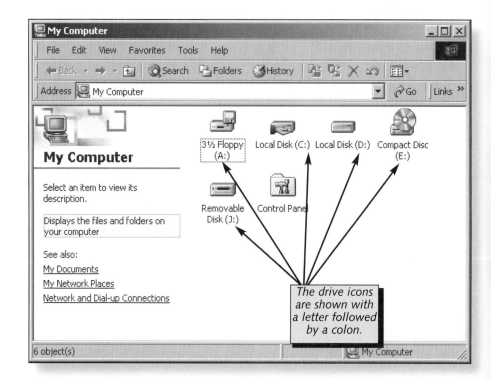

Figure 3.1
The My Computer window

Storage Devices

The My Computer window displays a *drive icon* for each of the storage devices attached to your computer system. Below each of these device icons is the alphabetical letter (followed by a colon) used to identify that device. Table 3.1 lists the most common storage devices and the device icons that represent them.

Table 3.1	Storage Device Icons
ICON	**DEVICE TYPE**
	Floppy disk drives
	Hard, or fixed, disk drives not shared
	Shared drive
	Removable disk drive
	CD-ROM drive

Your floppy disk drive is usually assigned to drive letter A:. If your computer has a second floppy disk drive, this drive is probably labeled B:. Your primary hard disk drive is C:. Additional hard disk drives, removable disk drives, CD-ROM drives, Zip drives, and so on, have their own letters. If your computer is connected to other storage devices via a network, icons and letters also represent these devices. The hand that seems to be holding the disk drive means that the drive is shared. A *shared drive* is a disk drive attached to your computer that other users who are on the network can access. A *network drive* is a storage drive you can use, even though this drive is physically attached to another computer.

Files

Three basic kinds of files exist: system files, program files, and document files. *System files* are the files that collectively make up your Windows 2000 operating system. *Program files* are the application software that you use to perform tasks on your computer. *Document files* (or data files) are the work that you create while you are using your computer. Each different file type has its own characteristic *file icons.*

Table 3.2 shows a few of the file icons you will see on your computer.

Table 3.2	File Icons
ICON	**FILE TYPE**
	Setup files for installing software
	Application software files (Microsoft Word)
	Text document files
	Sound document files
	Picture document files

File Windows

Two basic types of windows exist: *application windows* and *document windows.* Application windows appear when you run a program. Document windows let you perform separate jobs within an application window. For example, to type a letter, you would open a word processing program application window. To work with several letters, you would open a document window for each letter.

Folders

Storage disks contain files and folders. A *folder* is a named icon that contains files and folders. You use folders to organize files and folders. An organized hard disk drive contains many folders. Each application software program creates one or more folders for its own use.

A few folder icons, such as **Printers** and **Control Panel** inside the My Computer window, are specially designed. The pictures on these folder icons tell you that these are not ordinary folders containing files and other folders. Rather, these special folders are part of the Windows 2000 operating system.

Some folders appear to be held by a hand. These folders are **shared folders.** Like shared drives, other users who are on the network can access shared folders.

Folders were called **directories** in previous versions of Windows before Windows 95. Folders inside of folders were called **subdirectories.** Following this convention, some Windows 2000 users call these nested folders **subfolders.**

HANDS On

Windows BASICS

Setting Folder Options

1. Click the Start button, point to Settings, and click Control Panel.

2. Double-click Folder Options.

3. Click the appropriate options to set the view in the General tab.

4. Click OK.

5. Click Close.

Setting Folder Options

Windows 2000 provides a variety of ways to view the contents of your storage devices. In this activity, you will set your view to match the screen illustrations in this tutorial.

1. **If necessary, log on to the Windows 2000 operating system and turn on the monitor.**

2. **Click the Start button** ![Start].

The Start menu appears.

3. **Point to Settings and click Control Panel.**

The Control Panel window opens.

4. **Double-click the Folder Options icon.**

The Folder Options window appears.

5. **Click the General tab.**

6. **Click the following option buttons:**

   ■ Enable Web content on my desktop

   ■ Enable Web content in folders

   ■ Open each folder in the same window

   ■ Double-click to open an item (single-click to select)

7. **Click OK.**

8. **Click the Close button** ![X].

These settings ensure that only one window will be open at a time and that your folder windows will look and work like those in the Hands On activities in this tutorial.

HANDS On

Windows BASICS

View Contents of a Drive

1. Open the My Computer icon.

2. Open the drive icon to be viewed.

3. Open a folder to see the contents.

Figure 3.2

A drive C: window

Windows 2000 provides keyboard substitutes for mouse clicks. See Appendix B for specific information.

Viewing the Contents of Your Hard Disk

In this activity, you will open the My Computer window and view the contents of your hard disk.

1. Open the My Computer icon 🖥️.

The My Computer window appears.

2. Open the drive C: icon.

A window appears, displaying the contents of drive C:, as shown in Figure 3.2.

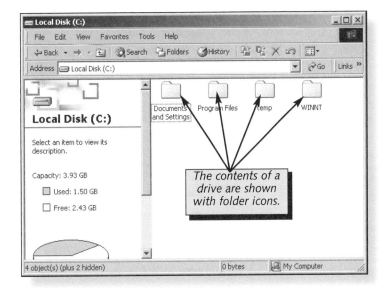

> *𝒩ote* — *Your drive C: window and your folders will probably contain different items. If you don't see the large icons as shown in Figure 3.2, click the View menu and select Large Icons.*

3. If necessary, scroll the contents of the window until you can see the *WINNT* folder.

4. Open the *WINNT* folder.

The **WINNT** folder window appears on the desktop. This folder contains the Windows 2000 operating system files, as shown in Figure 3.3.

Figure 3.3
The *WINNT* folder

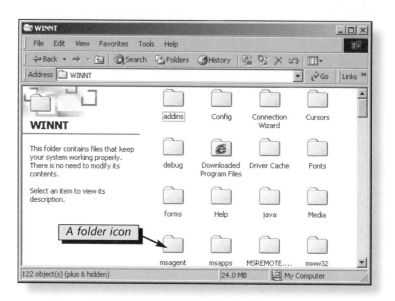

5. If necessary, maximize the *WINNT* folder window.

6. Click the **triangle button** beside the **Back button** ⟵ Back ▾ on the toolbar.

A drop-down list displays the previous windows you opened.

7. Select **My Computer**.

The My Computer window appears, maximized.

View Contents of a Drive

1. Open the My Computer icon.

2. Open the drive icon to be viewed.

3. Open a folder to see the contents.

Viewing the Contents of a Floppy Disk

In this activity, you will use the Student Data Disk that comes with this tutorial to view the contents of the diskette.

1. Insert your **Student Data Disk** into drive A: (or drive B:).

2. If your Student Data Disk is in drive A:, open the **drive A: icon** in the My Computer window; if your Student Data Disk is in drive B:, open the **drive B: icon**.

A window appears that displays the contents of your Student Data Disk, as shown in Figure 3.4.

3. Open the *Worksheets* folder.

A window appears that displays the contents of the *Worksheets* folder. Notice that diskettes also use folders to organize files.

4. Click the **Back button** ⟵ Back ▾ twice.

The My Computer window is now open.

Figure 3.4
The Student Data Disk
window

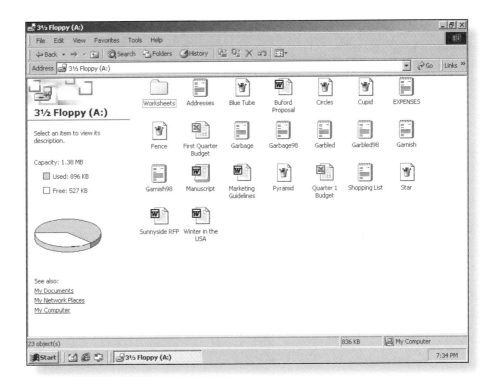

5. Remove your **Student Data Disk** from drive A: (or drive B:).

Your diskette drive should be empty.

6. Open your diskette drive icon in the My Computer window.

A window, such as the one in Figure 3.5 appears, asking you to insert a disk into drive A. You will see this reminder if you try to view a diskette drive without putting a diskette in first.

Figure 3.5
Empty diskette drive window

7. Insert your **Student Data Disk** in the diskette drive.

Wait while the disk loads and the contents appear in the Floppy window.

8. Close the Floppy window.

9. Remove the **Student Data Disk** from drive A: (or drive B:).

EXAMINING SYSTEM PROPERTIES

The Control Panel window is shown in Figure 3.6. Later in this tutorial, you will learn more about some of these programs. For now, you will continue the discovery of your computer system by examining your *system properties,* or system configuration settings.

Adding a hardware device to Apple Macintosh computers requires little more than plugging it in. It took the Windows 95 operating system to add a similar ease of use to PCs—more than 10 years later!

Figure 3.6
The Control Panel window

The System Properties Dialog Box

Double-clicking the System icon in the Control Panel window displays the System Properties dialog box, as shown in Figure 3.7. Five index tabs appear in this dialog box: General, Network Identification, Hardware, User Profiles, and Advanced.

Figure 3.7
The System Properties dialog box

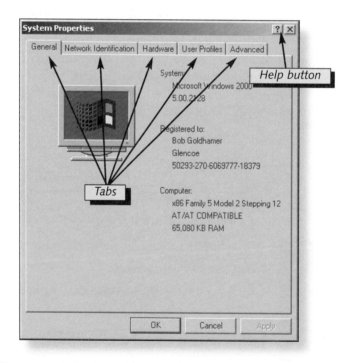

General Information

The General tab, as shown in Figure 3.7, displays the version of the Windows 2000 operating system used to boot your computer, who owns a license for the software, the type of processor (CPU) running your computer, and the amount of memory (RAM) the computer has. The General tab displays information only; you cannot set any options on the General tab.

Hints & Tips

Avoid manually changing the properties of the devices attached to your system to avoid conflicts. Windows 2000 automatically keeps all devices working together.

Viewing the General Properties on Your Computer

In this activity, you will open the System Properties dialog box from the Control Panel.

1. Click the Start button **on the taskbar.**

The Start menu appears.

2. Point to Settings.

The Settings menu pops up.

3. Click Control Panel.

The Control Panel window appears on the desktop.

4. Open the System icon.

The System Properties dialog box appears.

5. If necessary, click the General tab.

Your screen should resemble Figure 3.7.

Note *The information on the General tab will be specific to the computer you are using.*

6. Click the Help button [?] **that appears to the left of the Close button.**

The pointer changes shape to become a Help pointer, an arrow with a question mark. Clicking the Help pointer on an item on the screen displays a brief definition or an explanation about that item. If the item has no associated helpful information, the Help pointer disappears.

7. Click the center of the word Registered in *Registered to.*

The Help window displayed in Figure 3.8 appears.

Figure 3.8 ◀
"Registered to" Help passage

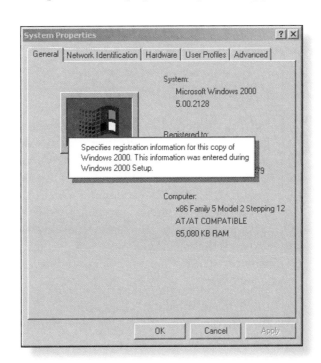

8. Click the **Help button** [?] again to learn more about the other information in the General tab of the System Properties dialog box.

9. When you are finished exploring the General tab, click outside the Help window to close the Help passage.

Hardware Options

The Hardware tab lets you view, add, remove, and otherwise control the hardware components of your system. There are four buttons on the Hardware window—the Hardware Wizard button lets you install, uninstall, change, and fix devices. The Hardware Profiles button allows you to set up your system for different purposes and users. The Driver Signing button allows you to protect your computer when installing new software. The Device Manager button displays information about the system, including devices connected to it, as shown in Figure 3.9. For the operating system to manage the hardware efficiently, Windows needs precise information about the input, output, storage, and processing equipment that make up your computer system.

Figure 3.9
Device Manager window

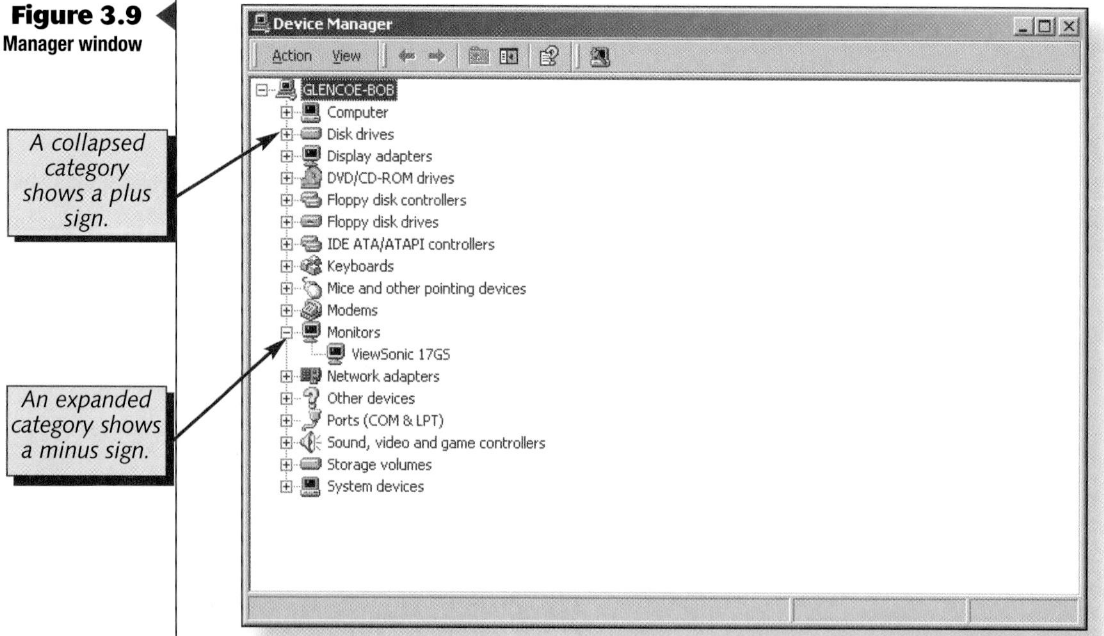

A collapsed category shows a plus sign.

An expanded category shows a minus sign.

Devices connected to the system appear in a ***tree,*** a structured list whose branches display and hide their contents as commanded. At the top of the list is the computer itself. Hardware device categories are indented below this level. The square to the left of each line contains either a plus sign (+) or a minus sign (-). These symbols indicate the amount of detail listed on the screen. A plus sign refers to a ***collapsed*** level. This means that you can display specific devices for a category that are currently hidden from view. To see (expand) the category, simply click the plus sign (+). When a category expands, the square displays a minus sign (-); this represents an ***expanded*** level.

While comprehensive descriptions of common hardware devices are beyond the scope of this tutorial, you can use the Device Manager to view information on any device. To do this, expand the category, right-click a device, and click Properties.

HANDS

Viewing the Devices on Your Computer

In this activity, you will examine the list of devices attached to your computer system.

Your goal in this activity is to examine the settings, not to change them. If you change any settings inappropriately, your system might operate poorly or not at all.

Windows BASICS

Viewing Your Device's Properties

1. Click the Start button, point to Settings, and click Control Panel.

2. Open the System icon.

3. Click the Hardware tab.

4. Click the Device Manager button.

5. Expand the category.

6. Right-click the device.

7. Click Properties; make no changes.

1. Open the Systems Properties dialog box, if necessary.

If necessary, repeat steps 1 through 4 of the previous activity.

2. Click the **Hardware tab**, if necessary.

3. Click the **Device Manager button**.

The Device Manager window appears, as shown in Figure 3.9.

4. Click the **plus sign (+)** to the left of the Disk Drives icon.

The disk drive branch expands, and you see a list of the disk drives attached to your system.

5. Click the **minus sign (-)** to the left of the Disk Drives icon.

The disk drive branch collapses, and you no longer see the list of disk drives.

6. Close the Device Manager window.

HANDS

Viewing Hardware Profiles

In this activity, you will examine the Hardware Profiles on your computer.

1. Open the Systems Properties dialog box, if necessary.

If necessary, repeat steps 1 through 4 of the activity on page 73.

Windows BASICS

Viewing the System Performance Properties

1. Click the Start button, point to Settings, and click Control Panel.

2. Open the System icon.

3. Click the Hardware tab.

4. Click the Hardware Profiles button.

2. Click the **Hardware tab**, if necessary.

3. Click the **Hardware Profiles button**.

Your computer may or may not show different hardware setups.

4. Click **Cancel**.

Device Installation

The Windows 2000 operating system automatically determines most of your computer's hardware settings, requiring no effort from the user. Windows 2000 **Plug and Play** feature means that you may install a new device by simply plugging the device into your computer and then turning on the device. Because the Windows 2000 operating system takes care of the settings for the device behind the scenes, the device works properly right away.

Companies such as Compaq, Intel, Microsoft, and Phoenix Technologies developed Plug and Play standards for IBM and compatible computers. For hardware to be Plug and Play compatible, the manufacturer must place the information Windows 2000 needs in the circuitry of the device.

A **modem** is a device that lets your computer communicate with other computers over public telephone lines. In the modem Properties dialog box, as shown in Figure 3.10, Windows 2000 has set up the modem's configuration and the hardware. Potential conflicts over memory usage and codes are eliminated before the device is used. The more advanced user can enter different settings manually.

Figure 3.10
The Properties dialog box
for a modem

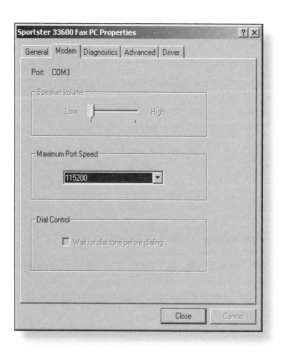

The Hardware Wizard button lets the user install hardware devices on a computer system. This button opens the Add/Remove Hardware Wizard dialog box, as shown in Figure 3.11. In Windows 2000, a **wizard** is an automated process that guides you through an operation with which you may be unfamiliar. A wizard presents a series of options from which you can select. Plug and Play hardware installs with little or no intervention on your part. However, with older, non-Plug and Play devices known as **legacy hardware,** you may have to inform Windows about the device by using the Add New Hardware wizard, or you may use the software provided by the manufacturer.

The first PCs to produce *letter quality* text printed like typewriters. Although the letters were high quality, the printer was incapable of printing graphics.

Figure 3.11
The Add/Remove Hardware
Wizard dialog box

Network, User, and Advanced Settings

The System Properties dialog box has three other tabs: the Network Identification tab, the User Profiles tab, and the Advanced tab.

Viewing the Advanced Settings

In this activity, you will examine the Advanced tab on your computer.

1. Click the **Advanced tab**.

2. Click the **Performance Options button** [Performance Options...].

The Performance Options dialog box appears.

3. Click **Change** on the right side of the dialog box.

The Virtual Memory dialog box appears. *Virtual memory* is hard disk drive space that Windows 2000 uses when more main memory is needed.

4. Click the **Cancel button** [Cancel].

The Virtual Memory dialog box disappears.

5. Click the **Cancel button** [Cancel].

The Performance Options dialog box closes.

6. Click the **Cancel button** [Cancel].

The System Properties dialog box closes.

7. Close the Control Panel window.

USING THE PRINTERS FOLDER

Whenever you are unsure about what a dialog box item means, click the Help button and click the Help pointer on the item.

As you learned with the Control Panel, Windows 2000 sometimes lets you run a program from more than one location. You can also access the *Printers* folder from either the Settings menu or the Control Panel window. Double-clicking the Control Panel's Printers icon displays the Printers window; an example is shown in Figure 3.12.

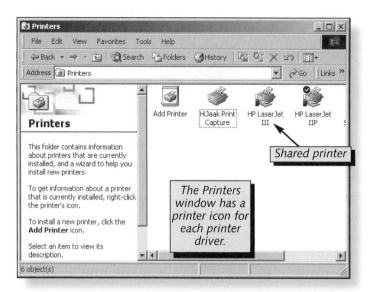

Figure 3.12
The Printers window

In the Printers window, you can select and set up the printer to which you want to send your output. The Printers window contains a printer icon for each of the printer drivers installed on your system. A *printer driver* is a program file that controls or regulates a specific printer. The Printers window also contains an Add Printer icon, which allows you to add (install) a new printer to your system. Printers that seem to be held by a hand are *shared printers.* Other users who are on the network can access shared printers.

When you open a printer icon, a status window appears with the name of the specific printer model in its title bar. Any document being printed appears in this window, as shown in Figure 3.13.

Figure 3.13
The status window for a printer

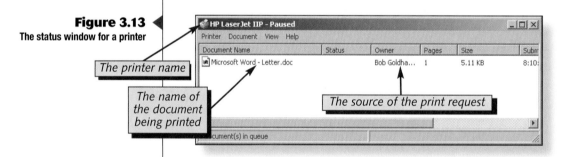

You can modify settings for a specific printer through the Properties dialog box. Three ways exist to access this dialog box. You can highlight the device icon for your printer in the Printers window, click the right mouse button, and then click Properties on the shortcut menu. Secondly, you can highlight the device icon for your printer in the Printers window and then click Properties on the File menu. Thirdly, you can open the device icon for your printer in the Printers window and click Properties on the Printer menu. The Properties window for each printer is a multi-tabbed dialog box similar to the one shown in Figure 3.14.

You will learn much more about controlling your printer in a later lesson in this tutorial.

You can right-click an item and select What's This? instead of clicking the Help pointer.

Figure 3.14 ◀
The Properties dialog box

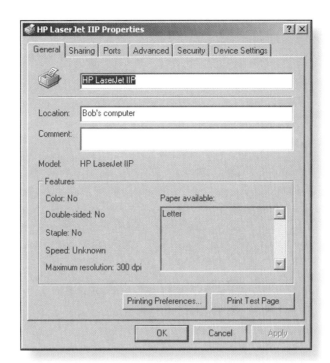

View Printer Properties

1. Open the Control Panel.

2. Open the Printers folder.

3. Select the printer device icon.

4. Click Properties on the File menu.

Viewing Printer Settings

In this activity, you will view the current print settings for the printer connected to your system.

1. **Open the Control Panel window.**

2. **Open the *Printers* folder.**

3. **Select the device icon for a printer connected to your computer system.**

4. **Click Properties on the File menu.**

The Properties dialog box for the printer you selected appears. Notice that its title bar displays the model name of the printer you are using.

5. **One at a time, click each of the tabs in the Properties dialog box to view the different categories of information for your printer. Use the Help pointer to learn more about any of the options.**

6. **Close the Properties dialog box.**

7. **Close the Printers and Control Panel windows.**

Device drivers are loaded into memory during the boot up procedure. That is why you usually have to reboot your computer after changing or installing a device driver.

 *You may explore Upgrading Device Drivers by continuing with the On the Web section that follows, or you may proceed directly to the exercises for this lesson. If you are finished with your computer session, log off the computer you are using.*

  Follow the "log off" procedures for your lab or school environment.

UPGRADING DEVICE DRIVERS

When you install Windows 2000 on your computer system, Windows uses specific software programs to match your hardware. These ***device drivers*** ensure that your printer, monitor, mouse, and other devices work optimally. As time passes, more efficient device drivers may become available. Hardware designed and manufactured more recently than the Windows 2000 program may not have device drivers on the disk. Hardware manufacturers often include device drivers on disk packaged along with the hardware. You may find updated drivers on the manufacturer's Web site or through Microsoft. In this activity, you will learn how to update a device driver by letting Windows 2000 search the Internet.

1. Open the System Properties dialog box, if necessary.

2. Click the **Hardware tab**.

3. Click the **Device Manager button**.

4. Click the **plus sign (+)** beside the Floppy disk controllers icon.

5. Right-click the **Floppy disk controller device**.

6. Click the **Properties option**.

7. Click the **Driver tab**, if necessary.

8. Click the **Update Driver button**.

The Upgrade Device Driver Wizard dialog box appears, as shown in Figure 3.15.

◀ **Figure 3.15**
The Upgrade Device Driver Wizard dialog box

9. Click **Next**.

The next wizard screen asks what you want Windows to do.

10. If necessary, click the **Search for a suitable driver for my device option**.

11. Click **Next**.

12. Check the **Microsoft Windows Update box**, if necessary, and make sure the other boxes are not checked.

13. Click **Next**.

 *A Microsoft Windows Update box may appear asking you to complete the Registration Wizard. If so, check with your instructor for instructions. The Update Wizard connects to the Internet, locates information regarding newer device drivers and lets you know whether a better driver can be found.*

 *Unless this is your computer or you have specific authorization, you should **not** replace your device driver, especially if your system is operating normally. Check with your instructor, computer lab assistant, or network administrator for instructions.*

14. Click **Cancel** in the Update Device Driver Wizard dialog box.

15. Disconnect from the Internet, if necessary.

16. Close all open windows.

The desktop is cleared.

17. You may proceed directly to the exercises for this lesson. If, however, you are finished with your computer session, log off the computer you are using.

 Follow the "log off" procedures for your lab or school environment.

Lesson Summary & Exercises

SUMMARY

After you complete this lesson, you should know how to do the following:

Working Inside the My Computer Window

- Select Folder Options from the Control Panel window to set up the way your folder windows look and work.
- Double-click the My Computer system icon to display your storage devices and the **Control Panel** folder.
- Double-click a storage icon to display its contents.
- Double-click a folder to display its contents.

Examining System Properties

- Double-click the **Systems** folder in the Control Panel to open the Systems Properties window.
- Click the Hardware tab and the Device Manager button to see a list of hardware categories.
- Click a plus sign to see the devices connected to your computer.

Using the Printers Folder

- Double-click the **Printers** folder in the Control Panel to see the printers connected to your computer.
- Select a printer, then click Properties on the File menu to open your printer's Properties window.

On the Web: Upgrading Device Drivers

- Click the Update Driver button in a device's Properties window to search the Internet for a newer device driver.

NEW TERMS TO REMEMBER

After you complete this lesson, you should know the meaning of these terms:

application window	file icon	shared folder
collapsed	folder	shared printer
device driver	legacy hardware	subdirectory
directory	modem	subfolder
document files	network drive	system files
document window	Plug and Play	system properties
drive icon	printer driver	tree
expanded	program files	virtual memory
file	shared drive	wizard

MATCHING EXERCISE

Match each of the terms with the definitions on the right:

Terms

1. document file

2. drive icon

3. file icon

4. folder

5. shared drive

6. expanded

7. program file

8. system files

9. printer driver

10. wizard

Definitions

a. A storage device on your computer that other users who are on the network can access

b. A container for files and other icons

c. The software that regulates the operation of your printer

d. The branch of a storage device tree, labeled (-), that shows its components

e. Icon that represents a storage device and activates a window displaying the files and folders stored on the device

f. Files that operate the computer

g. An automated process that guides you through a series of complex steps

h. Files that contain instructions used by application software

i. On-screen picture that represents information named and stored in a specific location

j. Named set of data that is created while working with an application and stored in a specific location

Lesson Summary & Exercises

COMPLETION EXERCISE

Fill in the missing word or phrase for each of the following:

1. In the device tree structure displayed on the Device Manager window, you can click a plus sign (+) to _____ the level.

2. Each named, ordered collection of information stored on a disk is called a(n) _____.

3. The first hard disk on your computer is named the _____ drive.

4. System configuration settings are called _____ _____ .

5. If you use a word processing application to type a memo, the text that makes up the memo is stored in a(n) _____ _____ .

6. On the tree structure of devices in the Device Manager window, a minus sign (-) represents an object that is _____.

7. Others on a network can use a _____ storage device, folder, or printer.

8. A(n)_____ is an automated process that guides the user through an unfamiliar operation.

9. The _____ _____ allows you to display a brief definition or an explanation about an on-screen item.

10. The_____ _____ is a program file that controls or regulates a specific printer.

SHORT-ANSWER QUESTIONS

Write a brief answer to each of the following questions:

1. How do you use the Windows 2000 contextual Help system?

2. What would happen if your computer only had files, but no folders?

3. List the three major file categories and the purpose of each.

4. What happens if you try to open a floppy drive icon without a disk in the drive?

5. What steps should you take to remedy the problem described in question 4?

6. Why does Windows 2000 have property windows?

7. What is a subfolder?

8. Why does each printer need a printer driver?

9. The contents of some windows are displayed in a tree structure. How do you use this structure?

10. From the information presented in this lesson, how could you learn the version of the Windows 2000 operating system you are using?

Lesson Summary & Exercises

APPLICATION PROJECTS

Perform the following actions to complete these projects:

1. Open the Keyboard icon located in the Control Panel. Use contextual Help to learn more about your keyboard properties.

 Warning *Do not change any settings.*

Close all open windows.

2. Suppose you were able to purchase a new printer. List the steps, in logical order, you would expect to perform to install the device properly. Be precise.

3. Display the settings for the sound card connected to your computer or network. Use contextual Help to learn more about the properties of your device.

 Warning *Do not change any settings.*

 **Note** *You can find information on the sound card by opening the Device Manager within the Hardware tab of the System Properties dialog box.*

4. Display the settings for the mouse connected to your computer or network. Use contextual Help to learn more about the properties of your mouse.

 Warning *Do not change any settings.*

 Note *Look for mouse settings in the Mouse icon in the Control Panel.*

5. What steps would you expect to go through if you purchased a non-Plug and Play device? Briefly describe the advantages or disadvantages of purchasing legacy hardware.

 6. You must be able to connect to the Internet to complete this On the Web project. Display the mouse properties of the computer you are using by selecting your mouse from the Device Manager window of the Hardware tab of the System Properties window. Click the Driver tab, and then click the Update Driver button. Follow the steps in the Upgrade Device Driver Wizard to find a newer version of your mouse driver on the Internet. Click Cancel if the Upgrade Device Driver Wizard suggests you replace your mouse driver.

Warning *Do not upgrade your mouse driver unless you have explicit permission to do so!*

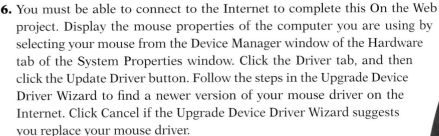

Exploring Disk Organization

CONTENTS

OBJECTIVES

After you complete this lesson, you will be able to do the following:

- Use the Windows Explorer to view and modify the structure of a disk.
- Modify the appearance of the Explorer window.
- Format a disk to prepare it to store information.
- Create folders and subfolders.
- Rename, delete, copy, and move folders.
- Design folder structures that suit different needs.
- Launch the Internet Explorer from the Windows Explorer.

Information is the computer's most important product. As a computer user, you must be able to locate and use stored information and to save ongoing work for future use. Protecting and updating that information requires careful organization. You must store data properly so that you can find the information later.

In Lesson 3, you learned that the file is the basic unit of disk storage; all the information that you store is in the form of files. In this lesson, you will use the Windows Explorer to analyze the organization of your hard disk and then apply that knowledge to the organization of a floppy disk.

WINDOWS in the workplace

USING THE WINDOWS EXPLORER

The Windows Explorer opens to display the Explorer window. With some features similar to that of My Computer, the Explorer window lets you search the storage system of your computer to examine its contents and organization. Figure 4.1 shows the Explorer window with all the components collapsed.

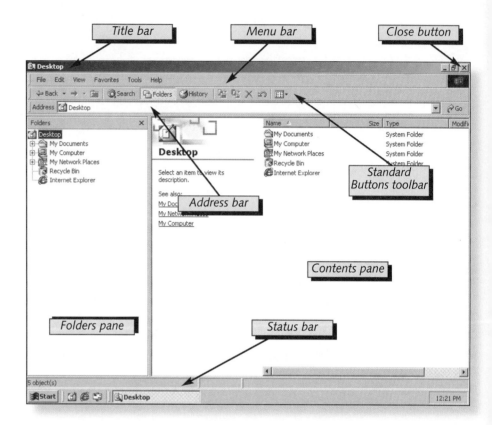

Figure 4.1
The Explorer window

As shown in Figure 4.1, the Explorer window has a title bar, a menu bar, and one or two toolbars. Below these bars, the Explorer window divides vertically into two panes: Folders and Contents. At the bottom of the window is the ***status bar.*** The status bar provides information about the selected objects in the panes. You will soon see that the Explorer window has many different views. You will learn how to adjust your view to your needs later in this lesson.

The Folders Pane

On the left section of the Explorer window is the Folders pane. This pane shows a tree of folders that displays the hierarchical organization of available disks. When you select an icon in the Folders pane, the name appears in the title bar. Notice that Desktop appears in the title bar in Figure 4.1, and Desktop is highlighted in the Folders pane.

The root or base of the entire Windows 2000 tree is the Desktop. In Figure 4.1, the Explorer window displays the Desktop icon at the top of the Folders pane, with each Windows 2000 icon listed below. Since the purpose of the Explorer window is to display the contents of all files to which you have access, you may see different icons when you explore the desktop of your computer.

Expanding a branch in the Folders pane displays the folders for that branch. Figure 4.2 shows how the Folders pane changes by expanding the My Computer branch. Icons for the available disk drives appear along with a system folder.

Although each drive icon has the shape of the drive it represents, each drive icon is also a main or top-level folder. Each **main folder** can hold files and subfolders. The main folder is also called the **root directory.**

Figure 4.2
The Explorer window with
My Computer expanded

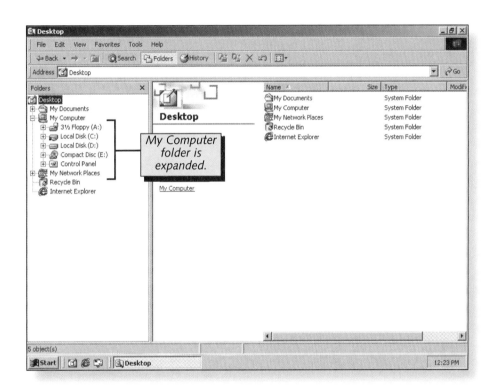

Disconnect from the Internet when you are finished. If you share hardware with other users, their access to the Internet may be slowed down or blocked. Likewise, if you access the Internet over phone lines, incoming or outgoing voice calls will be prevented.

Note *In spite of the technical distinction between main folders and subfolders, many people refer to them both simply as folders.*

Figure 4.3 shows how the Folders pane changes by expanding the C: branch. Notice that some folder levels display a plus sign (+). Remember that the plus sign indicates that the folder contains one or more other folders (or subfolders). Folders without a plus sign are empty or contain only files.

Figure 4.3
The Explorer window with
C: branch expanded

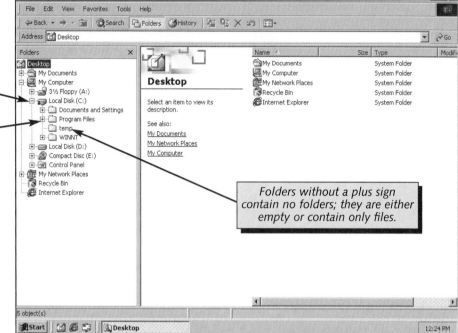

C: folder is expanded.

A plus sign indicates the folder contains one or more folders.

Folders without a plus sign contain no folders; they are either empty or contain only files.

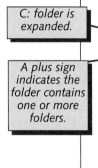

DOS users typed commands like MKDIR to create a folder (or directory) and RMDIR to delete a folder (or directory). Windows 2000 users click a folder to see the contents— DOS users typed CHDIR followed by the name of the folder and then DIR to see a list of the folder's contents.

The Contents Pane

When you click a folder in the Folders pane, the Contents pane (on the right) will display the contents of the selected folder. In Figures 4.1, 4.2, and 4.3, the Contents pane does not change, because the selected folder in each figure is the Desktop. Figure 4.4 shows the Explorer window with C: selected. Compare the title bar and Contents pane of Figure 4.4 with that of Figure 4.3. The Contents pane in Figure 4.4 shows icons of the objects contained in the C: drive.

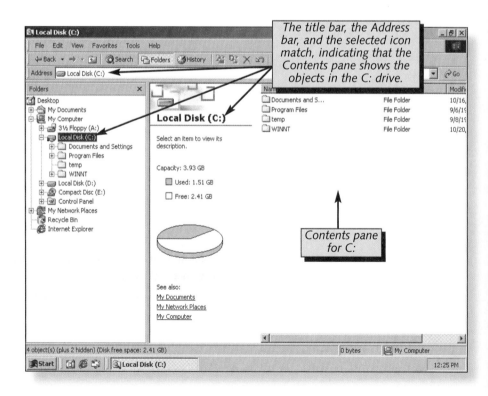

The title bar, the Address bar, and the selected icon match, indicating that the Contents pane shows the objects in the C: drive.

Contents pane for C:

Figure 4.4
The Explorer window with
C: selected

HANDS On

Exploring Your Hard Disk

In this activity, you will open the Explorer window, select various objects, and expand and collapse several folders to view the hierarchical structure of the hard disk.

1. **If necessary, turn on the computer to log on to the Windows 2000 operating system. If the monitor has a separate power switch, turn it on.**

2. **Insert your Student Data Disk into drive A: (or drive B:).**

3. **Click the Start button 🎬Start.**

4. **Point to Programs, then Accessories, and click Windows Explorer.**

The Explorer window appears.

5. **Adjust the Explorer window to resemble Figure 4.4.**

   a. **If Desktop is not the top object in the Folders pane, drag the vertical scroll box in the Folders pane to the top of the scroll bar.**

   b. **To ensure that your Explorer window is set up to follow the Hands On activities in this tutorial, click Folder Options from the Tools menu to display the Folder Options dialog box. On the View tab, make sure the same boxes are checked as shown in Figure 4.5. Then click OK.**

Figure 4.5 ◀
The Explorer window's Options dialog box

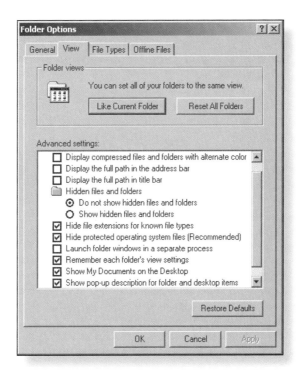

   c. **If a plus sign (+) appears beside the My Computer icon, click the plus sign to expand the sublevels. Then expand the C: drive.**

   d. **Click Details from the View menu to display objects in columns in the Contents pane.**

   e. **Click to place a check mark next to Status Bar on the View menu to display the status bar in the Explorer window, if necessary.**

f. Right-click an empty area of the menu bar. Make sure you have a check mark next to Standard Buttons and Address Bar on the shortcut menu. Then click outside the shortcut menu to close it.

g. Maximize the Explorer window.

h. Click the *WINNT* folder in the Folders pane.

i. If prompted, click the **Show Files link** to view the contents of the *WINNT* folder.

The title bar says *WINNT.* The Contents pane displays the objects in the *WINNT* folder.

6. Click the My Computer icon's **minus sign (-)** to collapse the My Computer level.

My Computer is now selected. The title bar says *My Computer.* The drive icons and system folders appear in the Contents pane, and a plus sign (+) appears beside the My Computer icon.

7. Press .

The My Computer level in the Folders pane expands.

Note *The left and right arrow keys on the keyboard can substitute for mouse clicks to expand or collapse a selected folder.*

8. Press ⬇ until you select drive C:.

Your C: drive may have a name beside it. The folders and/or files in the main folder for drive C: appear in the Contents pane.

Note *The ⬇ allows you to move down the Folders tree. Each time you press ⬇, the object just below the currently selected one highlights, the object's name appears in the Explorer title bar, and the object's contents are displayed in the Contents pane.*

9. Alternating between the keyboard and the mouse, expand and collapse the various folders in the Folders pane until you are well acquainted with the hierarchical organization of your computer system.

When you first work with an unfamiliar computer system that runs Windows 2000, the Windows Explorer can help you to understand its file organization quickly.

10. Select the device icon for the disk drive that contains your Student Data Disk (drive A: or B:) in the Folders pane.

The contents of the Student Data Disk appear in the Contents pane. Notice that you do not need to expand a folder in the Folders pane to see its details in the Contents pane.

11. Remove the **Student Data Disk** from the disk drive.

CUSTOMIZING THE EXPLORER WINDOW

Your preliminary investigation of the Windows Explorer demonstrates its benefit. When you customize the Explorer, however, it becomes even more useful. The Explorer customization commands are on the View menu.

View Options

Figure 4.6 shows the View menu options. These options control the way the Explorer window looks and works. Some options vary the appearance of items in the Contents pane, while others determine the order in which they appear. For example, you can have the Contents pane display objects alphabetically, by the date they were created, by their size, or by their type. File *type* is the category to which the object belongs—document, graphics image, program, and so on. The View menu options are explained in Table 4.1.

Figure 4.6
The Explorer window's
View menu

Table 4.1	Explorer View Menu Commands
OPTION	**DESCRIPTION**
Toolbars	Displays or hides sets of buttons just below the menu bar with shortcuts for common menu commands.
Status Bar	Displays or hides a bar at the bottom of the window that explains selected objects or menu commands.
Explorer Bar	Lets you change the options in the Folders pane—particularly useful for accessing the Internet.
Large Icons	Changes the Contents pane. A large icon appears above each folder or file name. First folders, then files, are arranged in rows and columns. You can drag objects to different locations.

Table 4.1	Explorer View Menu Commands—cont.
OPTION	**DESCRIPTION**
Small Icons	Changes the Contents pane. A small icon appears to the left of each folder and file name. First folders, then files, are arranged in rows and columns. You can drag objects to different locations.
List	Changes the Contents pane. Small icons appear to the left of each folder and file name. The listing is in columns from top to bottom. Dragging an object within the pane does not change its location.
Details	Changes the Contents pane. Small icons appear to the left of each folder and file name. The listing is in a single column. To the right of each file name are the size and type of file and the date the file was last saved.
Thumbnails	Displays a miniature version of the graphics or picture document files.
Arrange Icons	Lets you determine the order in which the files appear, by name, type, size, or date. AutoArrange keeps objects aligned as you drag them around the window.
Line Up Icons	Aligns objects in columns and/or rows after you have dragged them around the window.
Choose Columns	Lets you decide the order and categories of information you want while in the Detail view.
Customize this folder	Enables you to change the overall appearance, including the background of the Explorer window.
GoTo	Redisplays previously viewed Explorer windows.
Refresh	Updates the information displayed in the window to reflect the most current changes.

HANDS On

Changing Window Pane Views

In this activity, you will change several of the Explorer window's View options and observe the way the objects change in the Explorer window.

1. **With the Explorer window maximized and active on the desktop, select the C: drive icon in the Folders pane.**

2. **Verify that the Standard Buttons toolbar is visible in the Explorer window.**

The Explorer Standard Buttons toolbar is toggled on. Figure 4.7 identifies the Standard Buttons toolbar.

Figure 4.7
The Standard Buttons toolbar

 *If labels do not appear beside the buttons on your toolbar, click View, Toolbars, Customize. Select* Selective text on right *from the Text Options drop-down list.*

3. Click the **Views button** .

The Views button lets you change the appearance of files and folders in the Contents pane.

4. Click **Large Icons** from the drop-down list.

If you have trouble using the mouse, check Appendix B for information on adjusting the mouse settings.

5. Click the **Views button** four more times. Each time, select a different option from the drop-down list.

The five views you cycled through are explained in Table 4.2.

Table 4.2	Contents Pane Views
OPTION	**DESCRIPTION**
Large Icons	Displays the Contents objects as large icons in columns and rows. Large Icons view lets you drag objects into custom locations in the Contents pane.
Small Icons	Displays the Contents objects as small icons in columns and rows. Small Icons view lets you drag objects into custom locations in the Contents pane.
List	Displays the Contents objects as small icons without any details.
Details	Displays the Contents objects as in List but includes detailed information about each object.
Thumbnails	Creates a box around each icon. Images appear inside graphics or picture file types.

Changing Contents Pane Appearance

1. Click the Views triangle button on the toolbar and select a Contents pane option.

2. Click View, Arrange Icons, and select a Contents pane option.

6. Click the **Views button** and select **Details**.

7. Click **Arrange Icons** from the View menu.

The Arrange Icons menu shown in Figure 4.8 appears beside the View menu.

Figure 4.8
The Arrange Icons menu

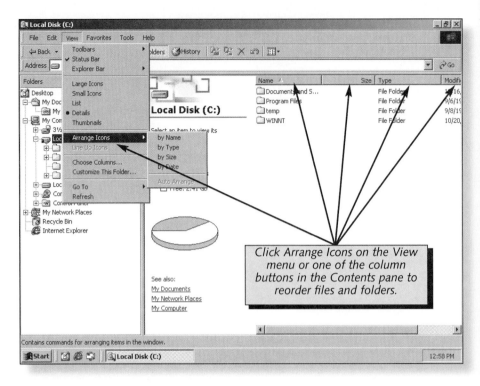

Click Arrange Icons on the View menu or one of the column buttons in the Contents pane to reorder files and folders.

8. Click By Date.

The Contents pane list rearranges. Objects are now organized by date (modified) from oldest to newest.

9. Click View, Arrange Icons, By Size.

The Contents pane list rearranges. Objects are now organized by file size from smallest to biggest.

 *Folders are listed in alphabetical order before the files.*

10. Click View, Arrange Icons, By Type.

The Contents pane list rearranges. Objects are now organized first by file type, and then alphabetically within each object category.

If you click any of these buttons a second time, you will arrange the files in the opposite order, that is, from last to first or first to last.

11. Click the word Name above the names of the folders and files in the Contents pane.

The Contents pane arranges its object list into computer alphabetical order; numbers precede letters. Notice how the folders and the files are grouped separately. Instead of accessing icon arrangement from the View menu, you can simply click the Name, Size, Type, and Modified buttons near the top of the Contents pane to arrange icons accordingly. (See Figure 4.8.)

Changing to the Windows Classic View

1. Click the Tools menu.

2. Click Folder Options.

3. Click the Use Windows classic folders option button.

4. Click OK.

Back in the 1960s and 1970s, programmers typed their program instructions onto punched cards. A stray hole could completely ruin the intent of the program—hence the phrase *Do not fold, spindle, or mutilate.*

Viewing the Contents Pane Without Web Content

In this activity, you will switch your Contents pane to remove the Web content. In this view, more files and details can be displayed.

1. With the Windows Explorer open, click the **Tools menu**.

2. Click **Folder Options**.

3. Click the **Use Windows classic folders option button**.

4. Click **OK**.

Your Contents pane changes in appearance. In the Details view, you should see the Date Modified column. In other views, you will see more folders and files.

WINDOW PANES

Another way to customize the Explorer window is to move the ***separator line,*** the thick vertical line that divides the window panes. Dragging the separator line left or right makes one pane wider and the other narrower. When an object such as the C: folder contains several levels of subfolders, widening the Folders pane lets you expand some or all of its branches without scrolling. When an object, such as the ***WINNT*** folder, contains many other objects, widening the Contents pane displays items differently.

Sizing Explorer Window Panes

In this activity, you will use your mouse to change the widths of the Folders and Contents panes, and you will also adjust the Contents pane's details columns (Name, Size, Type, Modified) to display information differently.

1. With the Explorer window maximized and active on the desktop and the Student Data Disk in the floppy drive, select the floppy disk drive in the Folders pane.

2. Point to the separator line between the Folders and Contents panes.

When the pointer is directly on the separator line, the pointer becomes a horizontal, double-headed arrow.

3. Resize the pane as shown in Figure 4.9.

As you drag the mouse, the Contents pane widens. Now the Contents pane has more room to display its details.

Figure 4.9 ◀
The resized Explorer panes

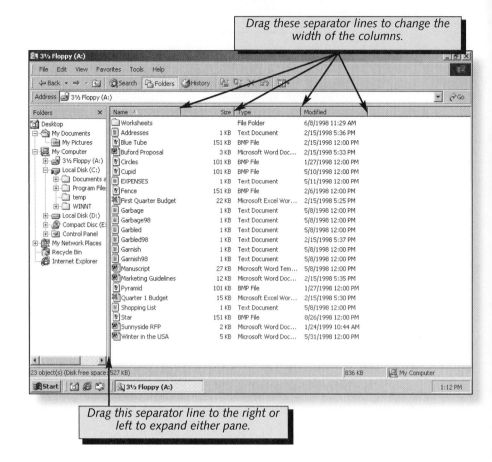

Drag these separator lines to change the width of the columns.

Drag this separator line to the right or left to expand either pane.

Widening a Pane and Its Columns

1. Click the Views triangle button.

2. Click Details, if necessary.

3. Drag the separator line between the panes to the desired pane size.

4. Drag the separator line between the column headings to the desired column size.

Next you will size the Details columns.

> **4.** Point to the vertical separator line between the headings *Name* and *Size* in the Contents pane.

When the pointer is directly on the separator line, the pointer becomes a double-headed arrow with a thick vertical line.

> **5.** Drag the separator line to display information as shown in Figure 4.10.

Move the separator line until the longer names in the *Name* column are cut off or ***truncated,*** such as "Buford Propo...", as shown in Figure 4.10. When Windows 2000 truncates text, such as a file name or a type description, an ellipsis (...) appears at the end of the line to indicate that the entire text passage is not displayed.

> **6.** Drag the separator line between *Name* and *Size* to the right until you remove the ellipsis from the files in the *Name* column.

The file names should display fully in the *Name* column.

> **7.** Close the Explorer window.

> **8.** Remove your **Student Data Disk** from the drive.

Keep your mouse rolling on a mouse pad. The ball can easily pick up dirt, dust, and hairs, preventing the pointer from moving smoothly on the screen.

Figure 4.10
Truncated Name and Type
descriptions

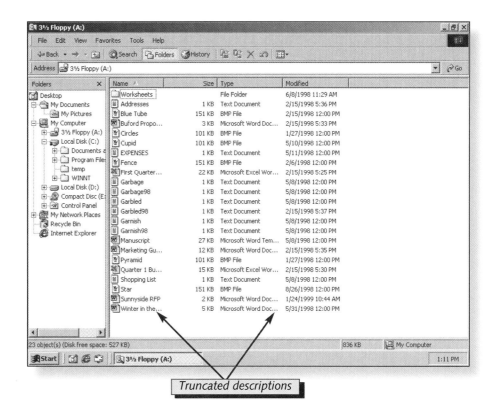

Truncated descriptions

FORMATTING DISKS

Before a disk can hold files and folders, the disk must be formatted. The *formatting* process erases any files already stored on the disk, scans the surface of the disk for errors, and then copies onto the disk information that the operating system uses to read data from and write data to the disk. This information includes the size of the disk, the number of characters that each sector can hold, and the location of each file. The method the operating system uses to control access to the disk is called the *file system.* There are several different kinds of file systems used by Windows 2000. The two most common file systems are *FAT* and *NTFS*. Old versions of DOS and the Windows 95/98 operating systems use the File Allocation Table (FAT) file system. (FAT32 is a variation of FAT that stores data more efficiently on large hard drives.) NT File System (NTFS) is a file system unique to Windows 2000.

In addition to performing the tasks of any file system, NTFS stores information more efficiently than FAT. NTFS also provides greater security for stored files. Network administrators can tightly control which users have access to individual files under NTFS. One look at the Properties dialog box lets you see the major difference between FAT and NTFS. In Figure 4.11, an NTFS disk's Properties dialog box includes tabs named Security and Quota. The FAT disk's Properties dialog box shown in Figure 4.12 does not have these tabs. Diskettes always use the FAT method.

If you try to view the contents of a diskette and you see a message telling you the disk needs to be formatted, you may have lost the data stored on the diskette. You might try using a third-party utility program to salvage the files.

Figure 4.11

NTFS hard drive Properties
dialog box

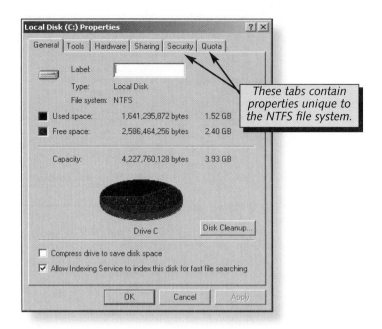

These tabs contain properties unique to the NTFS file system.

Figure 4.12

FAT 32 hard drive Properties
dialog box

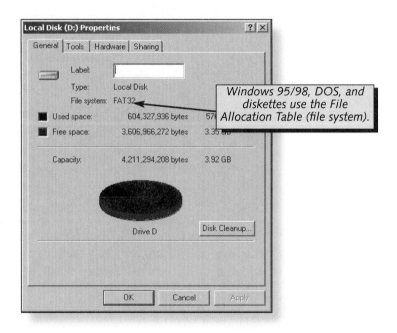

Windows 95/98, DOS, and diskettes use the File Allocation Table (file system).

The FAT contains the name of each file on the disk, as well as the size, creation date, the date the file was last modified or accessed, the type, and the location. Although you can reformat disks, they are usually formatted only once, when they are first purchased.

When you want to format a disk, click the appropriate drive in the My Computer window, and then click Format on the File menu. In the Format dialog box, you must specify the disk drive and the capacity of the disk. Both capacity types, 5.25-inch and 3.5-inch floppy disks, can be double density or high density.

 Warning   *Formatting a disk permanently erases the information on a disk. Use care when formatting a disk to make certain you don't mistakenly format a disk containing information you want to keep. Never format your hard drive!*

Formatting a Disk

In this activity, you will format a disk to use throughout this tutorial.

For this Hands On activity, you must obtain a disk that fits the drive you will use. You may use a disk that has unneeded data if you are absolutely sure you will never want the files again. Remember that when you format a disk, you erase all data on that disk.

1. Insert the floppy disk into drive A: (or drive B:).

2. Open the **My Computer icon** 🖳.

The My Computer window appears on the desktop.

3. Click the icon for the drive that contains the disk (drive A: or B:).

The icon is highlighted.

4. Click **Format** on the File menu.

The Format dialog box appears. Notice that its title bar displays the type of disk drive you have selected, as shown in Figure 4.13.

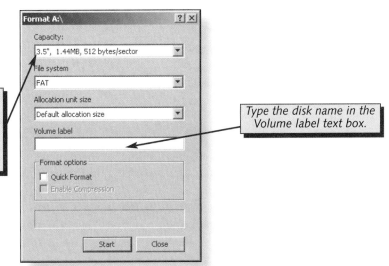

You must specify the correct capacity for the disk you are using.

Type the disk name in the Volume label text box.

Figure 4.13
The Format dialog box

5. Match the Capacity selection with the type of disk you inserted in the disk drive.

6. Uncheck the **Quick Format box**, if necessary.

You can use the Quick Format option to reformat a disk that has already been formatted. The disk is not checked for surface errors, however.

7. Click the **Volume label box**.

An insertion point appears in the text box.

8. **Type** WorkingCopy **in the text box.**

9. **Click Start.**

A warning box appears, reminding you that formatting erases all data.

10. **Click OK.**

As Windows 2000 begins the disk formatting operation, a progress bar fills from left to right at the bottom of the Format dialog box. When the bar is filled, a window appears informing you that the formatting operation is finished.

11. **Click OK.**

 *Occasionally, a disk will not format. If this happens, try to format the same disk on a different computer. If it still will not format, the disk is probably defective. Return it for a new one or throw it away.*

12. **Click Close.**

13. **Close all open windows and dialog boxes to clear the desktop.**

14. **Remove your newly formatted disk from the disk drive, and attach a disk label to the disk.**

15. **Write** Working Copy Disk **and your name on the disk label.**

CREATING FOLDERS AND SUBFOLDERS

A newly formatted disk contains no folders. Without folders, all files on the disk appear in the Contents list together. When you have many files on a disk, you will have difficulty keeping track of them without folders. Folders allow users to organize files in a meaningful way by grouping related files together.

To create a folder, you must first select the icon for the drive you want to use in the Explorer window. Then, click the New command on either the short-cut menu or on the Explorer window File menu. When the submenu appears, click the Folder option and type a name for the folder. So that you can find the files easily, always use a meaningful name that describes the files you will keep in the folder.

If you want to create a folder within a folder, you must first open the folder that will be the parent folder for the new folder. A ***parent folder*** is any folder that contains one or more folders. With a parent folder opened in the Explorer window's Folders or Contents pane, you can click New and then Folder from the Explorer window File menu, and then create the folder as previously described.

For years, PC users organized disks into *directories* and *subdirectories*, while Mac users called them *folders*. Starting with Windows 95, *folders* became the name used on both platforms.

Building Folder Structures

Creating a meaningful folder structure requires planning. The kind of structure you build depends on the way you use your computer and the number of people who share the information on the disk. The relationship of folders to subfolders is called the **disk structure.**

In an **application-oriented structure,** each program's folder contains one or more subfolders. For example, if your word processing program files are in a **Word** folder, you might create subfolders such as **Memos, Letters,** and so on, in the **Word** folder. An application-oriented structure is illustrated in Figure 4.14.

Figure 4.14
An application-oriented structure

Each program folder has subfolders.

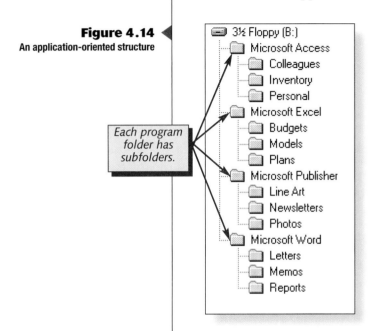

A **project-oriented structure** has separate folders for each of the tasks you do—regardless of the programs you use to create those files. For example, if you were producing a newsletter, you might collect all the stories and art for the newsletter in one folder.

When more than one person uses a computer, consider a **user-oriented structure.** Here, each user saves his or her work in a separate folder. Within each personal folder, the user can create and structure subfolders according to his or her needs.

In many cases, a combination of the three folder structures is used. For example, the subfolders within a user-oriented structure can be project- or application-oriented. Figure 4.15 shows examples of the different kinds of folder structures: project-oriented, user-oriented, and combined user-application and user-project structures.

Figure 4.15
Types of folder structures

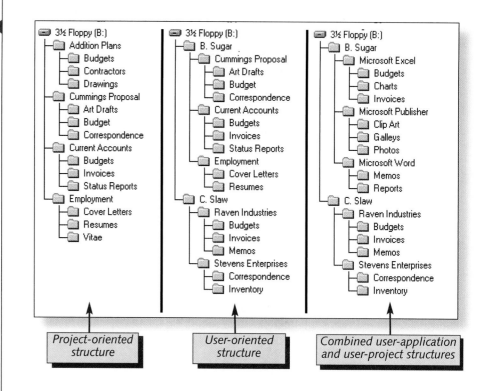

Project-oriented structure

User-oriented structure

Combined user-application and user-project structures

Creating Folders

1. Open Windows Explorer.

2. Click the device icon you will use. (Select a folder on the device icon if you are creating a subfolder.)

3. Point to New on the File menu.

4. Click Folder.

5. Type the name of the folder and press ⟦Enter⟵⟧.

Creating Folders

In this activity, you will create two folders on your newly formatted floppy disk named *Working Copy Disk*.

1. **Insert the Working Copy Disk into your disk drive.**

2. **Open and maximize Windows Explorer.**

3. **Scroll the Folders pane to the top, if necessary, and click the device icon for the disk drive that contains the floppy disk.**

The Contents pane displays nothing because the disk is empty.

4. **Click Details on the View menu, if necessary.**

5. **Point to New on the File menu.**

The New menu appears.

6. **Click Folder.**

A new folder icon labeled *New Folder* appears in the main folder on the blank disk in the selected drive, as shown in Figure 4.16. The icon label is highlighted, ready for you to type a name for the folder.

7. **Type Worksheets and press ⟦Enter⟵⟧.**

The new folder is created, named, and placed in the main folder of the disk in the specified disk drive.

Figure 4.16

The *New Folder* icon

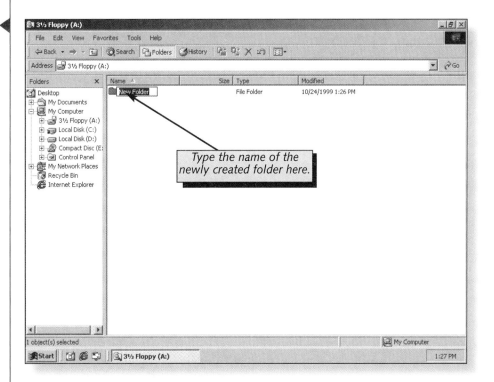

Type the name of the newly created folder here.

8. **Repeat steps 3 through 6.**

9. **Type** Documents **and press** `Enter ←┘`.

Now you have two folders, ***Documents*** and ***Worksheets***, in the main folder of your floppy disk.

Creating a Subfolder

In this activity, you will create a subfolder.

1. **In the Folders pane of the Explorer window, expand the device icon for the disk drive that holds your floppy disk.**

Icons for the two folders you created appear in the Folders pane.

2. **Click the *Documents* folder in the Folders pane.**

3. **Change to the Details view, if necessary.**

The Folders pane displays an open folder icon next to ***Documents***. On screen, there are three indicators that the ***Documents*** folder has no contents:

■ No plus or minus sign next to the Documents icon in the Folders pane

■ The empty Contents pane

■ 0 objects in the status bar

4. Right-click the **Contents pane**.

A shortcut menu appears.

5. Point to **New** and then click **Folder**.

The New Folder icon appears in the Contents pane.

6. Type Toss and press ⌈Enter⏎⌉.

The new folder is created and placed inside the ***Documents*** folder on the disk in the specified disk drive. The ***Documents*** folder now has a plus sign in the Folders pane, and the status bar says *1 object(s) selected,* as shown in Figure 4.17.

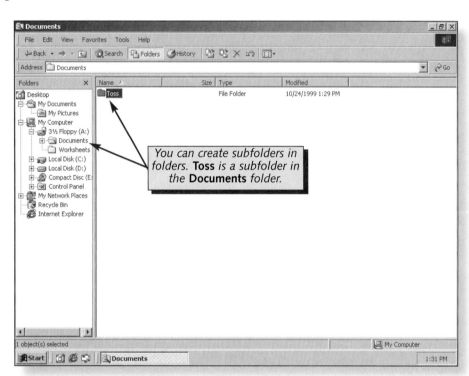

You can create subfolders in folders. **Toss** *is a subfolder in* the **Documents** *folder.*

Figure 4.17
New folder in the Explorer window

MANIPULATING FOLDERS

After you create folders, you can move, copy, delete, or rename them. Folder manipulation commands affect a folder and the subfolders and files contained in a folder.

Moving Folders

When you ***move*** a folder, Windows 2000 places the folder and all the contents in the new location and then deletes the folder and any contents from the original location. In this activity, you will learn to drag a folder from one location to another.

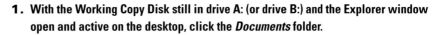

Manipulating Folders

1. Select the folder to be changed.

2. To move a folder to a new location, drag the folder.

3. To copy a folder to a new folder, drag the folder with the right mouse button to a new location and click Copy Here.

4. To rename a folder, click the folder, wait, click again, and type the new name.

5. To delete a folder, select the folder, press Delete, and click Yes.

1. With the Working Copy Disk still in drive A: (or drive B:) and the Explorer window open and active on the desktop, click the *Documents* folder.

2. Point to the *Toss* folder icon in the Contents pane.

 *Do not select the* **Toss** *folder.*

3. Drag the *Toss* folder to the *Worksheets* folder icon in the Folders pane.

4. When the *Worksheets* folder highlights, release the mouse button.

The *Toss* folder moves from the original location (the *Documents* folder) to the *Worksheets* folder. Notice that the Contents pane for the *Documents* folder is now blank.

5. Click the *Worksheets* folder icon in the Folders pane.

The folder opens, and its contents appear in the Contents pane. Notice that the *Worksheets* folder contains the *Toss* folder you just moved from the *Documents* folder.

 Be aware that you can easily "drop" an object into the wrong folder as you drag across the desktop. If that happens to you, click the toolbar's Undo button to return the dropped object to its original location and then try again.

HANDS On

Hints & Tips

When you drag a folder, don't release the mouse button until you are sure that you have selected the right destination. If the processor is busy when you drag, there may be a slight pause before the correct destination is highlighted.

Copying Folders

When you *copy* a folder, Windows 2000 duplicates that folder and its contents to the location you indicate; the original folder and contents remain where they were. In this activity, you will copy a folder from one location to another.

1. With the Working Copy Disk still in drive A: (or drive B:) and the Explorer window open, point to the *Toss* folder.

2. Drag the folder with the right mouse button to the *Documents* folder in the Folders pane.

3. Release the right mouse button.

A shortcut menu appears with options to move or copy the folder.

4. Click the **Copy Here** option.

Both the *Worksheets* and *Documents* folders have a *Toss* subfolder in them.

Deleting Folders

When you **delete** a folder from the C: drive, Windows 2000 removes the folder and the contents from the original location and places it in a holding area called the Recycle Bin, whose icon appears on your desktop. From the Recycle Bin, you can remove objects permanently from storage or restore them to their original locations. You'll learn more about the Recycle Bin in the next lesson. In this activity, you will delete a folder.

 Because any object that you delete from a floppy disk *is gone permanently, be sure you want to delete the folder or folders you intend to delete. It's not a good idea to delete folders that you have not created. Other users or application software may require these folders.*

1. **With the Working Copy Disk in its drive and the Explorer window open, click the** *Documents* **folder icon in the Folders pane.**

The folder opens and its contents appear in the Contents pane.

2. **Click the** *Toss* **folder icon in the Contents pane.**

The selected folder icon highlights.

3. **Press** `Delete`.

Since the Delete command permanently removes objects from storage, the Confirm Folder Delete dialog box appears asking "Are you sure you want to remove the folder 'Toss' and all its contents?"

4. **Click Yes or press** `Enter ←`.

The selected folder is deleted from its parent folder, **Documents**. Notice that the plus sign before the **Documents** folder in the Folders pane disappeared and the Contents pane is now empty.

If you accidentally delete a file or folder, take a deep breath, think about what you have done, and try the Undo button. If this doesn't work, ask for help. Pressing buttons and keys in a state of panic may make your mistake irreversible.

Renaming Folders

When you **rename** a folder, you change its name. The File menu's Rename command allows you to change the name of any selected icon. Alternately, you can simply click an icon's name two times (that is, click, wait, click—not a double-click), and type the new name. In this activity, you will use both of these techniques to rename a folder.

1. **Again working with the Working Copy Disk in your disk drive and the Explorer window open, click the** *Worksheets* **folder icon in the Folders pane.**

The folder opens and its contents appear in the Contents pane.

2. Click the *Toss* folder icon in the Contents pane.

The icon highlights.

3. Click **Rename** on the File menu.

The highlighted folder's name appears in a text box with a blinking insertion point.

4. Type Budgets-2000 **and press** .

The folder is renamed.

5. Point anywhere over the highlighted file name *Budgets-2000* in the Contents pane, and click the file name.

The highlighted folder's name appears in a text box with a blinking insertion point.

6. Type Budgets-2001 **and press** Enter.

7. Remove your **Working Copy Disk** from your computer.

Note   *You may explore Switching from One Explorer to Another in the On the Web section that follows, or you may proceed directly to the exercises for this lesson. If you are finished with your computing session, log off the computer you are using.*

Warning   *Follow the "log off" procedures for your lab or school environment.*

ON*the*WEB

SWITCHING FROM ONE EXPLORER TO ANOTHER

Windows 2000 has two Explorers: Windows Explorer and Internet Explorer. In this lesson, you have been working with Windows Explorer. Windows Explorer lets you locate files and folders on disks to which you are directly connected—either on the computer or on the network you are using. In Lesson 1, you saw how the Internet Explorer lets you find information located on the Internet. In later lessons, you will have other opportunities to use Internet Explorer. In this activity, you will see how easily you can launch Internet Explorer from Windows Explorer—one more example of the integration between the desktop and the Internet in Windows 2000.

You can change the left pane of Windows Explorer to display objects other than folders. Using the View menu and pointing to the Explorer Bar reveals the options Search, Favorites, History, Folders, and Tip of the Day. Thus far, you have used the Folders option to uncover the objects within your computer system in the Contents pane. You will use Search and History in later lessons. Tip of the Day displays keystroke combinations and mouse clicks that aid your use of the software. In this activity, you will use the Favorites option to switch from one Explorer to another.

1. **Open Windows Explorer, if necessary.**

2. **Click the View menu, point to Explorer Bar, and click Favorites.**

The left pane of Windows Explorer no longer displays your disk's folders, but rather the folders *Links*, *Media*, and *My Documents*, and also some Web pages, as shown in Figure 4.18.

Figure 4.18 ◄
The Favorites pane in
Windows Explorer

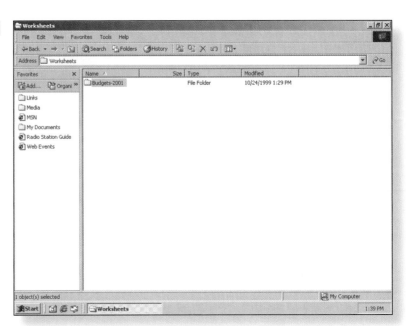

The ***Links*** and ***Media*** folders contain Web page links created when Windows 2000 was installed. The ***My Documents*** folder holds pages you (or another user of your computer) saved.

 *Some of the Web page icons in the Favorites pane may have been saved when other users explored and added objects through the Add to Favorites option.*

3. Click the MSN Web page icon.

Your computer should connect to the Internet, and the Contents pane of the Explorer window changes to display the MSN (Microsoft Network) start page, similar to the one illustrated in Figure 4.19. This page contains dozens of links.

Figure 4.19 ◀
The Contents pane showing the MSN start page

4. Type your ZIP Code in the text box and click [Enter↵].

Local weather and links to news stories in your community appear.

5. Explore sites by clicking the links on the screen. Use the Back [← Back ▾] and Forward [→ ▾] buttons to view previously visited sites.

6. Click View, point to Explorer Bar, and click Folders.

Your left pane reverts to the familiar Folders view.

7. Disconnect from the Internet, if necessary, and close the Explorer window.

8. You may proceed directly to the exercises for this lesson. If, however, you are finished with your computer session, log off the computer you are using.

 Follow the "log off" procedures for your lab or school environment.

Lesson Summary & Exercises

SUMMARY

After you complete this lesson, you should know how to do the following:

Using the Windows Explorer

■ The Windows Explorer lets you examine the contents of disks and folders on your computer.

■ Click Start, Programs, Accessories, Windows Explorer to run the Windows Explorer.

■ Click a disk and/or folder in the Folders pane to see its files and sub-folders in the Contents pane.

■ Click a folder icon's plus sign to see its subfolders; click the minus sign to hide the subfolders.

Customizing the Explorer Window

■ Select an option from the Views button to change the appearance of the Contents pane.

■ Choose the Arrange Icons option of the View menu to select the order in which objects appear in the Contents pane.

■ Click Use Windows classic folders from the Folder Options on the Tools menu to remove Web content from your Contents pane.

Window Panes

■ Drag the line separating panes to change their relative widths.

■ Drag the line separating column headings in Details view to change the column's width.

Formatting Disks

■ The formatting process erases any files already stored on a disk, scans the surface of the disk for errors, and then copies onto the disk information that the operating system uses to read data from and to write data to the disk.

■ The two most common file systems used by Windows 2000 are FAT and NTFS. The system called File Allocation Table (FAT) is used for diskettes and contains the name of each file on the disk, its size, creation date, the date the file was last modified or accessed, its type, and its location. The NT File System (NTFS), which is unique to Windows 2000, stores information more efficiently than FAT and provides greater security for stored files, especially on a network.

■ To format a disk, click the appropriate drive in the My Computer window and click Format on the File menu.

Creating Folders and Subfolders

■ A disk structure is a hierarchy of folders and subfolders organized in an efficient order.

■ With a folder selected, click File, New, Folder to create a subfolder within that folder. Type a name for the new folder and press `Enter ←`.

Manipulating Folders

■ To maintain a proper disk structure, you must be able to change the names and locations of folders.

- To move a folder, drag and drop it to a new location.
- To copy a folder, drag and drop with the right mouse button and select Copy Here.
- To remove a folder, select it and press [Delete].
- To rename a folder, click, wait, and click again. Type the new name for the folder and press [Enter←].

On the Web: Switching From One Explorer to Another

- Click the View menu, point to Explorer Bar, and click Favorites to explore the Internet from within Windows Explorer.
- Click a Web page icon to display the page in the Contents pane.

NEW TERMS TO REMEMBER

After you complete this lesson, you should know the meaning of these terms:

application-oriented structure	formatting	root directory
	main folder	separator line
copy	move	status bar
delete	NTFS	truncated
disk structure	parent folder	type
FAT	project-oriented structure	user-oriented structure
file system	rename	

MATCHING EXERCISE

Match each of the terms with the definitions on the right:

Terms

1. copy
2. delete
3. pane
4. truncate
5. format
6. main folder
7. parent folder
8. disk structure
9. status bar
10. type

Definitions

a. Process by which a new, blank disk is prepared properly for operation in a personal computer

b. Cut off the end of the name of an object when it is too long to be displayed

c. A top level folder, or root directory, on a disk

d. The category to which a file belongs

e. Operation in which data stored in a file or folder is duplicated so that the original remains and the duplicate is stored in another disk location

f. Remove an object from storage

g. A part of a window

h. The relationship of folders to subfolders

i. A folder which contains other folders

j. An area at the bottom of a window that explains selected objects or menu commands

Lesson Summary & Exercises

COMPLETION EXERCISE

Fill in the missing word or phrase for each of the following:

1. The _____ _____ is the method used to control access to a disk.

2. To view the maximum number of objects in a window without scrolling and still be able to drag them around the window, choose this view: _____.

3. The _____ in which folders on a disk are organized varies from system to system, depending on a user's preferences.

4. One way to move a file or folder from one disk location to another is to _____ the object's _____.

5. The root of the entire Windows filing system is the _____ .

6. The _____ _____ _____ is a strip of tool buttons just below the menu bar.

7. To expand a collapsed folder in the Explorer's Folders pane, click the _____ _____ .

8. The Explorer window's _____ pane displays the folders and files stored in the active or open folder.

9. The _____ view option displays the name, size, type, and date of each object in the Contents pane.

10. To _____ a file or folder, click the file or folder, wait, click again, and then type the new name.

SHORT-ANSWER QUESTIONS

Write a brief answer to each of the following questions:

1. Suppose your projects involve creating documents from a variety of data types—such as text, graphics, and numeric calculations. Which type of folder structure would likely work best for organizing your work? Why?

2. List and describe briefly what occurs when you format a disk.

3. What is the best thing to do with a disk that does not format properly?

4. Differentiate among these five view options: large icons, small icons, list, details, and thumbnail. Explain when each view option might be useful.

5. Discuss briefly the various ways in which you can customize the Explorer window.

6. What are the steps to delete a folder?

7. What are the steps to move a folder?

8. What are the steps to copy a folder?

9. What steps do you follow to rename a folder?

10. What are the steps to change the width of the Explorer window's Folder pane?

Lesson Summary & Exercises

APPLICATION PROJECTS

Perform the following actions to complete these projects:

1. Format several disks and save them for your future use. Be sure to select the proper disk capacity and type of format options and place a label on each disk.

2. Open your Explorer window and modify its appearance so that it looks similar to the Explorer window shown in Figure 4.20. Then make any adjustments you desire to customize its appearance to suit your needs.

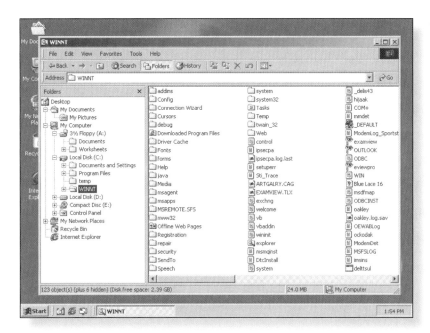

Figure 4.20
The customized Explorer window

3. Create a set of parent folders on a floppy disk and then create some folders within them. Practice the various operations available for manipulating the folders: copy, move, rename, and delete. Practice using both the mouse and the appropriate Edit menu commands to accomplish the move and copy tasks.

4. On a blank, formatted disk, create an application-oriented folder structure that a small business might use. Begin by creating a set of new folders and name them accordingly. A small business might use a word processing application for letters and reports, a spreadsheet application to prepare budgets and cost analyses, and a database application to maintain ledgers and payroll.

5. On the disk you used for Application Project 4, create a user-oriented folder structure. You can set up the structure for yourself only or for several users. Create and name the folders accordingly.

6. You must be able to connect to the Internet to complete this On the Web project. Start Windows Explorer, change the left pane to Favorites, and view the MSN start page. Click the Change Content tab on the MSN start page to change your Explorer window view. Follow the on-screen directions to personalize your view. Experiment with various options. When finished, disconnect from the Internet, if necessary.

Managing Your Files

CONTENTS

OBJECTIVES

After you complete this lesson, you will be able to do the following:

- Understand why you must manage disk storage.
- Recognize the names and types of files contained within folders.
- Recognize file types and their icons in Windows Explorer.
- Copy one or more files into a different folder or drive.
- Move files from one folder to another.
- Delete files from a disk.
- Rename files.
- Search for files by name, date, size, and location.
- Use a search engine to find information on the Internet.

Creating, copying, moving, editing, and deleting files are all part of managing information so that you can work productively. Duplicating important files is essential to safe computing. You or another user may accidentally delete or destroy information stored in a single location on the computer you are using. You can store duplicate disks away from your computer in case something happens to the original files stored on the hard drive.

File organization begins with the creation of a disk structure. In Lesson 4, you learned how to manipulate folders within a disk structure. Now you will learn how to create and manipulate files within those folders.

MANAGING FILES

File management is the process of organizing and caring for your disks and files. It involves much more than just creating files or deleting the ones you don't need. You may want to share a letter or picture you create with a friend or colleague. You may accidentally delete or destroy information stored in a single location. When you know how to copy files, you can easily duplicate the contents of a file onto another disk or into another folder. Copying lets you ***back up*** or duplicate files onto floppy disks or other storage media. You can store the ***backup*** disks away from your computer in case something happens to the original files stored on the hard drive. You can also rename and move files on disk. You can accomplish all of these file management tasks—delete, copy, rename, and move—with the keyboard or the mouse. You can manage files individually or in groups. Search methods help you locate files stored on your computer. You will master all of these techniques in the exercises in this lesson, using the Windows Explorer.

Many of the exercises in this lesson can also be done in the My Computer window, but the Explorer window is more convenient because you can work with multiple disks and folders in the same window.

CREATING FILES

Storing data properly means placing information on the correct disk drive so that you can find it later. To store information efficiently, in the form of files, you tell the operating system:

- On which *drive* to store the file
- In which *folder* to put the file
- By what *name* to identify the file
- By what *type* to create the file

File Names

File names consist of two primary parts: the ***file name,*** which is a descriptive name that a user assigns to a data file, and an optional ***extension*** that follows the file name and specifies the type of data stored in the file. In the Windows 2000 environment, file names follow two sets of rules.

MS-DOS File Names

Files created within the MS-DOS operating system are named according to the following rules, known as ***file-naming conventions:***

- The file name must contain at least one character but no more than eight characters.
- A period or *dot* separates the file name and the extension.
- The optional extension may have from one to three characters.

■ Valid characters for the file name and extension are letters of the alphabet (A-Z), digits (0-9), and the following punctuation symbols:

$	Dollar sign		^	Circumflex or caret
_	Underscore		#	Pound sign
-	Hyphen		%	Percent sign
!	Exclamation point		&	Ampersand
{}	Braces		~	Tilde
()	Parentheses			

■ Invalid characters include the following symbols:

	Space character		:	Colon
\	Backslash		+	Plus sign
/	Slash		=	Equal sign
<	Less-than sign		;	Semicolon
>	Greater-than sign		,	Comma
|	Pipe		?	Question mark
"	Quotation mark		*	Asterisk
[ ]	Square brackets		.	Period

■ The extensions .EXE, .COM, .BAT, and .SYS are reserved for program files and files that contain instructions for operating system commands.

■ File names can be entered with either uppercase or lowercase letters. Thus, **LETTER1.DOC** is the same file as **Letter1.doc** or **letter1.doc**; the MS-DOS operating system converts all file names to uppercase characters.

The limitations on the length of and type of characters in file names force users to be creative when naming files. A memo written to J. Smith concerning a billing error, for instance, might be stored in a file named **SMITHERR.MEM.**

Windows 2000 File Names

The Windows 2000 operating system provides much more descriptive freedom. File names can be up to 255 characters long, with spaces, and with more than one period. Only these nine characters are prohibited:

\	Backslash		|	Pipe
/	Slash		"	Quotation mark
<	Less-than sign		*	Asterisk
>	Greater-than sign		?	Question mark
:	Colon			

File extensions are still used, but they are not always displayed. Rather, the software that creates the file automatically assigns an extension. While Windows 2000 supports both old and new file-naming standards, not all versions of application software support both. Therefore, you must follow the old rules for MS-DOS file names when you are working with applications developed and released before the release of the Windows 95 operating system—or if you share files with someone whose system uses MS-DOS.

HANDS

Windows
BASICS

Creating and Saving Files

1. Start your application.

2. Enter the data.

3. Select Save As from the File menu.

4. Choose the location for the file.

5. Enter the file name.

Making a File

Remember that the three basic kinds of files are system files, program files, and document files. Unless you are a programmer, the files that you create are document files, the work that you do using a particular program.

The Notepad is a ***desktop accessory,*** a small program built into Windows 2000. Notepad allows you to create or view short, unformatted text documents. In this activity, you will create a Notepad file and save the file to your Working Copy Disk.

1. If necessary, log on to your system.

2. Insert your Working Copy Disk into the floppy disk drive.

3. Click the Start button and point to Programs and then Accessories.

4. Click Notepad.

Figure 5.1 shows how to get to the desktop accessory, Notepad.

Figure 5.1 ◀
Opening Notepad

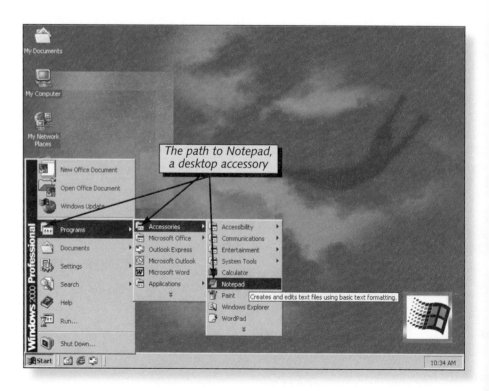

The Notepad program opens to display a window like the one shown in Figure 5.2.

Figure 5.2
The Notepad window with an
unsaved document

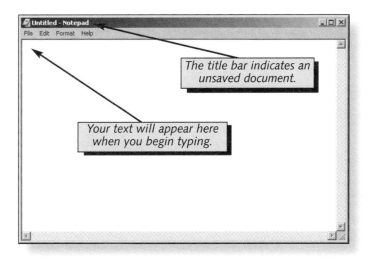

The title bar indicates an unsaved document.

Your text will appear here when you begin typing.

The title bar says *Untitled - Notepad*. The word *Untitled* indicates that the document in this window is unsaved; the document exists in the computer's memory but its file has not been stored. The ***insertion point*** (blinking vertical line) in the document window shows where the next text you type will appear.

Do not assign your own extensions to files if you want Windows 2000 to recognize the program that created the file. Instead, let the software assign its own extension when you save the file.

5. **Type the following sentences:**

> Remember to pick up bread on the way home.
> I have a dentist appointment on Tuesday at 4:40 p.m.
> Set the VCR to record at 11:30 p.m. on Channel 6.

The text you type appears in the Notepad document window.

6. **Click Save As on the File menu.**

The Save As dialog box appears for you to provide the information Windows 2000 needs to save your file: the location and name of the file. Figure 5.3 identifies the dialog box areas in which you provide this information.

7. **Click the triangle button to the right of the Save In text box.**

Figure 5.3
The Save As dialog box

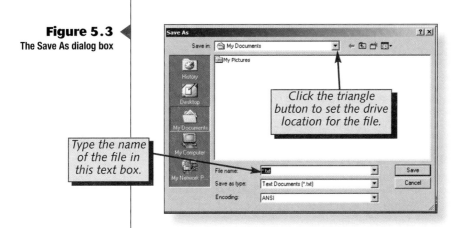

Click the triangle button to set the drive location for the file.

Type the name of the file in this text box.

A drop-down list of the storage devices attached to your computer appears. The Save In box allows you to set the drive location for the file you want to save.

8. Click the icon of the floppy drive that holds your Working Copy Disk.

The drive location appears in the Save In text box. The ***Documents*** and ***Worksheets*** folders (and possibly others) that you created appear in the Contents box immediately below the Save In text box.

9. Double-click the *Documents* folder.

The ***Documents*** folder appears in the Save In text box. If you were to save the file now, Windows 2000 would place the file in the ***Documents*** folder of your floppy disk.

10. Click the triangle button to the right of the Save In text box.

A menu, such as the one shown in Figure 5.4, drops down. This menu shows the file organization of the selected Save In location.

Figure 5.4 ◄
The Save In drop-down list

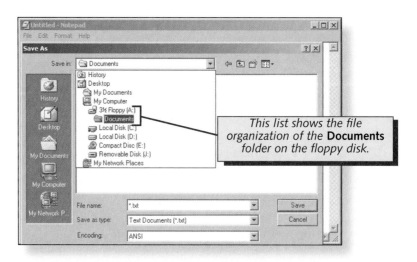

*This list shows the file organization of the **Documents** folder on the floppy disk.*

11. Click outside the menu to close it without making a choice.

12. Press ⌨Tab three times, first to move to the Folders area, then the Contents box, and finally to move to the File Name text box.

The text in the File Name box highlights, ready for you to enter a new name.

13. Type My Note in the File Name box.

My Note replaces **.txt* in the File Name box.

14. Click the Save button.

Windows 2000 saves the ***My Note*** document into the ***Documents*** folder on your floppy disk. The dialog box closes, and the Notepad title bar changes to say *My Note - Notepad*.

Press ⌨Tab to move from one option box to another in nearly every dialog box in Windows 2000. Or, you may use the mouse to place the pointer in the option box in which you want to type.

Right-click the Start button to display a shortcut menu. Click Explore to open the Windows Explorer.

15. Close the Notepad window.

16. Open the **Windows Explorer** and click the *Documents* folder on your floppy disk.

17. Verify that the Contents view is set to **Details**.

Your Explorer window should resemble Figure 5.5. The Folders pane shows the organization of your disk with the addition of your saved file. The Contents pane shows the name, size, type, and modification date of your newly saved file.

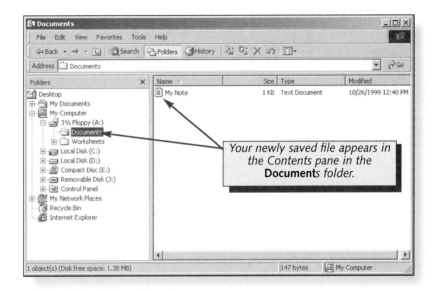

Figure 5.5
The Explorer window

18. Close the Explorer window.

19. Remove your **Working Copy Disk** from the disk drive.

WORKING WITH FILE TYPES

At the bottom of Figure 5.4 on page 122, the Save As dialog box option shows the Save As Type option. File type is a functional category—such as text document file, bitmapped image, document application file, or system file. Every file on your system has a file type. Windows 2000 recognizes dozens of file types when the operating system is first installed. As application software is added to the system, additional file types are created.

Viewing File Types

In this activity, you will examine the types of files on your Student Data Disk.

1. Insert your **Student Data Disk** into the floppy disk drive.

2. Open the **Windows Explorer** and maximize the window, if necessary.

3. In the Folders pane, click the icon of your floppy drive to display the contents in the Contents pane.

Viewing File Types

1. Open Windows Explorer.

2. Click the icon of the drive you want to view.

3. Set Contents view to Details.

4. View details of each file.

4. Verify that the Contents view is set to **Details**.

5. Drag to enlarge the Name heading until you can see all of the file names in their entirety.

6. Click the **Type heading**.

Notice how similar type files are grouped together in alphabetical order. When you click the Type heading in the Contents pane of the Explorer window, you organize the contents by type. Your Student Data Disk contains six different kinds of objects.

COPYING FILES

The same techniques that you used to copy *folders* in Lesson 4 apply to copying *files*:

■ Dragging a file or folder from one disk to another disk copies that object.

■ Using the right mouse button to drag a file or folder from one folder to another folder on the same disk copies that object.

You may also use a third method to copy folders and files that was not covered in Lesson 4—Copy and Paste. In this method, you select the file you want to copy, choose the Copy command, select the folder in which you want to place the file, and choose the Paste command. Both the Copy and Paste commands can be found in the Edit menu of the Explorer window.

HANDS On

Copying Files

Copy and paste method:

1. In Windows Explorer, select the file or files to be copied.

2. Click Copy from the Edit menu.

3. Select the destination folder.

4. Click Paste from the Edit menu.

Copying a File

In this activity, you will use the Copy and Paste commands to duplicate a file into another folder.

1. With the Windows Explorer active and maximized and your Student Data Disk in the floppy disk drive, open the icon for the floppy disk.

2. Select the *First Quarter Budget* file.

3. On the Edit menu, click the **Copy command**.

Nothing seems to happen! Actually, information about the file has been copied into memory—waiting for you to Paste into another location.

4. Expand the floppy drive icon to display the folders.

5. Click the *Worksheets* folder in the Folders pane.

6. On the Edit menu, click the **Paste command**.

Within a few moments, the *First Quarter Budget* file is added to the Contents pane of the *Worksheets* folder.

HANDS

Windows
BASICS

Copying Files

Copy to: button method:

1. In Windows Explorer, select the file or files to be copied.

2. Click the Copy to: button.

3. Select the destination folder.

4. Click OK.

Copying Identically Named Files

Thus far, you have copied folders and files from one disk or folder to another. If you want two copies of a file in the same folder, the copy must have a different name. In this activity, you will see what happens when you copy a file into a folder that already contains a file with that name.

1. Maximize the Windows Explorer, displaying your Student Data Disk in Details view, with the root folder selected.

2. Select the *First Quarter Budget* file.

3. Click the **Copy to: button** [image] on the toolbar.

The Browse For Folder window appears, as shown in Figure 5.6. In this window, you select the folder into which you want to copy the file.

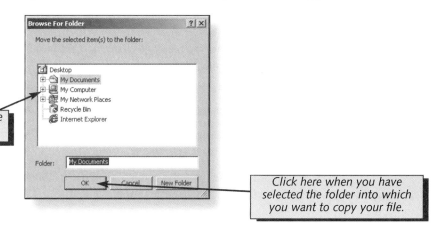

Click here to display the storage devices available to you.

Figure 5.6 ◄
The Browse For Folder window

Click here when you have selected the folder into which you want to copy your file.

4. Click the **plus sign** beside My Computer.

Your computer's storage device icons appear.

5. Expand the drive icon for your floppy disk.

6. Click the *Worksheets* folder.

7. Click **OK**.

The Confirm File Replace dialog box appears, as shown in Figure 5.7. The sizes and creation dates of the files are displayed in the dialog box to help you decide whether to replace the file. If you click Yes, the existing file is erased and replaced with the one you selected.

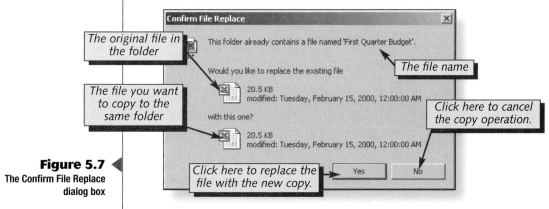

The original file in the folder

The file you want to copy to the same folder

The file name

Click here to cancel the copy operation.

Figure 5.7 ◄
The Confirm File Replace dialog box

Click here to replace the file with the new copy.

8. Click **No**.

Selecting Multiple Objects

Often you may want to manipulate a group of files at the same time. When you want to copy, move, or otherwise handle several files, you select them as a group, and then manipulate them all together. The following mouse and keyboard techniques let you select more than one file at a time.

Windows 2000 lets you create keyboard substitutions for mouse actions. See Appendix B for specific information.

- To select consecutive files, click the first file, hold down `⇧ Shift`, and then click the last file in the list. You will select all the files between the first and last files.

- To select noncontiguous files, click the first file, hold down `Ctrl`, and then click each of the files you want. You will select only the files you click.

Copying Multiple Files

In this activity, you will select and copy a group of files.

1. **Make sure the Windows Explorer is maximized, displaying the Student Data Disk in Details view.**

2. **Select the root folder of the floppy drive, if necessary.**

3. **Click the file name *Buford Proposal*.**

4. **Press and hold `⇧ Shift`, click the file name *Manuscript*, and then release `⇧ Shift` and the mouse button.**

All consecutively listed files from ***Buford Proposal*** through ***Manuscript*** are selected, as shown in Figure 5.8.

Copying Files

Right-click and drag method:

1. In Windows Explorer, select the file or files to be copied.

2. Right-click and drag to the destination folder.

3. Release the mouse button and select Copy Here.

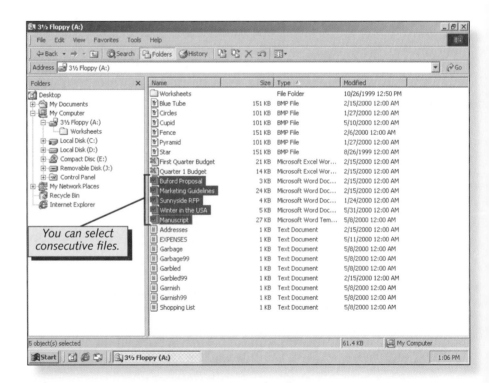

You can select consecutive files.

Figure 5.8
Consecutively highlighted files

5. **Click anywhere in the Contents pane to deselect the files.**

6. **Click the file *Buford Proposal*.**

You know two dragging techniques for copying folders and files—right-click dragging and holding [Ctrl] while dragging with the left mouse button. Right-click dragging is safer, since you can confirm your intentions after you drag on the shortcut menu. If you use [Ctrl] and the left mouse button, be sure to release the button before you release [Ctrl]. Otherwise, you will move the file, not copy the file—if you are trying to copy the file to another location *on the same disk*.

7. Press [Ctrl], select the file name *Sunnyside RFP*, then release [Ctrl].

The two noncontiguous files—***Buford Proposal*** and ***Sunnyside RFP***—are selected.

 *When selecting noncontiguous files, click the first file without [Ctrl], then hold down [Ctrl] and click to select the additional files.*

8. Click anywhere in the Contents pane to deselect the files.
9. Select this group of files: *Buford Proposal, Manuscript, Marketing Guidelines, Sunnyside RFP,* and *Winter in the USA.*
10. Point to one of the selected files.
11. Press and hold [Ctrl] and drag the group of selected files to the *Worksheets* folder in the Contents pane.

The pointer becomes an Object Copy pointer, ready to copy the selected files.

12. Release the mouse button; then release [Ctrl].

The Copying dialog box appears as the selected files copy to the *Worksheets* folder on the Student Data Disk. Each copy will have the same name as the original file on the Student Data Disk's main folder.

Note *If you did not see the Copying dialog box, you may not have held down [Ctrl] as you dragged. Or, you may have released [Ctrl] before you released the mouse button. Click Undo Move on the Edit menu and try again.*

13. Double-click the *Worksheets* folder in the Contents pane.

The Contents pane displays these five copied file names: ***Buford Proposal, Manuscript, Marketing Guidelines, Sunnyside RFP,*** and ***Winter in the USA***, in addition to the worksheet files that were already present.

MOVING FILES

When you move files on a disk, you aren't moving the contents of the file. You are changing only the location of the file as maintained by the filing system.

Sometimes you will want to move a file from one folder to another. For example, when you have a folder for current projects and another for recently completed projects, you may want to move files you have finished working with into the completed projects folder. You may also want to move files that you rarely use to a floppy disk so they don't occupy valuable hard disk space.

The methods used to move files are similar to those you learned when copying files. You can use the Cut and Paste commands from the Edit menu or the Move to: button [image] on the toolbar to remove a file from its current folder and place it in another folder. Alternatively, you can drag the file from one folder to another, *without* holding down [Ctrl].

Moving Files

Click and drag method:

1. In Windows Explorer, select the file or files to be moved.

2. Drag to the destination folder.

Cut and paste method:

1. In Windows Explorer, select the file or files to be moved.

2. Click Cut from the Edit menu.

3. Select the destination folder.

4. Click Paste from the Edit menu.

Move to: button method:

1. In Windows Explorer, select the file or files to be moved.

2. Click the Move to: button.

3. Select the destination folder.

4. Click OK.

Moving Files in the Explorer Window

In this activity, you will move a file from the root folder to another folder on the same disk. Then, you will move a file from a subfolder to the root folder of a disk.

1. With your Student Data Disk still in the floppy disk drive and the Explorer window open and maximized, select the *Worksheets* folder, if necessary.

The floppy disk has two levels, the root folder level and the ***Worksheets*** folder level.

2. Click the Up One Level button 🖻 on the toolbar.

The Up One Level button takes you from the current folder (the ***Worksheets*** folder) to its parent folder (the root folder). The root folder level is now selected. The Contents pane displays the contents of the root folder on the Student Data Disk.

3. Drag the *Addresses* file into the *Worksheets* folder icon in the Contents pane.

The selected file moves into the ***Worksheets*** folder on your Student Data Disk.

4. Select the *Worksheets* folder in the Folders pane.

Notice that the Contents pane displays the ***Addresses*** file.

5. Click the Up One Level button 🖻 on the toolbar.

Notice that the file name ***Addresses*** no longer appears in the main folder on the Student Data Disk.

6. Select the *Worksheets* folder in the Folders pane.

The contents of the selected folder appear in the Contents pane.

7. Point to the *Addresses* file.

8. Drag the file onto the icon for the floppy disk drive that contains your Student Data Disk. Release the mouse button when the drive icon highlights.

The file is moved from the ***Worksheets*** folder to the root folder of the Student Data Disk.

9. Select the icon for the drive that contains your Student Data Disk.

The contents of the root folder appear in the Contents pane. Notice that the *Addresses* file appears in the list.

 *When you drag a file from one disk to another, the files are copied, even if you don't hold* Ctrl *. If you want to move the file instead, right-click and drag. When you release the mouse button, choose the Move Here option.*

DELETING FILES

Files that you no longer need can quickly fill up even the largest hard disk drive, so you should delete files from time to time. Deleting a file removes the data from the disk. If you find that you have accidentally deleted a file you need, you may be able to recover the deleted file if you act soon after you deleted it. You will learn how to restore deleted files later in this lesson.

You may safely delete a file you named and created, after the file has served its purpose, with little concern. However, files placed on the hard drive during the software installation process are often critical to the operation of the software. A good rule to follow is to avoid removing any files in a program folder whose name or function you do not recognize. To remove the program itself, use either the program's uninstall feature (if available) or the Add/Remove Programs program in the Windows *Control Panel* folder.

 Before you delete a software program, scan its folder to make sure you have stored no personal work there. Develop the habit of storing no personal files in an application folder.

When you want to delete a file from a folder, select the file and press Delete . A warning box appears, as shown in Figure 5.9, asking you to confirm that you want to remove the file from the disk.

Click Select All on the Edit menu to select all the files in the active folder. The Invert Selection option de-selects any files you have selected and selects all the others; that is, it reverses the highlighting in the Contents area of the Explorer window.

Figure 5.9
Confirm File Delete dialog box

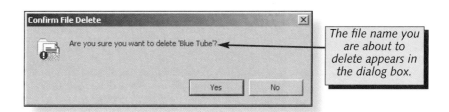

The file name you are about to delete appears in the dialog box.

Windows
BASICS

Deleting Files

1. Select the file or files to be deleted.

2. Press Delete.

3. Click Yes.

Hints & Tips

Deleting Multiple Files

In this activity, you will select multiple files in the Contents pane and delete them.

1. **With the Student Data Disk still in the drive and the Explorer window open, click the device icon for the floppy drive, if necessary.**

2. **Click the file name *Shopping List* in the Contents pane.**

3. **While pressing** Ctrl, **click the file name *First Quarter Budget*, then release** Ctrl.

The two files—***Shopping List*** and ***First Quarter Budget***—are selected.

When selecting nonconsecutive files, click the first file without Ctrl, *then hold down* Ctrl *and click to select the additional files.*

4. **Press** Delete.

The Confirm Multiple File Delete dialog box appears asking whether you want to delete these two items.

5. **Click Yes.**

The selected files are deleted from your floppy disk.

RESTORING DELETED FILES

When you delete a file from a floppy disk, it is immediately removed from storage. When you delete a file from a hard disk, however, the file icon is placed in the Recycle Bin, but the file itself remains in storage.

The Recycle Bin icon on the desktop resembles a wastebasket. When the Recycle Bin is empty, the wastebasket appears empty. When you delete items to the Recycle Bin, however, its icon appears to be full of pieces of paper. (This tells you the Recycle Bin is not empty!) To restore an item from the Recycle Bin, you open the Recycle Bin, as shown in Figure 5.10, click the item, and click Restore on the File menu.

Figure 5.10 ◄
The Recycle Bin window

To permanently clear all the contents of the Recycle Bin, click the Empty Recycle Bin command on the File menu. Check your Recycle Bin's contents periodically, especially any time you discover that your available hard disk space is getting low. Deleted files occupy disk space while they are stored in the Recycle Bin, so removing them from the Recycle Bin will free up hard disk space.

Checking Recycle Bin Settings

In this activity, you will verify that your Recycle Bin is configured to hold deleted files.

1. In the Folders pane, right-click **Recycle Bin** and click **Properties**.

This dialog box lets you control whether deleted files are placed in the Recycle Bin from all drives.

2. Click the **Global tab**, if necessary.

3. Click the **Use one setting for all drives button**.

4. Uncheck the **Do not move files to the Recycle Bin** and check the **Display delete confirmation box**, if necessary.

5. Click **OK**.

Checking Recycle Bin Settings

1. Right-click the Recycle Bin and click Properties.

2. Adjust settings as required.

Restoring a Deleted File

In this activity, you will copy a file to the C: drive, delete the file, and restore the file.

1. With the Student Data Disk still in the drive and the Explorer window open, select the root folder of the floppy drive.

2. Drag the *Pyramid* file from your Student Data Disk to the root folder of drive C:.

The file is copied, not moved, even though you didn't hold Ctrl when you dragged. When you drag from one *disk* to another, files are automatically copied.

3. Click **C:** in the Folders pane and locate *Pyramid* in the Contents pane.

4. Click *Pyramid* in the Contents pane and press Delete.

The Confirm File Delete dialog box appears asking "Are you sure you want to send 'Pyramid' to the Recycle Bin?"

5. Click **Yes**.

Restoring a Deleted File

1. Double-click the Recycle Bin icon.

2. Select the folders or files you want to restore.

3. Click the File menu and click Restore.

6. Click the **Show Desktop icon**  on the taskbar.

When your desktop appears, notice that the Recycle Bin icon now has papers in the wastebasket.

7. Double-click the **Recycle Bin icon**.

The Recycle Bin's contents appear in a window. Notice that the Recycle Bin contains *Pyramid*.

> *Note*   If additional files appear in the Recycle Bin window, other files have been deleted. You may need to scroll to find the **Pyramid** file.

8. Click the file *Pyramid*.

9. Click **Restore** on the File menu.

The file disappears from the Recycle Bin window.

10. Close the Recycle Bin window.

11. Click the **Local Disk (C:) taskbar button**.

The Explorer window appears and the *Pyramid* file appears in the Explorer window of the root folder of drive C:.

12. Select the *Pyramid* file in the Contents pane.

13. Hold down ⇧ Shift and press Delete.

The Confirm File Delete dialog box appears.

14. Click **Yes**.

The file is no longer on drive C:.

15. Click the **Show Desktop icon** on the taskbar.

16. Double-click the **Recycle Bin icon**.

17. Verify that the *Pyramid* file is not in the Recycle Bin.

> *Warning*   When you hold down ⇧ Shift and press Delete, *the file is* not *placed in the Recycle Bin. The file is instead permanently deleted.*

18. Close the Recycle Bin window.

RENAMING FILES

If you want to change the name of a file, do so with the Rename command or change the name of the file directly in the Explorer window. As with deleting and removing files, you must use caution. You should only rename those files you created, since program files have specific meaning to the software that uses them.

Renaming a file involves two separate, single-click mouse actions. First, you select the file whose name you wish to change. Then you click the file name again. When you do this, the highlighted file name appears in a text box along with the insertion point. If you now type a new file name, the new name completely replaces the old name. Alternatively, you can press → or ← to move the insertion point to a specific character in the file name and make minor changes to the file name without replacing the entire name. Table 5.1 lists the keystrokes you can use to move the insertion point for editing (renaming) a file name.

Table 5.1	Moving the Insertion Point
KEY	**PURPOSE**
←	Moves the insertion point one space to the left
→	Moves the insertion point one space to the right
Home	Moves the insertion point to the left of the first character
End	Moves the insertion point to the right of the last character
Ctrl + ←	Moves the insertion point to the beginning of the previous word
Ctrl + →	Moves the insertion point to the beginning of the next word
Delete	Removes the character to the right of the insertion point
Backspace	Removes the character to the left of the insertion point
Ctrl + Delete	Removes all characters to the right of the insertion point

Renaming a File in the Explorer Window

In this activity, you will select and rename a file.

1. **Display the contents of the root folder of your Student Data Disk in the Contents pane of the Explorer window.**

2. Click the file name *Circles*.

The name will be highlighted.

3. Click the highlighted file name *Circles* a second time.

A box now surrounds the file name, which appears highlighted, as shown in Figure 5.11. Notice that a blinking insertion point appears at the end of the name of the file.

Figure 5.11
The highlighted file name

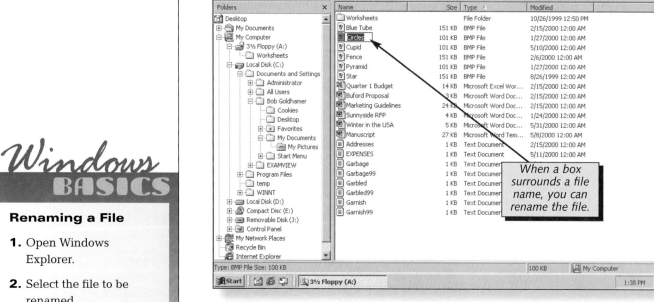

Renaming a File

1. Open Windows Explorer.

2. Select the file to be renamed.

3. Click the file a second time *or* select Rename from the File menu.

4. Edit the existing name or type a new name.

5. Press .

 Warning *Click, wait, click is not the same command sequence as a double-click. If you double-click **Circles**, the Paint program associated with this graphics file will open. Click Exit on the File menu to close both the document and the application that created it.*

4. Type Color Rings **and press** **.**

The file name is changed. Notice that the file name remains selected.

Note *If file extensions are not hidden on the View tab of the Folder Options dialog box, you will see the file as **Circles.BMP**. In this case, you must type the same extension when you rename the file (**Color Rings.BMP**). If the extensions are hidden, Windows 2000 will add the extension automatically.*

Renaming a File with the Rename Command

Some people prefer to use the Rename command to rename a file instead of accidentally double-clicking and opening an application. In this activity, you will use the Rename command on the File menu to change a file name.

1. **Display the contents of the root folder of your Student Data Disk in the Contents pane of the Explorer window.**
2. **Click the file name *Winter in the USA*.**
3. **Click the File menu in the Explorer window.**
4. **Click Rename.**

A box surrounds the highlighted file name.

5. **Type Poem and press Enter.**

The file name is changed.

SEARCHING FOR FILES

Disk drives may contain thousands of files in dozens of folders. Additionally, many computers have more than one disk drive and each drive can be divided into one or more partitions. A ***partition*** is a portion of a disk drive that has its own drive letter. Finding a file can be a tedious process if you cannot remember the name of the file, the folder in which it is located, or the disk drive on which it is stored. Fortunately, you can search for files using Windows Explorer. The more you know about the name, folder, date, size, or type of file, the easier it is to locate the file. Even if you know none of this information, you can locate a file if you can specify some of the text that the file contains. In this section, you will use the Search option of the Explorer Bar to locate files on your computer.

Searching Based on Name and Location

When you select the Search option of the Explorer Bar, the Windows Explorer left pane changes, as shown in Figure 5.12. The Search for Files and Folders pane shows text boxes, buttons, and drop-down lists that aid you in your hunt for missing files. You can initiate a search by entering all or part of the file name for which you are looking and the drives and/or folders to be searched.

By default, the search begins at the specified drive's root folder and continues to search the drive's subfolders.

HANDS On

Searching for a File

1. Open Windows Explorer.

2. Click View, point to Explorer Bar, and click Search.

3. Select the drive(s) in which to search from the *Look in:* drop-down list.

4. Type as much of the file name as you know in the appropriate text box. If necessary, click appropriate check boxes in the Search Options area to further identify your missing file.

5. Click Search Now.

Finding Files by Name and Location

In this activity, you will find files by typing only a part of the file name.

1. **Display the contents of the root folder on your Student Data Disk in the Contents pane of the Explorer window.**

2. **Point to Explorer Bar on the View menu and click Search.**

There are two other ways to change the left pane of the Explorer window. Depending on the current Explorer Bar option, you will see other choices on the Standard Buttons toolbar. You can also use Ctrl *+ E for Search or* Ctrl *+ I for Favorites.*

The Search for Files and Folders pane opens, as shown in Figure 5.12. Your floppy disk drive appears in the *Look in:* box.

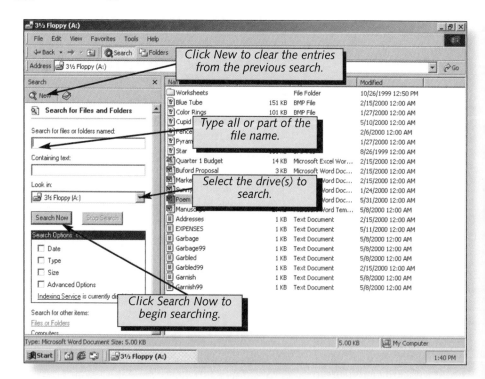

Figure 5.12
The Search for Files and Folders pane of the Explorer window

3. **Type gar in the *Search for files or folders named:* text box.**

4. **Click Search Now.**

Windows Explorer searches for all files and folders in the selected location that have the characters *gar* anywhere in their name. The Contents pane shows the results of the search—in this case, six files.

5. **Click New** New .

The text box and the Contents pane clear, and you are ready to search for another file.

Choosing to Exclude Subfolders from the Search

When subfolders are included in a search, the process can take a long time or produce numerous matching files. In this activity, you will limit your search to a single folder.

1. **Open the Search for Files and Folders pane.**

2. **Click the Look in: box triangle button and select your floppy disk drive letter, if necessary.**

3. **Select the root folder of your floppy disk drive. (If the *Worksheets* folder is selected, click the Up One Level toolbar button.)**

4. **Type *budget* in the *Search for files or folders named:* text box.**

5. **Click Search Now.**

Four files appear in the Contents pane—one from the root folder and three from the *Worksheets* subfolder.

6. **Click the Advanced Options check box.**

Additional search options appear, as shown in Figure 5.13.

Figure 5.13 ◀
Advanced search options

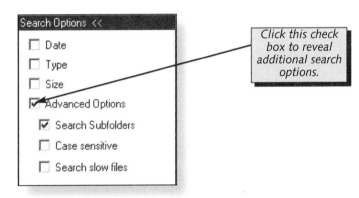

7. **Click the Search Subfolders check box to deselect it.**

8. **Click Search Now.**

This time only one file appears in the Contents pane—the file containing the word *budget* in the root folder, not the three files in the subfolder.

9. **Click New $\boxed{\text{α New}}$ to clear the text box and the Advanced Options check box.**

Searching by Date

Even if you remember nothing of the name, location, or contents of a file, Windows Explorer can find the file if you remember when you created or last used the file. Clicking the Date check box in the Search for Files and Folders pane displays the options shown in Figure 5.14.

You can also access the Search pane by clicking Start, Search, For Files and Folders.

When you use meaningful file names and well-designed folder structures, you minimize the number of times you have to search for a missing file.

Figure 5.14

Date check box options

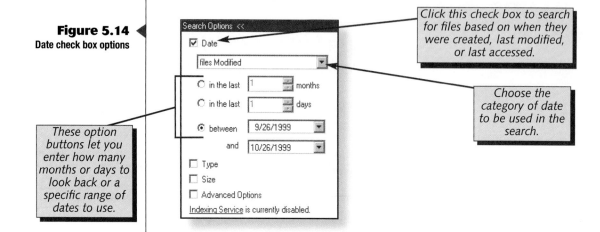

Click this check box to search for files based on when they were created, last modified, or last accessed.

Choose the category of date to be used in the search.

These option buttons let you enter how many months or days to look back or a specific range of dates to use.

The file system maintains several dates regarding each file—the date the file was created, the date the file was last modified (or saved) and the date the file was last accessed (or viewed). The Date check box section has a drop-down list box that lets you choose which of these dates you want to use. By default, the modified date is selected. You can choose from the three option buttons to search back a certain number of months, days, or range of dates.

Note *You can use a combination of the search methods illustrated in this lesson. For example, you can type a partial file name and the date you believe it was last modified before you start the search.*

HANDS

Finding Files by Date

In this activity, you will find files that were modified during a specific range of dates.

1. **Open the Search for Files and Folders pane in Windows Explorer.**

2. **Click the Look in: box triangle button and select your floppy disk drive letter, if necessary.**

3. **Click the Date check box.**

The Date options appear as shown in Figure 5.14.

4. **Drag the separator bar to widen the left pane so that you can see all of the date options text.**

5. **Click the between option button.**

The date exactly one month ago and the current date appear in the two boxes.

6. Click the text inside the first date text box.

7. Type 1/25/00.

8. Press [Tab].

The text inside the second date text box highlights. You could type the second date here. Instead, you will use the triangle button to display and choose a date from a calendar window.

9. Click the **triangle button** beside the second date text box.

A calendar of the current month and year displays, with today's date highlighted.

10. Click the **arrow button** at the top of the calendar to move to January, 2000.

11. Click **28**.

The date 1/28/2000 appears in the text box.

12. Click **Search Now**.

Windows 2000 searches your Student Data Disk and displays two files in the Contents pane that were modified between the specified dates.

13. Close Windows Explorer.

14. Remove your Student Data Disk from the floppy disk drive.

You may explore Searching on the Internet in the On the Web section that follows, or you may proceed directly to the exercises for this lesson. If you are finished with your computer session, log off the computer you are using.

Follow the "log off" procedures for your lab or school environment.

When using the Internet for research, make sure you identify the date of any Web pages that you include in your bibliography. The contents of the Internet are in a constant state of change and today's Web page may be unavailable or quite different tomorrow.

ON*the*WEB

SEARCHING ON THE INTERNET

Many times the information or file you are looking for is not located on any of your disk drives. If you are on a network, the search feature lets you look for other computers that might have the data you need. If you have access to the Internet, the Windows Explorer Search pane lets you search millions of computers!

To find a specific location, or Web site, you must know its Web address, called the *Uniform Resource Locator,* or *URL.* URLs are listed in magazine, newspaper, and television advertisements, on boxes of software packages, and within many Help screens on your computer. *Search engines* let you find pages of interest by entering words or phrases, called *keywords.* Much of the Web is in a constant state of flux—addresses and pages change daily. Search engines let you find a Web site that has moved since your last access. You can also use a search engine and online telephone directories to find addresses and telephone numbers for a company or an individual.

In this activity, you will use Windows Explorer to find information on the Internet.

1. Open **Windows Explorer**, if necessary.
2. Click **View, Toolbars**.
3. Make sure the **Address Bar option** is checked.

The Address toolbar lets you see and enter URLs, disk drives, networked computers, and folders.

4. Click the **Tools menu**, point to **Explorer Bar**, and click **Search**.
5. Click the **Internet link** at the bottom of the Search pane. (You may have to scroll to the bottom of the pane to see it.)

After your computer connects to the Internet, the contents of the Search pane changes.

6. Click the **Find a business option button**.
7. Type McGraw-Hill in the *Business:* text box.
8. Type Columbus in the *City:* text box and OH in the *State:* text box.
9. Click **Search**.

The Search pane shows the results of the search, as shown in Figure 5.15.

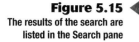

ON*the***WEB**

Figure 5.15 ◀
The results of the search are
listed in the Search pane

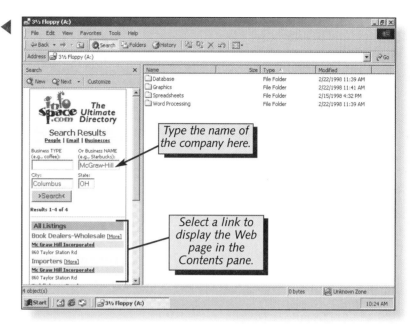

10. Click the **New button** ⟨ New ⟩.

11. Click the **Find a Web page option button**.

12. Type McGraw-Hill in the *Find a Web page containing:* text box.

13. Click **Search**.

The Search pane shows the links to the Web pages for McGraw-Hill.

14. Click the <u>**McGraw-Hill**</u> **link** to jump to the company's home page.

15. Close the Search pane to see more of the Web page.

16. Click links to explore the Web site.

17. Close all open windows and disconnect from the Internet, if necessary.

18. You may proceed directly to the exercises for this lesson. If, however, you
    are finished with your computer session, log off the computer you are using.

*Follow the "log off" procedures for your lab or
school environment.*

Lesson Summary & Exercises

SUMMARY

After you complete this lesson, you should know how to do the following:

Managing Files

- File management is the process of organizing and caring for your disks and files.
- You may create, copy, move, and delete files and folders.
- Develop the habit of creating a backup copy of your files to avoid data loss.

Creating Files

- Use the Save As dialog box to set the drive, folder, name, and type of a file.
- To name files, follow the Windows 2000 or MS-DOS file-naming conventions.

Working with File Types

- Use Windows Explorer to identify the file type of an object.

Copying Files

- Use the Copy and Paste commands to copy a file from one folder to another.
- Hold down Ctrl and drag a file or folder to copy an object from one folder to another on the same disk.
- Click the Copy to: button and select a destination folder to duplicate files.
- To select consecutive or contiguous files, click the first file in the Contents pane, hold down Shift, and click the last file.
- To select noncontiguous files, click the first file, hold down Ctrl, and click each file you want to select.

Moving Files

- To move an object elsewhere on the same disk, drag the file or folder to another folder.
- To move an object to the root folder on the same disk, select the file or folder and drag the file or folder onto the drive icon.

Deleting Files

- You should delete files when they are no longer needed to clear space on your hard drive.
- A file deleted from a floppy disk is permanently erased.
- A file deleted from the hard drive is moved to the Recycle Bin on your desktop.
- Select the file to be deleted and press Delete. To confirm the deletion, click Yes in the Confirm File Delete dialog box.
- To permanently clear all contents of the Recycle Bin, click the Empty Recycle Bin command on the File menu.

Lesson Summary & Exercises

Restoring Deleted Files

■ To restore deleted files, double-click the Recycle Bin desktop icon, select the files to be undeleted, and click the Restore option on the File menu.

Renaming Files

■ To rename a file, click the file name once to select it and again to change it. Type a new name or edit the name that appears in the box.

Searching for Files

■ To search for a file, use the Explorer Bar, Search option on the View menu.

■ Enter the name of the file, the drive in which to search, or the level of folders to be searched.

■ Click the Date check box to limit the search within particular dates.

On the Web: Searching on the Internet

■ Use the Internet link in the Explorer's Search pane to find Web sites related to a topic.

■ Click the Find a business option button, enter the business name, city, and state and click Search to display links to that company's data.

■ Click the Find a Web page option button to locate a company's Web site.

NEW TERMS TO REMEMBER

After you complete this lesson, you should know the meaning of these terms:

back up	file-naming conventions
backup	insertion point
desktop accessory (or accessory)	keyword
extension	partition
file management	search engine
file name	Uniform Resource Locator (URL)

Lesson Summary & Exercises

MATCHING EXERCISE

Match each of the terms with the definitions on the right:

Terms

1. back up
2. copy
3. delete
4. partition
5. insertion point
6. move
7. rename
8. search engine
9. extension
10. file name

Definitions

a. Procedure for changing the name of a file

b. Portion of a disk drive that has its own drive letter

c. Software that lets you find information on the Internet by entering keywords

d. Procedure for creating a duplicate set of data that you can use if the original data is destroyed

e. Procedure for removing entirely a set of data from a disk

f. Procedure for creating an exact duplicate of data stored in a file and placing it in another disk location with either the same name as the original file or a different name

g. Under old MS-DOS rules, a part of a file name that is from one to eight characters and that tells the user the contents of the file

h. Procedure for removing data from its original disk location to another disk location

i. A three-character part of a file name that identifies the type of data stored in the file

j. Blinking line in a text or an edit box that you can position to insert, delete, or type characters

Lesson Summary & Exercises

COMPLETION EXERCISE

Fill in the missing word or phrase for each of the following:

1. A small program built into Windows 2000 is known as a(n) _____.

2. One way that Windows 2000 allows you to copy or move a file is by _____ the file to another disk or folder.

3. You can _____ a file to remove it from a disk.

4. When you _____ a file, you change its name but the data remains unaltered.

5. Clicking a selected file name or folder name causes a(n) _____ to appear, which allows you to edit the file or folder name.

6. When you _____ _____ data by copying it to another disk, you are safeguarding it in case you lose the original data.

7. Windows 2000 allows you to _____ a file based on its name, location, or the date it was last modified.

8. The _____ _____ _____ is an address that lets you view a page from a Web site on the Internet.

9. A(n) _____ _____ is software that helps you find information on the Internet by allowing you to enter keywords or to choose categories.

10. The Windows operating system now makes it possible for users to create _____ _____ that are up to 255 characters.

Lesson Summary & Exercises

SHORT-ANSWER QUESTIONS

Write a brief answer to each of the following questions:

1. What is the name of the Windows 2000 program that you use primarily for managing data stored on disks?

2. Why is the Copy operation the most commonly used file management procedure?

3. Describe two methods that Windows 2000 provides for moving a file or folder from one disk location to another.

4. List the precautions you should take before deleting a file.

5. Suppose you cannot remember the name of a file (or which folder it is in) with which you last worked one week ago. Describe how you would locate the file.

6. What information does the operating system need in order to save a file?

7. What characters are prohibited in a Windows 2000 file name?

8. What happens if you drag a file into a folder that already has the same file name?

9. How do you select a group of consecutive objects in a list window? A group of noncontiguous objects?

10. What steps should you follow if the object that you are trying to rename accidentally opens? Why does this sometimes happen?

Lesson Summary & Exercises

APPLICATION PROJECTS

Insert your Student Data Disk into drive A: (or drive B:). Perform the following actions to complete these projects:

1. Use the Explorer window to create three new folders on your Student Data Disk: **Word Processing, Database**, and **Graphics**, respectively. Rename the **Worksheets** folder, **Spreadsheets**. Click the Details button, if necessary, to view a detailed list of your Student Data Disk. Copy the **Buford Proposal, Marketing Guidelines, Poem, Sunnyside RFP,** and **Manuscript** files to the **Word Processing** folder. Move the **Blue Tube, Color Rings, Cupid, Fence, Pyramid**, and **Star** files to the **Graphics** folder. Move the **Addresses** file to the **Database** folder. Move the **Quarter 1 Budget** file into the **Spreadsheets** folder. Delete the five files you copied into the **Word Processing** folder from the root folder.

2. Open the Explorer window, if necessary. Open the **Word Processing** folder on your Student Data Disk and create a subfolder labeled **Text**. Move **Expenses** from the root folder to the **Text** subfolder. Move all of the **Garbage, Garbled**, and **Garnish** files to the **Text** folder. Expand the disk icon to see its hierarchy in the Folders pane.

3. Open the Notepad desktop accessory. Write a memo to someone and save it as **My Memo**. When you save the file, set its location to the **Text** folder you created in Application Project 2 for this lesson.

4. Open the Explorer window, if necessary. Open the **Spreadsheets** folder. Select the **Shitake Budget** file and rename it **Shitake Budget 2000**. Move the **Instruments** and **Phone List** files from the **Spreadsheets** folder to the **Database** folder. Delete these files from the **Spreadsheets** folder: **Buford Proposal, Manuscript, Marketing Guidelines, Sunnyside RFP**, and **Winter in the USA**.

5. Open the Explorer window, if necessary. Use the Search pane to locate all files on your Student Data Disk that have a file name containing "99." How many files did you find? Now use the search operation again to search for all files on your Student Data Disk that were modified between May 8, 2000 and June 30, 2000. How many files did you find?

6. You must be able to connect to the Internet to complete this On the Web project. In Windows Explorer, use the Search pane to search for and display your address and phone number. Use the Find a person's address option button, and enter your name, city, and state.

If you do not have a phone number listed in your name or you have an unlisted phone number, your name will probably not appear. Choose a name of someone else who has a listed number to complete this project.

Windows 2000 Accessories

CONTENTS

OBJECTIVES

After you complete this lesson, you will be able to do the
following:

■ Identify the Accessories categories
included in Windows 2000.

■ Use the Calculator to perform simple
calculations.

■ Create, save, open, edit, and set options
for both text and formatted documents with
WordPad.

■ Draw pictures using Paint.

■ Recognize the Communications
accessories used to send and receive data
through a network, telephone, computer,
or fax.

■ Use a browser to explore the World Wide
Web.

The first personal computer operating systems met the basic requirements of booting the computer, managing system resources, managing file storage, and running application software. Users who had to type documents—simple or complex—purchased word processing programs. Spreadsheet and database management software, games, educational programs, and data communications all required separate purchases. If the program met a central need of the user, the expense ($100-$500) was cost-effective. For the person who typed one or two letters a month, however, the price of a full-featured word processor was too high.

Software manufacturers filled this gap by offering inexpensive software (often less than $100). As operating systems evolved, more of these features have been provided with the operating system. Lesson 6 introduces you to many of the small application programs that are included with Windows 2000.

EXPLORING ACCESSORIES

As you learned in Lesson 5, the small application programs are called accessories. Several categories of accessories—also called *applets*—are available in Windows 2000.

> *Note*   *Accessories are added to your system during the installation of Windows 2000. You can also add individual accessories later on. Your computer may have a different set of accessories than those shown in the figures in this lesson.*

General-Purpose Accessories

Applets in the general-purpose category range from serious (a small word processor) to not so serious (a drawing program) to recreational (games). Table 6.1 lists some of these programs and their functions.

Table 6.1	**General-Purpose Accessories**
NAME	**FUNCTION**
Synchronization	A file management tool that allows you to synchronize the files stored on different computers. You can connect the computers with cables or use floppy disks or telephone connections to synchronize files when the computers are in different locations.
Calculator	An on-screen calculator that allows you to perform both simple arithmetic and more complex scientific calculations.
Imaging	A program that lets you view and edit scanned images and fax documents.
Notepad	A text editing program that allows you to create and view short, unformatted text documents.
Paint	A painting program that allows you to create and modify images in black-and-white or color.
WordPad	A word/text processing program that allows you to type formatted letters, memos, and other text documents. WordPad also lets you revise text files used by the operating system.
Screen Savers	A set of moving images that helps prevent damage to the monitor's screen when the computer has been idle for a long time.
Backup	A utility program that duplicates data on your hard disk. Files that have been backed up can be recovered if they are accidentally deleted or damaged.

Communications Accessories

Windows 2000 includes several applets to assist you in sending and receiving digital information from one computer to another. To run some of these applications, you must have a modem installed on your computer. Table 6.2 summarizes these accessories.

Table 6.2	Communications Accessories
NAME	**FUNCTION**
Network and Dial-Up Connection	Enables your computer to connect to remote computer networks using your modem or cables.
Fax Service Management	Helps you manage fax devices on your computer or network.
HyperTerminal	Connects your computer to another computer, even if the other computer isn't running Windows. Requires a modem.
Phone Dialer	Places telephone calls from your computer through a modem.
Outlook Express	An e-mail program that can be used to exchange electronic mail or newsgroup messages.
NetMeeting	Lets you connect to several users, exchange audio and video images, send files, and sketch on a whiteboard.
Internet Connection Wizard	Lets you set up your computer to access the Internet through the network, cable, or telephone lines to which your computer is attached.
Address Book	Lets you store information about people you regularly contact, such as names, addresses, phone numbers, and e-mail addresses.

Entertainment Accessories

Multimedia consists of sound, text, graphics, animation, and video combined into a single application software package. The accessories in this group allow you to control any multimedia hardware devices attached to your computer system, such as CD-ROM drives, speakers, video players, or sound cards. Table 6.3 briefly describes these applets.

Table 6.3	Multimedia Accessories
NAME	**FUNCTION**
CD Player	Plays audio compact disks from a CD-ROM drive connected to your computer.
Windows Media Player	Plays audio and video clips. Controls multimedia hardware devices.
Sound Recorder	Records, edits, and plays back sound files. Lets you insert sound files into documents.
Volume Control	Controls volume and balance of a sound card.

Windows 2000 has two other categories of accessories. Accessibility applets make using the computer easier for users with special learning needs or specific disabilities. System tools accessories allow you to more easily control, update, and maintain your computer system, and manage the network to which it is connected.

Reading about Windows 2000 accessories is like listening to someone talk about how to drive a car. The only way to really learn to drive is to get behind the wheel and practice. In the following section, you will learn the basic functions of several Windows 2000 accessories.

USING THE CALCULATOR

The computer has enormous potential to do arithmetic quickly and accurately. The Windows 2000 Calculator puts a hand-held calculator right on your screen. The Calculator has two views: Standard and Scientific. In this tutorial you will use the Standard Calculator view, as shown in Figure 6.1. If your mathematical needs are more advanced, you most likely already know how to use the complex functions on the Scientific Calculator view, as shown in Figure 6.2.

Figure 6.1
The Standard Calculator view

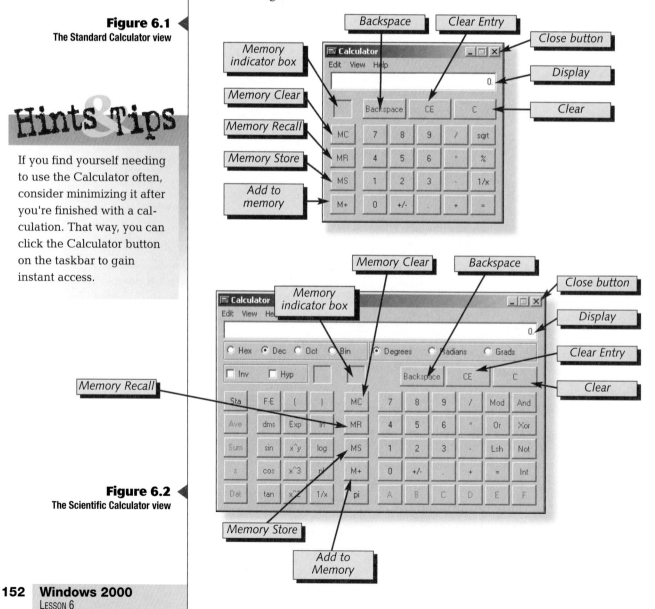

Hints & Tips

If you find yourself needing to use the Calculator often, consider minimizing it after you're finished with a calculation. That way, you can click the Calculator button on the taskbar to gain instant access.

Figure 6.2
The Scientific Calculator view

Entering Numbers

You can enter numbers with the keyboard or the mouse. Using the numeric keypad on the right side of your keyboard is usually easier. Make sure ⌨ is on before you start so the numeric keypad will enter numbers rather than activate the arrow keys. On most keyboards, an indicator light glows when ⌨ is active. Alternatively, you can use the mouse to click the digit buttons on the screen.

Clearing the Calculator

The Clear button ⌨ sets the Calculator back to zero to start a new calculation. The Clear Entry button ⌨ clears the last entry so you can rekey the entry without having to start over. The Backspace button ⌨ deletes the last digit you typed. The Memory Clear button ⌨ clears any number stored in the Calculator's memory.

Mathematical Operations

To perform various mathematical operations, use the following operators:

- Slash or diagonal (/) for division
- Multiplication sign (x) for multiplication
- Minus sign (-) for subtraction
- Plus sign (+) for addition
- Equal sign (=) to display the results

 *You can use on-screen Help to learn about other Calculator functions.*

Selecting the Calculator View

1. Click Start, Programs, Accessories, Calculator.

2. Click View.

3. Select Standard or Scientific.

Selecting the Calculator View

In this activity, you will switch back and forth between the Standard and Scientific Calculator views.

1. If necessary, log on to your system.

2. Click **Start** ⊞Start.

3. Point to **Programs** and then **Accessories**.

The Accessories menu shows the available programs.

4. Click **Calculator**.

The Calculator window appears on the desktop.

5. Click the **View menu** on the Calculator window.

Notice that two views appear and one is selected.

6. Click **Scientific**, if necessary.

The Scientific view of the Calculator appears.

7. Click the **View menu** and switch the window to **Standard view**.

Performing a Mathematical Calculation

In this activity, you will use the Standard Calculator view to perform a mathematical calculation.

1. Set the Calculator window to the Standard view.

2. Click **8**.

3. Click **x**.

4. Click **6**.

5. Click **=**.

The answer to the mathematical statement (8 x 6 =), 48, appears on the display.

Using the Memory Feature

In this activity, you will use the Memory feature to continue the calculation from the previous activity.

1. With the answer from the previous activity still showing on the Calculator's display, click **MS** [MS].

The displayed value is stored in memory, and an *M* appears in the memory indicator box (above the MC button).

2. Click **5**.

3. Click **+/-**.

4. Click **M+** [M+].

The displayed value, –5, is added to the value currently stored in memory.

5. Click **Clear Entry** [CE].

The displayed value is 0.

6. Click **MR** [MR].

The value 43—the result of adding 48 and -5 in the calculator's memory—appears on the display.

7. Click **MC** [MC].

The memory feature is cleared and the *M* disappears from the memory indicator box.

8. Close the Calculator.

The Calculator window no longer appears on the desktop.

USING TEXT APPLETS

Two basic kinds of text handling programs exist: text editors and word processors. A *text editor* creates unformatted or "plain vanilla" text files. *Text files,* or *unformatted files,* contain the characters you type and very little else. The Notepad accessory that you used in Lesson 5 is a text editor. When you save a Notepad document, its file type is Text.

Unformatted text files are used for the following purposes:

- To create and edit files that control computer startup functions and software settings.

- To transmit a file via modem. Since unformatted files are much smaller than formatted files, you may send data as text files quickly and cheaply.

- To transfer text from one program to another program. This is most often necessary when dealing with non-Windows or DOS-based software or with incompatible computers or operating systems.

A *word processor* allows you to not only produce text but also to enhance the appearance or formatting of the document. Formatting a document refers to applying fonts, indenting or aligning paragraphs, and using other features to make the document more appealing to readers. Such embellishments in a *formatted file* can make the document more attractive and easier to read. A text editor does not include these features in its unformatted files. Word processor files can have a generic file type, such as Rich Text Document, or a program-specific file type, such as a Microsoft Word document.

USING WORDPAD

The WordPad applet is two programs in one: a text editor and a word processor. When you create a new WordPad document, your choice of file type determines whether WordPad will be a text editor or a word processor. The New dialog box, as shown in Figure 6.3, lists four file type choices: Rich Text Document, Word 6 Document, Text Document, and Unicode Text Document.

Figure 6.3
The New dialog box

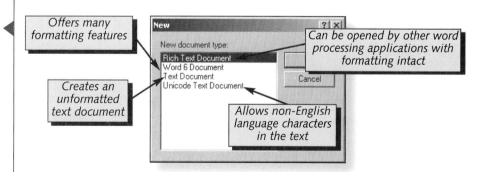

The Word 6 Document format provides formatting features compatible with Microsoft's full-featured word processing application. The Rich Text Document format allows a file to be read (opened) by other word processing applications maintaining a few of the more common formatting features. The Text Document format creates an unformatted text document. The Unicode Text Document allows you to include non-English language characters in the text.

HANDS On

Creating and Saving a New Text File

In this activity, you will use the WordPad accessory to create and save a text file.

1. Insert your **Student Data Disk** into drive A: (or drive B:).
2. Click **Start** and point to **Programs** and then **Accessories**.
3. Click **WordPad**.

The WordPad copyright box appears on the desktop briefly, and then the WordPad window appears, as shown in Figure 6.4.

Figure 6.4 ◀
Blank WordPad window

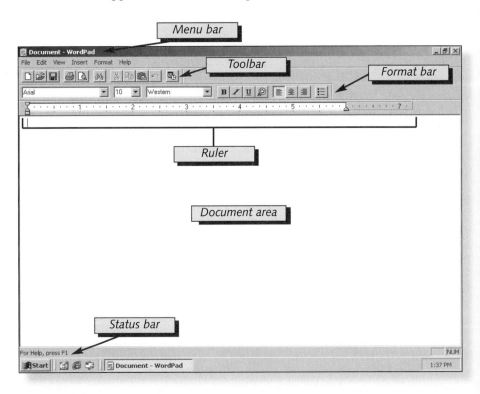

Windows BASICS

Creating and Saving a New Document with WordPad

1. Click Start, Programs, Accessories, WordPad.

2. Type your document.

3. Click Save on the toolbar.

4. Select the drive and/or folder in which to store your document.

5. Enter a name for your document.

6. Click Save.

The WordPad window resembles the Notepad window with three significant additions. Below the menu bar is the toolbar, with buttons for WordPad's most common program commands. The *format bar,* with buttons for WordPad's most common formatting commands, appears below the toolbar. The *ruler,* which is used to format paragraphs of text, appears below the format bar.

Figure 6.5
The WordPad window with typed text

4. Compare your WordPad window with Figure 6.4. If the toolbar, format bar, ruler, or status bar are not displayed, turn them on one at a time from the View menu.

The blinking insertion point below the ruler shows where text will appear as you type.

5. Type the following lines of text. Press Enter↵ after each line.

Regarding contractors

The bottom line: How much will it cost?

How much of that cost can we reduce by performing the labor ourselves?

Your text should appear similar to the text shown in Figure 6.5.

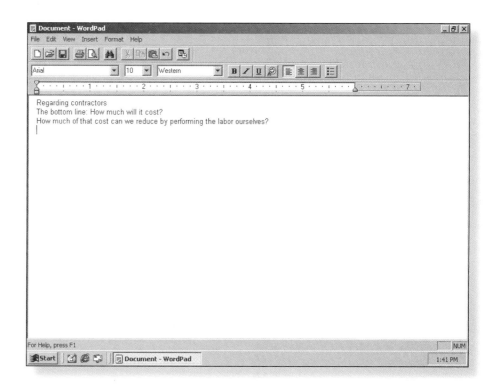

6. Click **Save** 🖫.

Note — *If you point to a toolbar button, a description box will appear that identifies the name of each button.*

The Save As dialog box appears, as shown in Figure 6.6.

7. Click the **triangle button** in the **Save in box**.

Figure 6.6
The Save As dialog box

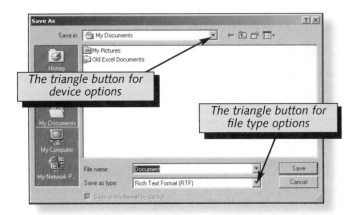

The drop-down list of device options appears.

8. Click the icon for the drive that contains your Student Data Disk (drive A: or B:).

9. Double-click the *Word Processing* folder.

10. Click the **triangle button** in the **Save as type box**.

A drop-down list of file type options appears.

11. Click **Text Document**.

12. Double-click the word **Document** in the File name text box to highlight it.

13. Type A note to myself in the File name text box.

 *Before you can save a new document, you must provide a file name.*

14. Click the **Save button** .

A dialog box appears asking if you really want a text document.

15. Click **Yes**.

The document is stored in a text file named ***A note to myself*** on the diskette. Notice that the title bar now shows the name of the file.

HANDS On

Click New to create a new document; click Open to use an existing document.

Opening Documents

WordPad can have only one document open at a time. In this activity, you will open a new and an existing document in the WordPad window.

1. With *A note to myself* still open in the WordPad window, click the **New button** 🗋.

The New dialog box appears, with the default file type, Rich Text Document.

Opening and Saving a WordPad Document

1. To create a new document, click the New button, then OK.

2. To open an existing document, click the Open button, select the drive and/or folder, and double-click the name.

3. Click the Save button to resave an existing document with your editing changes.

Or

Select Save As from the File menu to give a new name to a document, select the drive and/or folder in which to save the document, enter a new name, and select the file type.

HANDS On

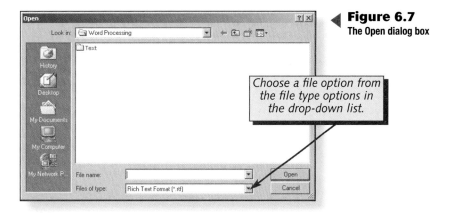
Hints&Tips

The better your keyboarding skills, the more efficiently you can use the computer. You can learn to type using self-teaching books, signing up for classes, or running keyboarding programs.

2. Click OK.

A new, blank document replaces the previously displayed text saved in the text file ***A note to myself***.

3. Click the Open button 🖾 **on the toolbar.**

The Open dialog box appears, as shown in Figure 6.7. The Look in box shows the ***Word Processing*** folder as the default location for your files.

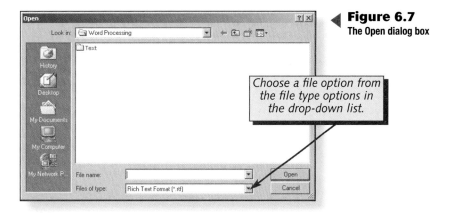

Figure 6.7
The Open dialog box

Choose a file option from the file type options in the drop-down list.

4. Click the Text Documents (*.txt) option from the Files of type drop-down list.

WordPad stores and recognizes file types based on the file extension: *.doc* is used for Word for Windows documents, *.rtf* for Rich Text Format, *.wri* for Windows Write, and *.txt* for the various forms of text documents.

5. Double-click the file name *A note to myself*.

The text saved in the selected file appears in the WordPad window.

Editing a Document

In this activity, you will edit or modify an existing text document and save the changes.

1. Make sure *A note to myself* (on your Student Data Disk) appears in the WordPad window.

2. Double-click the word Regarding in the first line of the document.

Double-clicking a word selects it. The word and the space character that follows it are highlighted.

3. Type Ask all bidding and do not press 🔲Spacebar**.**

Editing a File

1. Open the file.

2. Double-click words to select them.

3. Move the insertion point where you want to insert text.

4. Use Delete to remove characters to the right of the insertion point.

5. Click the Save button to store your changed document.

Figure 6.8
The modified text document

The new text replaces the existing text.

4. Press End **and type : (a colon).**

The insertion point moves to the end of the line when you press End.

5. Select the phrase The bottom line: , including the space character that follows the colon.

To select the text, click to the immediate left of the capital T, hold down the left mouse button, and drag through the space after the colon (:).

6. Press Delete **.**

The selected text is deleted, and the rest of the text in the line shifts to the left. The document should appear similar to the one shown in Figure 6.8.

7. Click the Save button 💾 **.**

8. Click Yes.

The modified version of the file is saved on the floppy disk with the same file name: *A note to myself*.

Printing a Document

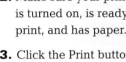

1. Open your document.

2. Make sure your printer is turned on, is ready to print, and has paper.

3. Click the Print button.

Printing a Document

In this activity, you will print the text document you've created, modified, and saved.

1. **Make sure your printer is turned on, ready to print, and has paper that is aligned properly.**

2. **Make sure *A note to myself* is still open.**

3. **Click the Print button 🖨 on the toolbar.**

A message appears briefly and the document in the WordPad window is sent to the printer. After a few moments, the printer should begin printing the document.

4. **Close WordPad.**

The WordPad window disappears from the desktop.

Opening and Modifying a Word for Windows Document File

WordPad's Word 6 Document format option provides a mini-version of a word processing program. The format bar lets you select the fonts (the style and size of lettering) and line appearance (centering a line of text, for example). The ruler is used to set tabs and margins. These features allow you to format or enhance the appearance of text and paragraphs. A feature called **word wrap** controls where lines of text end. As you type a paragraph, you can ignore the right margin. When text no longer fits on the current line, the text automatically continues on a new line; you just continue typing.

In this activity, you will open a Word for Windows 6.0 document and format the file.

1. **With your Student Data Disk still in the floppy drive, start WordPad.**

2. **Click the Open button 📂.**

The Open dialog box appears.

3. **If necessary, select drive A: (or drive B:) on the Look in drop-down list and choose Word for Windows from the Files of type drop-down list.**

4. **Open the *Word Processing* folder.**

5. **Click the file named *Sunnyside RFP* and then click Open.**

The document stored in the *Sunnyside RFP* file appears in the WordPad window.

6. **Maximize the WordPad window, if necessary.**

If some of the text scrolls off the screen to the right, select Options from the View menu, click the Word tab, click the Wrap to Ruler option button, and click OK.

7. Click the down scroll arrow until the line *Dear Ms. Canyon* appears at the top of the document window.

8. In the list following the first paragraph, point to the left of the *p* in *proposal document.*

The pointer becomes a right-pointing arrow.

9. Click.

The line highlights. When you click once to the left of a line of text, the entire line highlights.

10. With the pointer still positioned directly to the left of the highlighted line, drag straight down to select the three lines in the list, as shown in Figure 6.9.

Figure 6.9 ◄
Selected lines

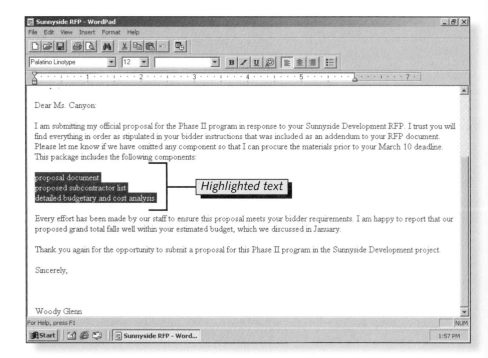

You must select text before you can format it.

11. Click the **Format menu**.

The Format menu appears.

12. Click **Bullet Style**.

The selected lines are formatted as bulleted paragraphs, each preceded by a bullet character (•).

13. Scroll to the bottom of the document.

14. Triple-click (click three times quickly) anywhere in the paragraph that begins *Thank you again...*

The paragraph highlights.

15. Press ⌷Delete twice.

The selected paragraph and the line space following the paragraph are deleted from the document.

16. Scroll to the top of the document and select the company name, **Woody Glenn**, in the letterhead.

17. Click the **Bold button** B on the format bar.

The selected text formats with the Bold attribute; the text becomes heavier and darker.

18. Click the **Save button** 🖫.

The latest changes are saved to the document stored in *Sunnyside RFP*.

19. Click the **Print button** 🖨.

The printer prints one copy of the *Sunnyside RFP* file.

20. Close WordPad.

WordPad disappears from your desktop.

USING PAINT

If a picture is worth a thousand words, think of the pages you save by adding graphics to explain or complement your written text. The Paint applet in Windows 2000 lets you create or edit a picture using a variety of tools. Figure 6.10 identifies some of the major parts of the Paint window.

Figure 6.10
The Windows 2000 Paint window

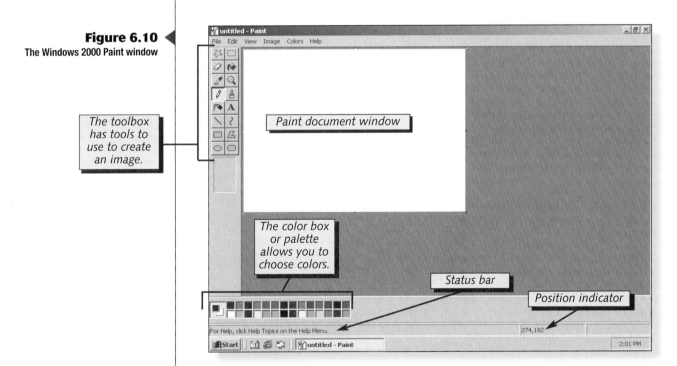

Exploring the Toolbox

On the left side of the Paint window is the *toolbox.* The toolbox contains the tool buttons that you use to create an image. To use a tool, click its button. To find out what a tool does, point to the tool without clicking. A *tool tip* will appear, providing the tool's name. Table 6.4 explains each of the Tool icons. When you choose certain Tool icons, other choices may appear below the toolbox, allowing you to pick the shape, size, and other characteristics of the selected tool.

Table 6.4		Tool Icons
ICON	**NAME**	**FUNCTION**
	Free-Form Select	Lets you choose an irregularly shaped part of the painting to copy, move, or edit.
	Select	Lets you choose a rectangular part of the painting to copy, move, or edit.
	Eraser/Color Eraser	Erases a part of the painting.
	Fill With Color	Fills an enclosed area with the selected color.
	Pick Color	Selects a color from the painting.
	Magnifier	Zooms in on a part of the painting for detailed work or examination.
	Pencil	Draws a thin free-form line or shape.
	Brush	Draws a brush stroke of the selected brush shape and size.
	Airbrush	Sprays the selected color onto the painting.
	Text	Lets you add text of varying styles and sizes directly into your painting.
	Line	Draws a straight line of the selected width.
	Curve	Draws a curved line of the selected width.
	Rectangle	Creates a rectangle of the selected line width and color.
	Polygon	Creates a multi-sided shape of the selected line width and color.
	Ellipse	Creates an oval using the selected line width and color.
	Rounded Rectangle	Creates a rounded rectangle using the selected line width and color.

Choosing Colors

On the bottom of the Paint window is the **color box** that contains a series of squares of colors. These color choices are called the **palette**. To select the color with which you want to draw or fill, click the color in the color box. To select a color from one already in the painting, use the Pick Color icon and click the desired color in the drawing.

HANDS On

Windows BASICS

Drawing with Paint

1. Click Start, Programs, Accessories, Paint.

2. Select a drawing tool from the toolbox.

3. Select a color from the color box.

4. Draw.

Creating and Editing an Image

In this activity, you will use the Paint accessory to create and edit a graphics image.

1. Click **Start** [Start] and point to **Programs** and then **Accessories**.

2. Click **Paint**.

The Paint window appears on the desktop.

3. Point to the **Ellipse tool** [○].

The tool tip appears as well as a functional description of the tool in the status bar.

4. Point to each of the tools in the toolbox to read the names and descriptions.

5. Maximize the Paint window, if necessary.

6. Verify that the black color chip is selected in the color box.

Note *In the box to the left of the color box are two color chips. The top color chip indicates the selected color; the bottom color chip indicates the background color. Click the black swatch in the color box, if necessary.*

7. Click the **Pencil tool** [✎].

8. Point to the upper-left corner of the Paint document window.

The pointer is shaped like a pencil, your current painting tool. The position indicator, as shown in Figure 6.11, at the bottom of the document window reflects the number of **pixels** from the upper-left corner of the window. For example, 10,12 means the pointer is 10 pixels from the left edge and 12 pixels down from the top of the window. Each pixel is one screen dot.

Figure 6.11
The position indicator

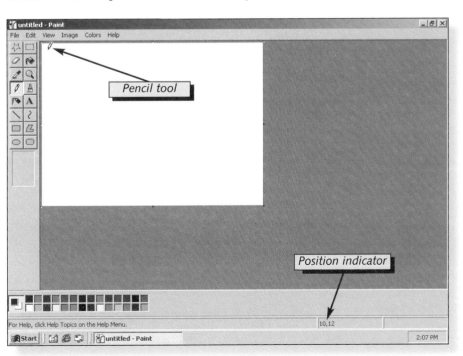

9. Without pressing the mouse button, roll the pointer around the document window.

Notice that the position indicator changes to reflect the pointer's changing position.

10. Press the mouse button to drag the pointer around the window.

The Pencil tool creates a free-form line.

11. Click **Select All** on the Edit menu.

Select All activates all the pixels in your window so that you can copy, move, delete, or modify them.

12. Press `Delete`.

The drawing area highlights, the pointer changes to a four-headed arrow, and the screen clears.

13. Use the **Pencil tool** ⟋ to draw a flower, such as the one shown in Figure 6.12.

Figure 6.12
Flower drawn with the Pencil tool

 You may find it difficult to draw with the mouse. Graphic artists use specialized input devices to draw on the computer. If desired, practice drawing for a few minutes to get the feel of drawing. Then clear the screen and repeat step 13.

 Be sure that each petal of the flower is closed off with no open edges.

14. Click the green color chip in the color box.

Green is now the selected color for any lines you paint. A green square appears at the far left of the color box.

Hints & Tips

Click Undo on the Edit menu to undo up to three changes.

15. Click the **Line tool** .

The Line tool is selected and its line width options appear near the bottom of the toolbar.

16. Click the bottom (thickest) line in the line width selector.

17. Point to the document window.

The pointer changes shape to become a cross pointer.

18. Point to the center of the flower.

19. Drag to draw a thick green line.

Now you have a stem for your flower, as shown in Figure 6.13.

Figure 6.13
The Line tool

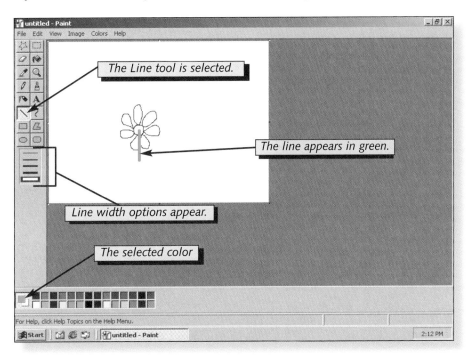

20. With your flower on the screen, click the **Fill With Color tool** in the toolbox.

When you point to the window, the pointer takes the shape of a spilling paint can. The drip of paint to the pointer's left is its active or "hot" spot.

21. In the color box, click a color for a petal of your flower.

22. Click one of the enclosed petals.

The enclosed area fills with the color you chose.

Warning

Before you click any part of the Paint window, be sure that this hot spot is inside an enclosed area. Otherwise, your entire background will fill with color. If the entire background fills with your chosen color, choose Undo from the Edit menu to remove the paint. You may have to reuse the Pencil tool to close off the petal.

23. Click a different color in the color box and fill another petal of your flower.

 Use the Undo command if you want to undo your changes and pick another color.

24. Click a different color to fill each petal in your flower.

Your flower should look something like the one shown in Figure 6.14.

Figure 6.14 ◀
Petals filled with colors

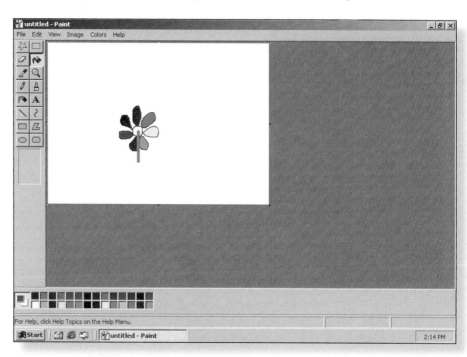

Moving and Copying Part of a Drawing

You can move and copy parts of your drawing if you select the object first.

1. With your drawing on the screen, click the **Select tool** ▢.

2. Point above and to the left of your flower.

Notice that the pointer changes to a crosshair (perpendicular lines with a small circle at the point of intersection). Whenever you see this pointer, the dot in the small circle is where the corner of the object should begin.

3. Drag down and right diagonally to enclose your entire flower.

As you drag the mouse, a selection rectangle like the one shown in Figure 6.15 appears. All the pixels inside the rectangle are selected.

Hints & Tips

Just as you learned in Lesson 5, you can use the Copy (or Cut) and Paste commands to duplicate (or move) images. Use the same pairs of commands to move or duplicate text in Notepad, WordPad, or most any Windows applications.

Figure 6.15
Flower selected

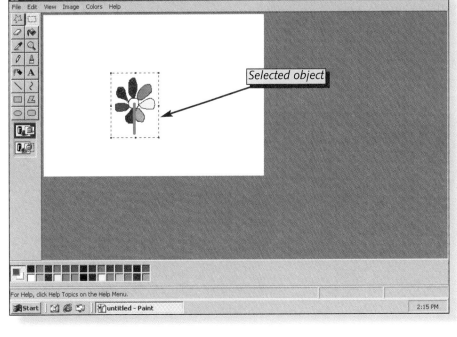

Moving and Copying Objects

1. Select the object to move or copy with the Select or Free-Form Select tool.

2. Click Cut from the Edit menu to move the image or Copy to duplicate the image.

3. Click Paste from the Edit menu.

4. Drag the object to the desired location.

5. Click outside the object to deselect it.

You can also hold Ctrl while dragging to copy the selected object.

4. **Point inside the selection rectangle.**

The pointer changes to a four-headed arrow. This pointer shape tells you that you can drag the rectangle to a new screen location.

5. **Drag the selection to the bottom left of the screen.**

As you drag, the image inside the selection rectangle moves.

6. **Make sure the flower is still selected and select Copy from the Edit menu.**

7. **Select Paste from the Edit menu.**

8. **Drag the image immediately to the right of the first flower, making sure you don't overlap any parts of the flowers.**

A second flower is copied.

9. **Continue to select Paste and drag to fill your screen with flowers, as shown in Figure 6.16.**

Saving and Printing the Image

In this activity, you will save and print your image.

1. **With your flowers still on the screen, click Save on the File menu.**

The Save As dialog box appears.

Figure 6.16
Moved and copied flowers

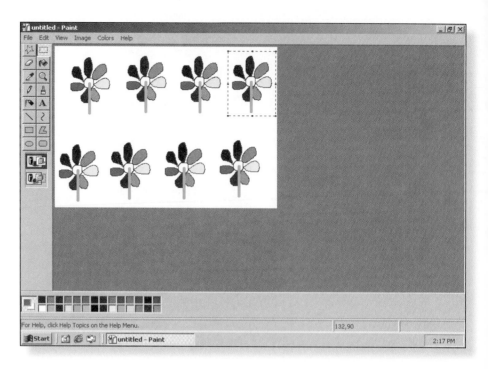

 *If you save an untitled document, Windows 2000 displays the Save As dialog box so that you can locate and name the document.*

2. Be sure the Save in box displays the correct location (drive) of your Student Data Disk.

3. Double-click the *Graphics* folder.

4. Activate the **File name text box**, if necessary, and type Flower Painting **as the file name.**

5. Click **Save**.

The image is saved and stored in a file named *Flower Painting*.

6. Be sure the printer connected to your system is turned on and ready to print.

7. Click **Print** on the File menu.

The Print dialog box appears.

8. Verify that the number of copies is set to **1**.

9. Click **OK**.

After a few moments, the image is sent to the printer and begins printing.

 *Your image will be in black and white unless you have a color printer.*

10. Close the Paint window.

11. Remove your **Student Data Disk** from the floppy drive.

Saving Images

1. With your image on the screen, select Save As from the File menu.

2. Select a location in which to save the image.

3. Type a name for your image.

4. Click Save.

UNDERSTANDING COMMUNICATIONS ACCESSORIES

The Communications accessories included in Windows 2000 let you and your computer send and receive **e-mail** (electronic mail) or faxes, which means sending information between your computer and:

- Another computer on the same network
- Another computer through a modem
- A fax device
- An intelligent telephone system

Few computers have all of the Windows 2000 Communications accessories installed. Network users may install only network-specific accessories. Users not on a network may install only fax- and modem-related accessories. An individual who has both a desktop and laptop computer may install accessories that help coordinate the files on the two computers. For more information on these accessories, refer to Help in Windows 2000.

 *You may explore Accessing the Internet by continuing with the On the Web section that follows, or you may proceed directly to the exercises for this lesson. If you are finished with your computing session, log off the computer you are using.*

 Follow the "log off" procedures for your lab or school environment.

ACCESSING THE INTERNET

In previous lessons, you explored portions of the Internet by clicking links from the taskbar, Windows Explorer, the Device Manager, and Windows 2000 Help. In this section, you will learn more about this online world by directly launching your browser from the desktop. The Internet consists of several components that allow the exchange of different kinds of information, such as files, electronic mail, electronic conversation, and so on. Each of these exchanges requires the user to have hardware and software to access the Internet.

Most individual users have a modem connected to a telephone line that carries signals between their computer and the Internet. Network users may share modems with other users. Faster connections use more expensive technology that not only transfers files faster but also allows for the exchange of audio and video conversations known as *video-conferencing.*

Some large businesses and universities are part of the Internet *backbone*—the computers that make up the Internet. Other users must connect to the Internet indirectly, through *Internet service providers (ISPs)* or *online services.*

To share information over the Internet and to explore all components of the Internet, you need browser software such as Microsoft Internet Explorer.

Many individuals feel that the most exciting component of the Internet is the World Wide Web. The Web consists of screens, or *Web pages,* that contain text, graphics, animation, sound, and video. Companies advertise and sell products on the Web and individuals may create their own Web pages.

To find a specific location, or *Web site,* you must know its Web address, or URL. URLs are listed in magazine, newspaper, and television advertisements, on boxes of software packages, and within many help screens on your computer. Search engines let you find pages of interest by entering keywords. Much of the Web is in a constant state of flux—addresses and pages change daily. In this activity, you will access the Internet's World Wide Web using your browser.

1. If you are using Microsoft Internet Explorer, double-click the Internet Explorer desktop icon .

Note *If you are using another browser, see your instructor for help on launching your browser.*

Your browser will load and display your default or *home page*. The document window displays the home page.

2. Click the **Address text box** above the document window.

The home page address is highlighted.

3. Type http://www.glencoe.com **and press** Enter ←.

After a short pause, you should see the Glencoe/McGraw-Hill home page, as shown in Figure 6.17.

Figure 6.17 ◄
The Glencoe/McGraw-Hill
home page

4. Move your mouse pointer over the home page.

Your mouse pointer changes to the shape of a hand when you pass over certain text or graphics areas. As you learned in Lesson 1, these locations are called links. When you click a link, your browser jumps to (a) another location on the Web page; (b) another page at the current site; (c) another Web site; or (d) another part of the Internet, such as e-mail.

5. Click the **Postsecondary Education** link.

6. Click **Back** ⇐ Back ▾.

7. Click other links to explore this Web site.

8. Close your browser and disconnect from the Internet.

9. You may proceed directly to the exercises for this lesson. If, however, you are finished with your computer session, log off the computer you are using.

Follow the "log off" procedures for your lab or school environment.

Lesson Summary & Exercises

SUMMARY

After you complete this lesson, you should know how to do the following:

Exploring Accessories

■ Separate accessories into categories depending on their function.

Using the Calculator

■ The Calculator has two views: Standard and Scientific.

■ To switch between Calculator types, select Standard or Scientific from the View menu.

■ To perform a calculation, enter numbers, click arithmetic operators, and click =.

■ To add numbers to memory, click M+.

■ To display the number stored in memory, click MR.

Using Text Applets

■ Text editors produce unformatted text files and word processors produce formatted text files.

■ To save a document as an unformatted file, select Text Document from the Save as type drop-down list.

Using WordPad

■ To save a WordPad document, select Save As from the File menu and enter a name, location, and file type for the document.

■ To open a WordPad document, click the Open button, choose the location and file type, and double-click the document name.

■ To remove text from a document, select the text and press Delete.

■ To emphasize text, select the text and click the Bold button.

■ To create a bulleted list of items, click the Bullets button.

Using Paint

■ To create a graphics image, select a drawing tool from the toolbox and a color from the palette, and drag with the mouse.

■ To move an object, select it with a Select tool and drag it to the desired location.

■ To copy an object, select it, select Copy and then Paste from the Edit menu.

■ To save a graphics image, select Save from the File menu, choose a location, and type a name.

Understanding Communications Accessories

■ Use the Windows 2000 Help feature to find out the specific functions and features of accessories that exchange data between computers.

On the Web: Accessing the Internet

■ Double-click the Internet Explorer desktop icon to launch the Web browser, connect to the Internet, and load the home page.

■ To load a specific Web page, enter an address in the Address text box.

■ Click a link to jump to another location on the same page or to another page.

Lesson Summary & Exercises

NEW TERMS TO REMEMBER

After you complete this lesson, you should know the meaning of these terms:

applets	home page	pixel	unformatted file
backbone	Internet service	ruler	video-conferencing
color box	providers (ISPs)	text editor	Web pages
e-mail	multimedia	text file	Web site
format bar	online services	toolbox	word processor
formatted file	palette	tool tip	word wrap

MATCHING EXERCISE

Match each of the terms with the definitions on the right:

Term

1. accessories
2. applets
3. color box
4. e-mail
5. formatted file
6. palette
7. pixel
8. toolbox
9. word wrap
10. unformatted file

Definitions

a. Feature of word processors in which typed text automatically drops to the next line when the insertion point reaches the right margin

b. Pure, unenhanced text file

c. Device within the Windows 2000 Paint accessory that allows you to select from a variety of drawing tools

d. Another term for accessory programs

e. Another name for the color box

f. Short for electronic mail, a means of transmitting written information via telephone lines between computers equipped with modems

g. A single dot on the computer screen

h. Ancillary programs for specific tasks that are included with the Windows 2000 operating system

i. Device from which color options can be selected

j. Document file that stores formatting characteristics—such as fonts, indentation, and so forth—along with text

COMPLETION EXERCISE

Fill in the missing word or phrase for each of the following:

1. The _____ feature in word processors allows you to type text without having to press ⌷Enter⏎⌷ at the end of each line.

2. The toolbox in the Windows 2000 _____ accessory allows you to select a variety of painting tools.

3. The WordPad accessory allows you to create, view, and edit both _____ files, which contain text only, and _____ files.

Lesson Summary & Exercises

4. If you need to find the square root of a number, you can do so with the _____ accessory.

5. The Windows 2000 accessory that functions like a word processing program is called _____ .

6. You can find a Web site by using a search engine or by typing its _____ _____ _____ .

7. When creating or editing an image using the Paint accessory, you can choose from a variety of colors on the _____, also called the _____.

8. The joining of text, graphics, sound, and sometimes animation into the same application software package is called _____.

9. To send an e-mail message to another computer, you need to use one or more of the _____ accessories.

10. Small application programs provided with the Windows 2000 operating system are referred to as either a(n) _____ or a(n)_____ .

SHORT-ANSWER QUESTIONS

Write a brief answer to each of the following questions:

1. Why do operating systems often include accessory programs?

2. Differentiate between a text editor and a word processor.

3. What are the file types for WordPad documents? How do you choose the one you want?

4. Differentiate among the WordPad toolbar, format bar, and ruler.

5. How do you view or hide each of the screen elements in question 4?

6. Which Windows 2000 accessory might be used to create a logo for a personal letterhead?

7. How do you select part of a Paint document? Why might you do this?

8. In Paint, how do you change the thickness of a line you plan to create? How do you change its color?

9. In Paint, why does the Fill With Color tool sometimes color your entire background when you try to color a part of your painting? What steps should you take to correct this problem?

10. The Windows 2000 Communications accessories allow your computer to send and receive information between your computer and other devices. Which devices might you want to access from your system, and why? (You can answer hypothetically or actually.)

APPLICATION PROJECTS

Insert your Student Data Disk into drive A: (or drive B:). Be sure to have a blank disk available in the event that your Student Data Disk becomes full. Perform the following actions to complete these projects:

1. Start WordPad and maximize its window. Open the Word document file named **Buford Proposal** in the **Word Processing** folder on your Student Data Disk. Position the insertion bar to the right of the label DATE:, press ⎢Tab⎥, and type today's date. Highlight the name *Myra* and type your name. Next, highlight the word *administrative* in the first body paragraph and delete it. Highlight the four lines that describe the budget allocation revisions, and then click the Bullets button on the format bar. Save the revised memo as a Word document named **Updated Proposal** in the **Word Processing** folder of your Student Data Disk. Your revised memo document should resemble the one shown in Figure 6.18. Print the document.

Figure 6.18 ◀
Revised memo

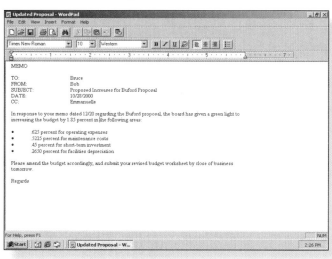

2. Use the Calculator to determine the answers to the following arithmetic problems. Remember to clear the Calculator between each calculation.

   a. 4521 + 865 + 975 + 36 =   **c.** 754891.562/829.67 =
   b. 86.29 - 75.68 =   **d.** 126.75 * 94.38/69 =

3. Start Paint. Use selected tools to create your own picture. Be creative; experiment with different shapes, options, and colors to create an attractive design. Save the design as **Project 6-3** in the **Graphics** folder on your Student Data Disk. Change the file type to 16 Color Bitmap to save space.

4. Start Paint. Open the image stored in the file named **Cupid** on your Student Data Disk. Use color palette selections and any tools you wish to enhance the image. Save the file as **Heart**. Change the file type to Monochrome Bitmap.

5. Start WordPad. Write a note to a friend and format its text as you choose. Be experimental. Save the document in a file with the name of your friend in the **Word Processing** folder of your Student Data Disk. Print the note.

6. You must be able to connect to the Internet to complete this On the Web project. Launch your browser and connect to the Internet. Click Search and select a search engine to find information about (a) your school, (b) employment in a company you would like to work for, (c) a book you would like to purchase. Write the results of your search, including the search engine you selected and the keyword or phrase that helped you locate the appropriate Web sites. Discuss the results of your research with other students in the class.

Controlling Printing Features

CONTENTS

OBJECTIVES

After you complete this lesson, you will be able to do the following:

- Control your print queue by deleting and pausing print jobs.
- View and select fonts to enhance your printed output.
- Choose different sizes of paper for your printed output.
- Switch between portrait and landscape orientations.
- Choose the best resolution for your printed output.
- Locate and fix printer errors.
- Download fonts from the Internet.

Many years ago computers were believed to be ushering in a paperless society. Although that era may come someday, today's computers can and do produce vast amounts of printed output. Whether you create junk mail, letters, brochures, or greeting cards, your output quality is dependent upon your operating system, application software, design choices, and printer.

In Lesson 3, you viewed some of the properties of the printer attached to your computer system. As you may recall, you double-clicked the Printer icon from the *Printers* folder of the Control Panel window. In this lesson, you will learn to manage the output to your computer by changing these properties and by using other controls.

MANAGING YOUR PRINTER

When Windows was installed on your computer, information about the printer or printers available to your computer was stored. Whenever an application (or applet) prints a document, a "soft" copy of the output is temporarily stored on the hard disk first. This process, called ***print spooling,*** allows you to work on another project while the computer actually prints the ***hard copy*** of your document onto paper in the background. Without print spooling, you would have to wait until the printing process ends to perform any other computer tasks. This is true because the computer sends data to the printer much more slowly than a computer can process data.

Using the Print Spooler

Print spooling allows you to control your printer even after you print your work from the application window. Each print request sent to the print spool is placed in a print queue. The ***print queue*** is a list of print jobs waiting for the computer to send the jobs to a particular printer.

You can cancel or pause the jobs in the print queue. For example, if you send three documents to the queue, you do not have to print the documents in the order they were sent to the queue. You can select individual jobs and pause or cancel them before the computer sends the jobs to the printer. As a result, a long document doesn't have to tie up a printer. If you need to print a short memo immediately, you can pause a long document on the queue, print the short memo, and then resume printing the long document. You can even clear the entire print queue in one step—a technique known as ***purging.***

Opening Your Print Queue

In this activity, you will open the window (queue) for your printer so you can manage the print jobs as they are sent to the queue.

1. If necessary, log on to your system.
2. Insert your **Student Data Disk** in the floppy drive.
3. Point to **Settings** on the Start menu **Start**.
4. Click the *Printers* folder.
5. Double-click the device icon labeled with the name of the printer connected to your system.

Your printer's window appears.

6. Click the **Printer menu**, and then click **Pause Printing**.

As documents are printed, they will be held on the print queue.

7. Minimize your printer's window.

Your print queue is minimized and a printer button appears on the taskbar.

8. Close the *Printers* folder.

Sending a WordPad Document to the Print Queue

In this activity, you will start WordPad, open a document file, print the document, and view the print job on the print queue.

1. Start WordPad.

2. Click the Open button  .

3. Click the correct disk location for your Student Data Disk, if necessary, and open the Word document named *Sunnyside RFP* in the *Word Processing* folder.

> *If you have more than one Student Data Disk, you may have to check one or more disks to find the files you need for the activities in this tutorial. Remember to change the Files of type to Word for Windows.*

4. Click your printer's button on the taskbar.

The print queue window opens on top of the WordPad window.

5. Tile the WordPad and print queue windows horizontally.

6. Activate the WordPad window.

7. Click Print on the File menu.

Right-click a blank spot on the taskbar; choose Tile Horizontally from the shortcut menu.

The Print dialog box appears, as shown in Figure 7.1.

Figure 7.1 ◀
The Print dialog box

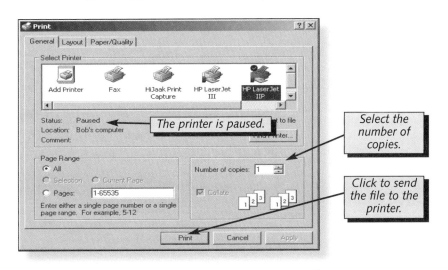

8. Click Print.

The document is sent to the printer. While the data is spooling, a message box appears briefly identifying the spooling document and the target printer.

9. Watch your printer's window.

As you watch, the job you just sent will become listed in the print queue, as shown in Figure 7.2.

Figure 7.2
The paused print queue
with a print job

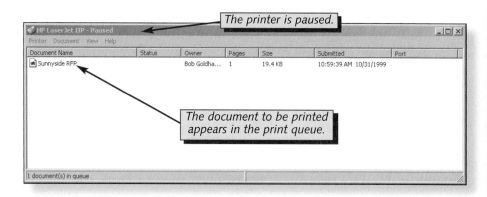

The printer is paused.

The document to be printed appears in the print queue.

 *Most, but not all, printers are set up with print spooling. If yours is not, your print jobs will go straight to the printer and nothing will appear in the print queue.*

10. Click the print job *Sunnyside RFP*.

11. Click Document, Pause.

The print job is paused, as indicated by the word *Paused* under the Status column. Now the job would not print, even if you resumed the print queue by unchecking the Printer, Pause Printing option. Point to the Printer button on the taskbar and notice also that the button displays the word *Paused*.

 *A printer icon appears next to the clock on the bottom right of the taskbar. You can double-click this icon to open the printer queue window whenever it appears.*

You can right-click the print job and select Pause Printing from the shortcut menu that appears.

Printing Another Document and Canceling the Printing

In this activity, you will return to the WordPad window, open another document, send it to the printer, and then delete it from the print queue.

1. Activate the WordPad window.

2. Click the Open button 📂 **.**

The Open dialog box appears.

3. **Open the *Buford Proposal* file.**

The document stored in the ***Buford Proposal*** file replaces the ***Sunnyside RFP*** document in the WordPad window.

4. **Click the Print button**  **.**

The current document is sent directly to the print queue.

You can right-click the print job and select Cancel from the shortcut menu that appears.

5. **Click the *Buford Proposal* print job listed in the print queue.**
6. **Click Cancel on the Document menu.**

The selected print job is canceled.

7. **Minimize your printer's window and close the WordPad window.**

Resuming Printing

In this activity, you will activate the printer window and resume the paused print job.

1. **Click your printer's taskbar button.**
2. **Click Pause Printing on the Printer menu.**

The check mark is removed from Pause Printing. The print job on the queue *does not* resume printing since it was specifically paused earlier.

3. **Click the *Sunnyside RFP* print job.**
4. **Click Pause on the Document menu.**

The document now prints.

5. **Close the printer's window.**

You can right-click the print job and select Pause Printing from the shortcut menu to resume printing the job.

SELECTING AND USING FONTS

The appearance of printed text is greatly enhanced by using different styles for the characters that make up the text. Many of the first printers had only a single style of lettering. Hardware additions and cartridges became available to change the style on later printers. Due to printer software, most printers can print more than one style in a single document, without any changes to the hardware.

In the early days of personal computing, the characters you saw on the screen only approximated the look of the printed output. With the coming of WYSIWYG, however, on-screen and printed characters look alike.

If you have trouble viewing the colors and fonts on your screen, Windows 2000 can display in high contrast for easier reading. See Appendix B for more information.

Any text that is printed on paper appears in a font. A *font* is a set of characters that appears with a specific typeface, one or more attributes, and a specific size. A *typeface* is a family for type or printed characters that is determined by particular design or style characteristics. For instance, the Times New Roman typeface looks very different from the Impact typeface, as shown in Figure 7.3. In fact, these two examples demonstrate the two general categories for typefaces: serif and sans serif.

Figure 7.3 ◄
Serif and sans serif typefaces

Serif Typefaces

Courier New
Bookman
Times New Roman

Sans Serif Typefaces

Arial
Impact
Tahoma

Windows
BASICS

Managing Your Print Queue

1. Click Start, Settings, Printers.

2. Open your printer's icon.

3. To hold output in the queue from printing, click Printer, Pause Printing.

4. To hold one job in the queue, select a print job and click Document, Pause.

5. To delete the print job, select a print job and click Document, Cancel.

6. To resume printing jobs from a paused print queue, click Printer, Pause Printing.

7. To resume printing a paused job in the queue, select a print job and click Document, Pause.

A *serif typeface* like Times New Roman is adorned with little lines and curves on the tips, or strokes, of each character—the *serifs.* The text you're reading now is another example of a serif typeface. In general, serif typefaces are better suited for paragraph text because the little lines and curves help your eyes to flow along each line more smoothly as you read the text. *Sans serif typefaces,* like Arial, on the other hand, do not have these lines and curves. Their appearance is more block-like. Sans serif typefaces generally work better for headings where reading ease is not as critical. Figure 7.3 illustrates several serif and sans serif typefaces.

Attributes for typefaces include characteristics such as bold, italic, or underlining. These features enhance the appearance of a typeface. The *weight* of printed characters—that is, the thickness of the characters and the spacing between characters—is also an attribute that affects the appearance of typefaces. Thicker character strokes and/or less letter spacing can make typefaces appear heavier; thinner character strokes and/or more letter spacing can make typefaces appear lighter or more airy.

The size of printed characters is another element that makes up a font. The most common unit of measurement for typefaces is the *point.* One point is equal to $\frac{1}{72}$ inch, and points are used to express vertical measurement. A line of characters in a 12-point typeface occupies approximately $\frac{1}{6}$ inch vertically because $\frac{12}{72}$ points equal $\frac{1}{6}$ inch. In general, body text appears in 10- to 12-point typefaces. Headlines and display type generally appear in bigger sizes, anywhere from 14 to 72 points or more.

When you put together a typeface, size, and one or more attributes, you have a font. For example, 12-point Courier, 10-point Times New Roman Bold, and 36-point Helvetica Condensed Italic are three fonts, but the term *font* is frequently used to refer more generally to the entire font family, for example, Courier, Times New Roman, or Arial.

Using Printer Fonts

Printers produce two types of fonts: scalable and bit-mapped (nonscalable) fonts. You can print **scalable fonts** in a range of sizes. This means you can select the point size from within the application. Windows 2000 provides several scalable **TrueType fonts** (which appear with the *TT* icon beside their names in the Windows 2000 environment). TrueType fonts are desirable for a graphical user interface because they display on screen as they look when printed on paper. **OpenType fonts** (which appear with an *O* in their icon) are a more recent version of scalable fonts. Other manufacturers of scalable, viewable fonts include Bitstream, Speedo, and Adobe. These fonts are supported by Windows 2000 and have their own file type icons.

Bit-mapped fonts (nonscalable fonts) which appear with the *A* icon beside their names in the Windows 2000 environment are usually built into the printer. Each character is composed of a dot pattern. Bit-mapped fonts are not scalable because each size requires its own pattern. When you select a bit-mapped font from within your application software, Windows 2000 tries to match it with a similar screen font.

Viewing and Printing Sample Fonts

In this activity, you will view some of the font options available on your computer system and then print a sampling of selected fonts.

1. Point to **Settings** on the Start menu ![Start] .

2. Click the *Control Panel* folder.

3. Scroll the Control Panel window, if necessary, to locate the *Fonts* folder.

4. Open the *Fonts* folder.

The Fonts window appears, as shown in Figure 7.4. Each font is contained in a separate file and represented by its own icon. TrueType font icons have blue and gray *TT* on their file icons; OpenType fonts have a green and black *O*; bit-mapped fonts have a red *A*.

The set of fonts available on the computer you are using depends on what software has been installed on the computer. Your computer will undoubtedly have a different set than the ones displayed in Figure 7.4.

5. Double-click the **Arial icon**.

The Arial window appears with an informational and sample screen of the selected font, as shown in Figure 7.5.

 *If the Arial (OpenType) font is not available on your system, select another sans serif option, such as Helvetica or MS Sans Serif.*

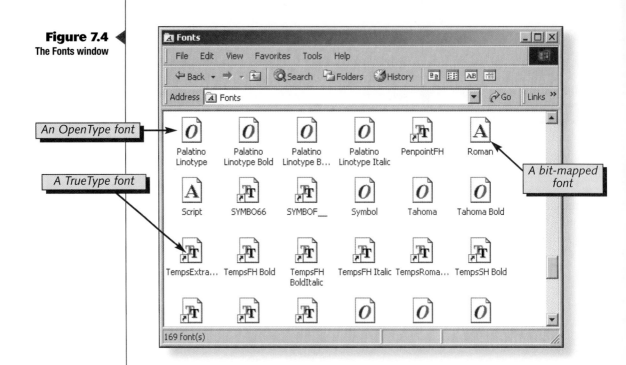

Figure 7.4 ◀
The Fonts window

An OpenType font →

A TrueType font →

A bit-mapped font

Figure 7.5 ◀
The Arial font window

Choose one or two fonts that suit your purpose—one for the body text and one for the title. Don't mix too many fonts or the appearance of your message will detract from what you want to say.

6. **Maximize the window, if necessary.**

7. **Scroll down the sample font window to see the screen display of larger-size type in the selected font.**

Size samples, up to 72 points, appear in the window.

8. **Click Print and then Print again when the Print dialog box appears.**

The font sample is sent to the printer and printed.

9. **Close the font sample (OpenType) window.**

10. **Double-click the Courier New icon in the Fonts window.**

The Courier New window appears with a sample of the selected font.

 *If the Courier New font is not available on your system, select another serif option, such as Times New Roman, Courier, or Bookman.*

11. **Click Print and then Print again.**
12. **Close the font sample window.**
13. **Open the font sample window for another font of your choice.**
14. **Print the sample.**
15. **Close the font sample window.**
16. **Close the Fonts and Control Panel windows.**

SELECTING PAPER AND PAGE CHARACTERISTICS

Print quality is affected not only by fonts but also by paper options. These options control the size, source, and orientation of the paper.

Feeding the Paper

The appearance of your printed output varies widely depending on your printer and the kind of paper on which it can print. Some printers can accept many different sizes of paper, while others are more limited. Usually, dot-matrix printers are either tractor fed (the printer pulls paper with holes on the sides through the printer) or paper fed (the printer pulls one sheet of paper at a time through the printer). Laser, inkjet, and bubble-jet printers use separate sheets of paper stored in trays or a hopper. Some trays or hoppers hold only one size of paper; others hold several sizes. If your printer holds more than one tray at a time, you can print various sized pages within the same document. Otherwise, you have to change trays or feed the paper manually. The Paper Source list in the Properties dialog box lets you select the location you want to use.

Choosing Paper Size

Not all documents must be printed on $8\frac{1}{2}$ x 11-inch paper. Most printers can accommodate various paper sizes. The Device Settings tab in the Properties dialog box lists available paper sizes for your printer. Figure 7.6 shows Paper Size options. Some of the most popular paper sizes are listed in Table 7.1.

 *Your paper size options will depend on your printer.*

Figure 7.6
Some paper options in the
Properties dialog box

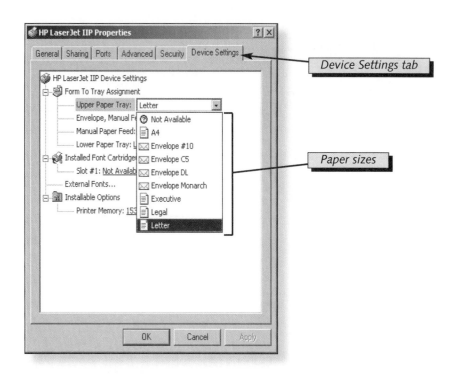

Table 7.1	**Paper Sizes**
SIZE	**DESCRIPTION**
$8\frac{1}{2}$ x 11 in.	Most common paper size. Also called Letter.
$8\frac{1}{2}$ x 14 in.	Longer than Letter paper. Also called Legal.
$7\frac{1}{2}$ x $10\frac{1}{2}$ in.	Executive size. Slightly narrower and shorter than Letter paper.
$3\frac{7}{8}$ x $8\frac{7}{8}$ in.	Envelope (#9).

Selecting the Orientation

Orientation refers to the layout of the image you want to print in relation to the dimensions of the page. You can print your document using one of two orientations—portrait or landscape. **Portrait orientation** is usually considered the "normal" orientation. That is, text and graphics are printed across the shorter width and down the longer length of the page (for example, $8\frac{1}{2}$ x 11 inches). In **landscape orientation,** the text and graphics are printed across the longer width and down the shorter length (for example, 11 x $8\frac{1}{2}$ inches). Figure 7.7 shows these orientations.

Setting Paper Size and Orientation

In this activity, you will view and change various printing options.

1. Open the *Printers* folder from Settings on the Start menu ![Start].

The Printers window appears.

Figure 7.7
Portrait and landscape
orientations

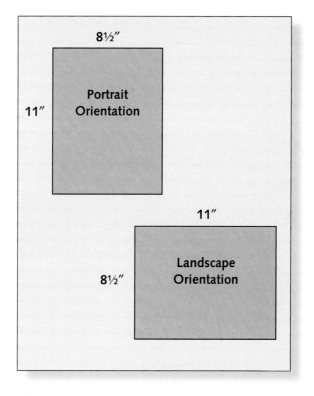

Windows
BASICS

Setting Paper Size and Orientation

1. Click Start, Settings, Printers.

2. Double-click your printer's icon.

3. Click Properties from the Printer menu.

4. Click the Device Settings tab.

5. Select paper size.

6. Click the General tab.

7. Click the Printing Preferences button.

8. Click the Layout tab.

9. Click the Landscape or Portrait button.

2. Double-click the icon named for the printer connected to your system.

3. Click **Properties** on the Printer menu.

The Properties window appears, with tabs for printer-specific options.

 *Your Properties window may show a different group of options than the ones shown in Figure 7.6—depending on your printer.*

4. Click the **Device Settings tab**.

5. Click the **Upper Paper Tray option** or **Auto Sheet feeder option**.

The set of paper options appears, as shown in Figure 7.6. The options are probably set to the defaults.

6. Click the **triangle button** and change the paper size to **Letter**, if necessary.

 If you click a paper size option, you will change the default paper size.

7. Click the **General tab**.

8. Click the **Printing Preferences button**.

A window with at least two tabs appears, as shown in Figure 7.8.

9. Click the **Layout tab**, if necessary.

10. Click the **Landscape option button**, if necessary.

Figure 7.8
The Printing Preferences
window

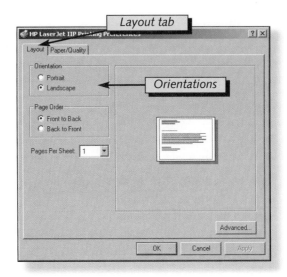

11. Click OK.

You have just changed the orientation to landscape. The next document you print will now appear in landscape orientation.

12. Close all open windows.

HANDS On

Printing a Document and Restoring Page Orientation

In this activity, you will drag and drop a document onto your Printer icon to print the document. Then, you will switch the page orientation setting to portrait.

1. Open the *Printers* folder.

2. Open the My Computer window and then open the drive containing your Student Data Disk.

Note   *Verify that your Student Data Disk is in the floppy drive.*

3. Open the *Graphics* folder.

You should only have two open windows on your desktop—the Printers window and the Graphics window.

4. Tile the open windows vertically.

5. Drag and drop the *Cupid* file icon from the *Graphics* folder to the icon for the printer attached to your system.

The file is sent to the printer. After a few moments, the printer will begin printing the image with landscape orientation, if your printer supports it.

6. In the Printers window, double-click the icon for the printer connected to your system.

7. Click Properties on the Printer menu.

Printing a Document

1. Open your Printers folder.

2. Open your document drive and folder.

3. Drag and drop your document icon onto your printer icon.

The Properties window for the printer appears on the desktop.

8. Click the **General tab**, if necessary.

9. Click the **Printing Preferences button**.

10. Click the **Portrait option button**.

11. Click **OK**.

12. Click **OK** again.

The orientation is now set for portrait orientation.

13. Close all open windows.

SETTING PRINTING RESOLUTION

Almost every printer produces text and images graphically—that is, as a series of dots. The more dots the printer can print in a given area, the higher the *resolution.* Many printers can print at several resolutions. As a rule, the higher the resolution, the clearer the hard copy appears and the longer the printer takes to print. High resolution printing also uses more ink. *Draft* is the lowest resolution, while *letter quality* is the highest resolution. You should print in draft mode when the quality of the output is not important or when you want a printout to proofread or edit. Use letter quality to create more attractive and readable hard copy.

Resolution is measured in the number of dots per inch *(dpi)*. Sometimes resolution for an inkjet or a dot-matrix printer is expressed as two numbers that correspond to the number of dots printed horizontally and vertically in a square inch. Thus, a resolution of 180 x 180 means the printer can print up to 180 dots horizontally and vertically in an inch. Laser printers usually express resolution with a single number in dots per inch (dpi) units, such as 600 or 1200 dpi. Many printers skip the numbering options altogether and express print quality as Fine or Letter Quality, Normal, Economy, or Draft.

Resetting Printing Resolution

In this activity, you will print two samples, each in a different resolution.

Note — *This activity is only meaningful if your printer supports multiple resolutions.*

1. Open the Printers window.

2. Open the icon of the printer connected to your system.

Setting Printing Resolution

1. Click Start, Settings, and Printers folder.

2. Double-click the printer you are using.

3. Select Properties from the Printer menu.

4. Click the Printing Preferences button.

5. Click the Advanced button.

6. Click the Print Quality triangle button.

7. Select a resolution and click OK.

3. Click **Properties** on the Printer menu.

Your printer's Properties dialog box appears.

4. Click the **Printing Preferences button**.

5. Click the **Advanced button**.

6. Click the **Print Quality option**.

7. Click the **triangle button** next to the **Print Quality box**.

If you are using a dot-matrix printer, then a set of Graphics options appears that is similar to the set shown in Figure 7.9. If you are using a laser printer, then a set of Graphics options similar to the one shown in Figure 7.10 appears.

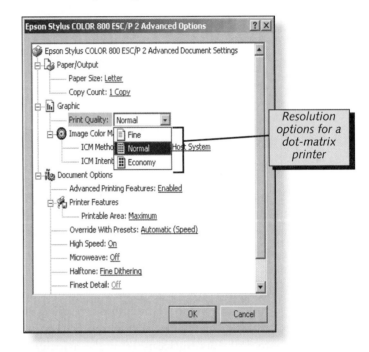

Figure 7.9
Graphics options for
a dot-matrix printer

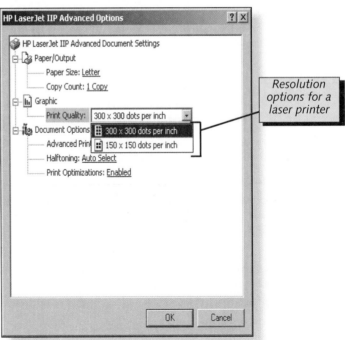

Figure 7.10
Graphics options for
a laser printer

8. Select the lowest numbers, Economy, Draft, or dpi for the Resolution setting.

9. Click **OK** three times to close the Properties windows.

10. Close the window for your printer.

11. Open the *Graphics* folder on your Student Data Disk.

12. Tile the Printers window and the *Graphics* folder.

13. Drag the *Star* file icon on your Student Data Disk to the icon for the printer connected to your system.

The selected file is sent to the printer.

14. Reset your printer to the highest resolution.

If necessary, review steps 1 through 10.

15. Print the *Star* file again.

16. Compare the results of the two printouts.

The last printout will be clearer than the first printout.

17. Reset your printer to the original resolution, if necessary.

18. Close all open windows.

19. Remove your **Student Data Disk** from the floppy drive.

TROUBLESHOOTING PRINTING PROBLEMS

In addition to the help techniques you discovered in Lesson 2, Windows 2000 has over 20 troubleshooters that let you diagnose and solve technical problems ranging from memory to sound to modem problems. You can run the troubleshooters whenever you want, or you can run one in response to a prompt when a problem occurs. By far, however, the most common hardware problem that affects PC users relates to printing errors. So many things can go wrong when you print—your printer may not be turned on, properly connected to the computer, have enough paper, be using the right driver, and so on. The Windows 2000 Print Troubleshooter guides you through a series of questions and possible solutions. By responding to the questions, new suggestions are made until either the problem is solved, or the problem is unsolvable by the troubleshooter, in which case you are asked to go online through Web Help in the Windows Help window.

When you run a troubleshooter, you should follow these guidelines:

■ Minimize all open windows using the Show Desktop icon 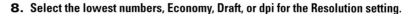 on the taskbar.

■ Resize the Help window and move it to the right side of the desktop.

■ Click Hide from the Options button to close the left pane of the Help window, if necessary.

■ Follow each step and read the suggestions and questions carefully.

HANDS

Running the Print Troubleshooter

In this activity, you will fix a printing problem using suggestions from the Windows 2000 Print Troubleshooter.

1. If your instructor tells you to do so, turn off your printer.

Warning *You may not want to turn off the printer if you are on a network or are otherwise sharing a printer. If not, go to step 2.*

2. Open your printer's Properties window.

3. Click **Print Test Page** from the General tab.

A dialog box opens asking if your test page printed correctly. If your printer is turned off, of course, your test page did not print at all. If your printer is on, the test page probably printed, or soon will.

4. Click **Troubleshoot**, whether the page printed or not.

The first Windows 2000 Print Troubleshooter window appears, as shown in Figure 7.11, asking what kind of print problem you are having. For the sake of this exercise, pretend that you don't know what the problem is.

Figure 7.11 ◄
The first Print Troubleshooter window

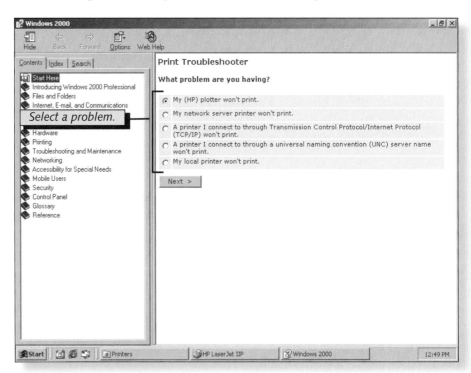

5. Maximize the window, if necessary.

6. Click **Hide**.

7. Click the **My local printer won't print option button**.

Running a Windows 2000 Troubleshooter

1. Respond to a prompt indicating a problem.

2. Click option buttons identifying your situation.

3. Click option buttons indicating whether suggestions worked or not.

4. Continue until the problem is solved.

8. Click **Next**.

The next Troubleshooter window appears asking another question.

9. Click **I am using a non-postscript printer**, and then click **Next**.

The next Troubleshooter window asks another question.

10. Click **I want to skip this step and try something else**, and then click **Next**.

11. Read the text in each window and respond by clicking **No** or **I want to skip this step**, and then clicking **Next**.

12. Continue until the Troubleshooter identifies your problem or gives up and asks you to contact your printer's manufacturer.

13. If you turned off your printer in step 1, turn the printer on now.

Your printer should print the test page.

14. Close the Troubleshooter window.

15. Close all open windows.

Always choose from a few fonts that appeal to your taste. Stick with those fonts. You will develop a style that makes your documents immediately recognizable.

You may explore Downloading Fonts by continuing with the On the Web activity that follows, or you may proceed directly to the exercises for this lesson. If you are finished with your computer session, log off the computer you are using.

Follow the "log off" procedures for your lab or school environment.

ON*the*WEB

DOWNLOADING FONTS

A good "starter set" of fonts—some of the fonts are good for head-lines, some for body text, others serving special purposes, such as casual fonts and symbol fonts—come with Windows 2000. Many software packages, like Microsoft Office, include additional fonts. You can purchase font sets from a wide variety of companies. The Internet is also a source for fonts.

Downloading is the process of copying files from another computer to yours. Once located, you can download programs, graphics, docu-ments, and even fonts onto your hard disk drive.

 Always secure permission from your instructor before you add a font to a computer that belongs to a school.

In this activity, you will download a font from a site on the Internet.

1. **Click the Launch Internet Explorer Browser button** ![e] **on your taskbar.**

You connect to the Internet and your home page appears.

 If your computer's home page is Microsoft, skip to step 3.

2. **Type** www.msn.com **in the Address box.**

The Microsoft home page appears.

3. **Type** font **in the Search the Web text box.**

4. **Click Go.**

A page appears with links to sites offering fonts.

5. **Scroll down, if necessary, and click the TrueType Core Fonts for Windows link.**

You see a page of fonts filled with examples and links, as shown in Figure 7.12.

6. **Find a font you like and click current server to download the file.**

You see a File Download dialog box. Your options are to run the file or to save it to disk and run it later.

ON_the_**WEB**

Figure 7.12 ◀
Microsoft Web page listing fonts
available for free downloading

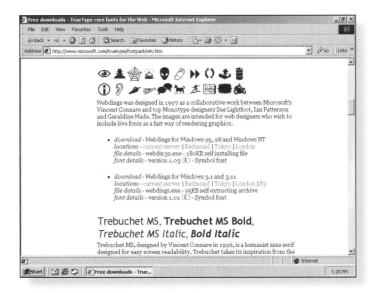

7. **Click the Run this program from its current location option button.**

8. **Click OK.**

Another File Download dialog box shows the progress of your font file transfer. When the file download is complete, you may see a Security Warning and then a License Agreement dialog box.

9. **Click Yes to the Security Warning dialog box and Yes to the License Agreement dialog box.**

A message box informs you that the new font has been installed on the computer you are using.

10. **Click OK.**

11. **Close the Internet Explorer.**

12. **Disconnect from the Internet, if necessary.**

13. **You may proceed directly to the exercises for this lesson. If, however, you are finished with your computer session, log off the computer you are using.**

Follow the "log off" procedures for your lab or school environment.

Lesson Summary & Exercises

SUMMARY

After you complete this lesson, you should know how to do the following:

Managing Your Printer

■ To open your printer's window, double-click your printer's icon in the **Printers** folder.

■ Select Pause to stop printing jobs from the print queue.

■ To cancel a job from the queue, select the job and click Cancel from the Document menu.

Selecting and Using Fonts

■ To display sample fonts, double-click the font icon in the **Fonts** folder window.

Selecting Paper and Page Characteristics

■ To set portrait or landscape orientation, click the Orientation option button in the printer's Properties, Device Settings, General tab, Printing Preferences window.

Setting Printing Resolution

■ To change resolution settings, click an option from the Print Quality drop-down list of the printer's Properties, Printing Preferences, Advanced window.

Troubleshooting Printing Problems

■ Run the Print Troubleshooter by responding to a prompt indicating a printing problem.

On the Web: Downloading Fonts

■ To download fonts, launch your browser and access the Microsoft home page. Search for fonts and click a link to a site offering free fonts. Click the font you want and then select the *Run this program from its current location* option button.

Lesson Summary & Exercises

NEW TERMS TO REMEMBER

After you complete this lesson, you should know the meaning of these terms:

attribute	letter quality	resolution
bit-mapped font	nonscalable font	sans serif typeface
downloading	OpenType font	scalable font
dpi	point	serif
draft	portrait orientation	serif typeface
font	print queue	TrueType font
hard copy	print spooling	typeface
landscape orientation	purging	weight

MATCHING EXERCISE

Match each of the terms with the definitions on the right:

Terms

1. draft

2. font

3. landscape

4. point

5. portrait

6. print queue

7. print spooling

8. resolution

9. scalable font

10. typeface

Definitions

a. Page orientation in which an image is printed across the $8\frac{1}{2}$-inch width of an $8\frac{1}{2}$ x 11-inch page

b. Process in which data sent for printer output is first sent to special files on the hard disk

c. Graphics quality of printed images determined by the number of dots per square inch that make up the image

d. Appearance of printed characters based on a specific typeface, size, and one or more specific attributes

e. Low-resolution print quality

f. Typeface, one or more attributes, and weight that a printer can print in any size

g. Family of design or style characteristics for printed characters

h. Unit of measurement for printed characters that equals $\frac{1}{72}$ inch

i. Page orientation in which an image is printed across the 11-inch width of an $8\frac{1}{2}$ x 11-inch page

j. Special area that stores print jobs temporarily and that allows for manipulating them before the data is sent to the printer

Lesson Summary & Exercises

COMPLETION EXERCISE

Fill in the missing word or phrase for each of the following questions:

1. The ability to type a memo in a word processing application while the printer prints a worksheet is possible because of Windows 2000's _____ _____.

2. _____ is a one-step technique for clearing the entire print queue.

3. Characters appearing in 12-point Arial Bold Italic are an example of a(n) _____.

4. As a general rule, _____ fonts are better suited for body text because they are easier for your eyes to follow as you read the text.

5. A higher point size number means a(n) _____ font.

6. Letter quality means a(n) _____ resolution than draft quality.

7. Bit-mapped fonts are generally built into _____ _____ printers.

8. _____ orientation means that text and graphics are printed across the length of a standard, $8\frac{1}{2}$ x 11-inch page.

9. Bold text has a heavier _____ than text that is not boldfaced.

10. The computer's printed output is known as _____ _____.

SHORT-ANSWER QUESTIONS

Write a brief answer to each of the following questions:

1. List and define the elements or characteristics that make up a font.

2. List the advantages of print spooling rather than sending data directly to a printer.

3. Describe briefly a situation in which you should use draft quality for printed output and a situation in which you should use letter quality.

4. As a general rule, which kind of typeface, serif or sans serif, would work best for large headlines? Why?

5. Briefly describe the procedure that you can use to cancel a print job.

6. Why might you want to cancel a print job?

7. Differentiate between scalable and nonscalable fonts.

8. How do you make and print font sample sheets?

9. What is the difference between portrait and landscape orientation? What steps do you follow to change default orientation?

10. How do you view and display the typefaces available to your system?

Lesson Summary & Exercises

APPLICATION PROJECTS

Insert your Student Data Disk into drive A: (or drive B:). Perform the following actions to complete these projects:

1. Start WordPad, and then open the file named **Buford Proposal** in the **Word Processing** folder. Open the window for the printer connected to your system and pause the printer. Use the appropriate command or button to print **Buford Proposal**. Then open the document stored in the **Sunnyside RFP** file in the **Word Processing** folder. Print this document. Activate your printer's window. Cancel the print job for the **Sunnyside RFP** document and resume printing **Buford Proposal** document. Close all open windows.

2. If your printer has more than one printer resolution, access the Print Quality options for your printer. (Otherwise, skip this project.) Set the appropriate options for low resolution and/or draft quality. Next, start WordPad and open the document stored in the **Sunnyside RFP** file in the **Word Processing** folder. Select the appropriate command or button to send the document to the printer. After the document prints, return to the printer's Print Quality options and set the appropriate options for high resolution and/or letter quality. Return to the WordPad program, send the document to the printer again, and compare the two printed images. Describe briefly any differences between the two printouts. Close all open windows.

3. Access your printer's Device Settings dialog box and select the Landscape orientation. Next, start Paint and open the **Fence** file in the **Graphics** folder. Send the image to the printer. Then return to the Device Settings dialog box for the printer and reset the orientation to Portrait. Print the image again. Close all open windows.

4. Open the window for your printer and pause the printer. Then start Paint. Quickly open and send to the printer at least three Paint images from the **Graphics** folder, such as **Blue Tube, Cupid**, and **Star**. Next, activate your printer's window and delete the second and third print jobs before they are sent to the printer. Allow the first print job to print, and then close all the windows.

5. Create print samples for at least three fonts in addition to the ones you sampled in Lesson 7. Keep these printouts to begin a font sample booklet that you can refer to for future font choices.

6. You must be able to connect to the Internet to complete this On the Web project. Launch your browser and connect to the Internet. Use any of the search engines to find fonts you can download. Try out your new font in a WordPad document. Name your document **New Font** and save it in the **Documents** folder of your Working Copy Disk.

Copying, Moving, Exchanging, and Sharing Data

CONTENTS

OBJECTIVES

After you complete this lesson, you will be able to do the following:

- Explain multitasking and how it facilitates data exchange.
- Describe the various ways that you can copy, move, and exchange data within and between files.
- Trace the development of data-sharing methods from importing and exporting, to converting, linking, and object embedding.
- Drag and drop data from one document to another in WordPad.
- Place data into the Clipboard and view it.
- Use the Clipboard commands—Cut, Copy, Paste—to move and copy data within and between files and to move and copy files within and between disks.
- Use OLE to copy objects from one application to another and edit the objects without exiting the client application.
- Share documents with other users through electronic mail.

In the early days of personal computers, combining data from two or more applications into one document was difficult or even impossible. Data created with different applications might be incompatible; and even when compatibility wasn't a problem, getting information from one document and into another required creativity and tedious, time-consuming procedures.

The Windows interface makes combining objects from different applications much easier. Now, since the release of Windows 95, users can take advantage of a new approach to data sharing—one that focuses specifically on the document and the tools used to create it. In this lesson, you will learn how to use several techniques to combine objects into one document.

SHARING DATA

Before the development of graphical user interfaces, working on multiple documents required a user to go to exhaustive lengths. For instance, combining a graphics image with a text document required a user to open a word processing application; create, edit, and format the text in the application's proprietary format; save the text in a file; close the application; and then open the graphics application to create, edit, and save the image. Then the user needed to convert the data in the image file to a format that the word processing application could recognize. The user had to then open the word processing program and file again. Different data formats often made it necessary to use a separate program to perform the data conversion.

Multitasking

As hardware became more powerful, computers could handle more than one task or program at a time. Working with more than one program or file at a time is called *multitasking.* Multitasking makes computing time-efficient. For instance, the computer can alphabetize a long list of names in the *background* or "invisibly" and still free up the screen so that you can open and use a different program to continue working. The print spooling that you used in Lesson 7 is another example of background processing.

Working within different applications to create different types of data characterizes an *application-centric approach* to computing. With this approach, each application has its own user interface, and no guarantee of consistency from one program to another exists.

USING APPLICATION-CENTRIC SHARING METHODS

Four types of application-centric file-sharing methods exist: importing and exporting data, converting data, linking data, and sharing data within integrated software packages.

- *Importing and Exporting Data.* One program saves its document in a format another program can use in a process called *exporting.* The other program opens the document by *importing* it.

- *Converting Data.* Small translation programs convert files from one format to another.

- *Linking Data.* **Linking** sets up an ongoing relationship between data and the program that created it, and eliminates the need to re-import the data every time the file is edited. One such technique is called *Dynamic Data Exchange (DDE).*

- *Using Integrated Software Packages.* Some programs combine word processing, spreadsheets, database, graphics, and communications into one program. Microsoft Office, Microsoft Works, and ClarisWorks are examples of software packages of this type.

USING DOCUMENT-CENTRIC METHODS

The developers of Windows realized that combining data created by different applications requires more than common user access, a graphical user interface, and multitasking. Instead, a way must exist to concentrate on the

single document—the final product—without being overly concerned with the programs that create each type of information within the document. This view of computer work is called a ***document-centric approach.*** There are several methods for data-sharing in Windows 2000.

- *Drag-and-drop.* The user selects text in one location and drags it to another.
- *The Clipboard.* The user selects text in one location, uses a special memory area to hold the data, and then deposits the data into another location.

Using Drag-and-Drop

Just as when you use the drag-and-drop methods to move or copy files and folders, you can do the same things with data. First you select the data. Then you drag and drop to move the data to a new location. If you hold down `Ctrl` while you drag, you will copy the selected text.

Moving Data with Drag-and-Drop

In this activity, you will use the drag-and-drop technique to move data within a document.

1. **Open WordPad.**
2. **Insert your Student Data Disk in the disk drive.**
3. **Open *Sunnyside RFP* from the *Word Processing* folder.**
4. **Click to the left of the *M* in the date, *March 1, 2000.***
5. **Hold down `⇧ Shift` and click to the right of the second zero in *March 1, 2000.***

The entire date is highlighted.

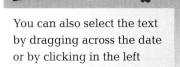
6. **Drag the date down to the line just above *Randi Canyon,* and then release the button.**

The date is now on the left margin.

7. **Click before the *R* in *Randi* and press `Enter ←`.**

You now have a blank line after the date.

8. **Click the Save button 💾 .**

Copying Data from One Document to Another

You can also drag data from one document to another. All you have to do is have both documents visible on the screen. In this activity, you will copy information from one letter to another.

1. **The WordPad window should still contain the *Sunnyside RFP* document.**

Using the Drag-and-Drop Method

1. Select the data to be moved or copied.

2. Drag the data to the new location.

3. Hold Ctrl and drag to copy the data.

2. Open WordPad.

A second copy of the WordPad accessory opens. The document window is blank.

 *Some programs, like Microsoft Word, let you work with more than one document at a time. To work on two documents with WordPad, however, you have to open the program twice.*

3. Right-click the taskbar and select **Tile Windows Vertically**.

Both copies of WordPad are now visible.

4. Click to the left of the first line *(Woody Glenn)* and drag down past the salutation *(Dear Ms. Canyon:)*.

The opening portion of the letter is selected.

5. Hold Ctrl and drag and drop the selection to the other WordPad window.

The selected text is duplicated in the second document, as shown in Figure 8.1. To write a new letter to Randi Canyon, you would just change the date and start typing!

Figure 8.1
Text copied from one document to another

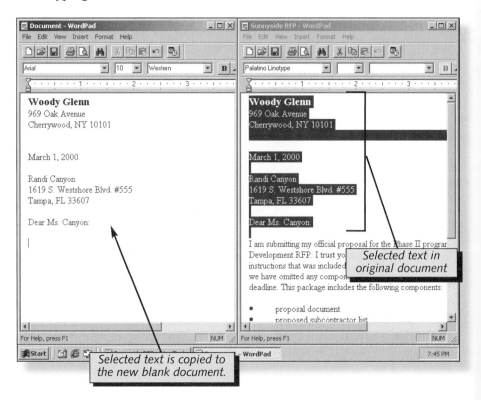

Selected text in original document

Selected text is copied to the new blank document.

6. Save the new letter as a Word for Windows document named *Randi Canyon* in the *Word Processing* folder of your Student Data Disk.

7. Close all open windows.

Protect the Clipboard.
When you cut or copy data
it replaces anything already
stored in the Clipboard.
Paste the Clipboard con-
tents *before* you put any
new data into it.

Using the Clipboard

When you use the Cut or Copy commands in Windows 2000, you place the selected information in a special area of main memory called the ***Clipboard.*** You can paste the data in the Clipboard elsewhere in the document window or in another document window, even if the second document window is in another application. If the programs support it, you can create a link to the software that placed the data in the Clipboard by using the Paste Link option on the Edit menu. Even if you cannot link the data, the Clipboard is an easy way to transfer information between any two applications—even between a Windows and a DOS program.

Note   *To edit linked data, use the Links option of the Edit menu.*

In previous lessons, you used the Cut/Copy and Paste commands to move or copy files (Lesson 5) and graphics (Lesson 6). Now that you know about the Clipboard, you can learn a more accurate description of these commands.

- ■ ***Copy*** places a replica of the selected object into the Clipboard and leaves the original alone.

- ■ ***Cut*** places a replica of the selected object into the Clipboard and removes it from its original location.

- ■ ***Paste*** inserts the contents of the Clipboard at the currently active location, such as the insertion point in a text file or the Contents pane in the Explorer window.

You must be made aware of two restrictions when you use the Clipboard. Every time you copy data to the Clipboard, the previous contents of the Clipboard are erased. And, like all memory, the contents of the Clipboard are erased when the computer is turned off.

Windows 2000 also has a ***ClipBook***. You use the ClipBook to store data from the Clipboard and to share that information with other users on your network. Unlike the Clipboard, which holds only one piece of information at a time, the ClipBook can save many pieces of information. Each piece of information is saved on a separate *page*. Pages in the ClipBook can be copied into the Clipboard and pasted into documents. You can also copy pages from other users' ClipBooks into your Clipboard.

Copying Data to the Clipboard

1. Select the data to copy.

2. Select Copy from the Edit menu.

Copying Data to the Clipboard

In this activity, you will copy data from a document into the Clipboard.

   1. Open WordPad.

   2. Insert your Student Data Disk in the disk drive, click the Open button 📂 **on the toolbar.**

   3. Open the *Word Processing* folder.

   4. Open the *Text* subfolder.

   5. Select the Text Documents (*.txt) option on the Files of type list.

   6. Open the *Expenses* file.

The data stored in text format appears in the WordPad window.

7. Click **Select All** on the Edit menu to select all of the text in the document.

The entire document highlights.

8. Click the **Copy button** 🖹 on the toolbar.

The selected text is copied to the Clipboard.

Viewing the Contents of the Clipboard

A special Windows accessory program called ClipBook Viewer lets you examine the contents of the Clipboard. The ClipBook Viewer helps you understand how the Clipboard commands work, and lets you save the contents of the Clipboard in a file for later use. In this activity, you will see the information that you just copied into the Clipboard.

1. Click **Run** from the Start menu 🟦 Start.

A dialog box opens. By entering the name of a program file in the text box, you can run an application—even if it has no desktop icon or Start menu entry.

2. Type clipbrd and click **OK**.

3. Maximize the Clipboard window in the bottom-left corner of the ClipBook window.

The data you copied from WordPad shows in the ClipBook Viewer, as shown in Figure 8.2.

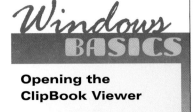
Figure 8.2 ◀
The ClipBook Viewer

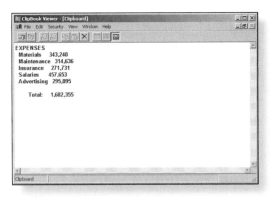

4. Tile the open windows horizontally.

Your screen should resemble Figure 8.3.

Pasting Between Documents

In this activity, you will paste the data you copied into a different document.

1. Click the WordPad's **Open button** 📂.

The Open dialog box appears.

Pasting Data to the Clipboard

1. Position your insertion pointer where you want to place the data.

2. Select Paste from the Edit menu.

Figure 8.3
ClipBook Viewer with text copied from WordPad

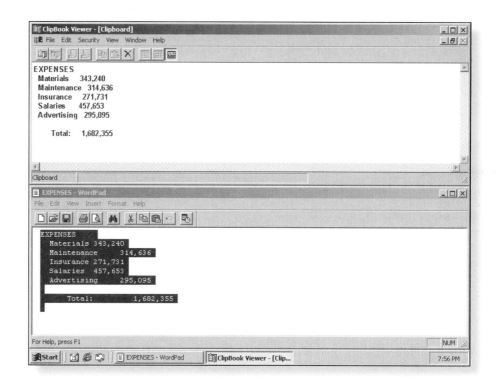

The shortcut key for Paste is Ctrl + v.

Data stored in RAM is held as a series of binary digits, or bits. Each character is made up of eight binary digits.

---

2. Make sure the disk location is set for the drive that contains your Student Data Disk.

3. Change the Files of type setting to **All Documents**.

4. Click the **Up One Level toolbar button** .

5. Open the *Buford Proposal* icon file in the *Word Processing* folder.

The file opens and the document appears in the WordPad window.

6. Maximize the WordPad window.

7. Move the insertion point to the line below *tomorrow* near the end of the document.

8. Click the **Paste button** on the toolbar.

The copied text is pasted into the document at the insertion point. Notice that the text has the same formatting as in the original document (Courier New).

9. Align the numbers by adding a tab or deleting spaces in front of each number.

10. Insert a blank line before the *Expenses* heading.

11. Click the **Save button** .

12. Print the document, if desired.

13. Restore the WordPad window so that you can see the ClipBook Viewer.

The ClipBook Viewer still contains the copied passage. This passage will remain here until you cut or copy another object or until you log off the computer you are using.

14. Close the ClipBook Viewer and WordPad.

USING OBJECT LINKING AND EMBEDDING

By far, the most flexible and document-centric method of sharing data involves **embedding** (or integrating) an object, such as an image or a block of text, from one program into another program. The program responsible for creating or editing the object is called the **server.** The program that will contain the embedded object is called the **client.**

Although several standards exist for embedding objects between server and client applications, **Object Linking and Embedding (OLE)** is the most common. To use OLE, both the client and server programs must support OLE.

In the most recent version, OLE 2.0, you can edit an embedded object directly in the client application. Double-clicking the object brings the server application's menu, icons, and other editing aids into the client application window. The File and Windows menus belong to the client, while the other menus come from the server. When you click outside the object, your client application menus and toolbars return to normal.

> *Note* *If both applications support it, you can use the drag-and-drop process to move an object from the server to the client window. While Windows 2000 supports OLE 2.0, not all application software on your computer supports the latest standard. Therefore, you may find yourself limited to the older OLE 1.0 standard in which you edit an object in the server program; when you double-click the object in the client program, the server program opens.*

HANDS On

Copying an Object

In this activity, you will open the Paint accessory program and copy an object to the Clipboard.

> *Note* *The steps to embedding an editable object into a document are the same as plain ordinary Copy and Paste. With OLE, however, the embedded object is editable, as you will see later.*

1. **Start WordPad with your Student Data Disk in the disk drive.**
2. **Open _Poem_ in the _Word Processing_ folder.**
3. **Start Paint.**

The Paint window opens and appears on the desktop.

4. **Maximize the Paint window, if necessary.**
5. **Open the image stored in the _Star_ file from the _Graphics_ folder.**

The shortcut key for Copy is Ctrl + c; the shortcut key for Cut is Ctrl + x.

6. **Click the Select tool and drag a selection outline around the star image.**

7. **Click Copy on the Edit menu.**

The selected image is copied to the Clipboard.

8. **Close Paint.**

Paint and the *Star* file are no longer in the computer's main memory.

Embedding an Object

In this activity, you will embed the copied bit-mapped star object in a WordPad document.

1. **With *Poem* open in WordPad, activate and maximize the WordPad window, if necessary.**

You can set up StickyKeys if you want to use ⇧ Shift, Ctrl, or Alt key combinations by pressing one key at a time. See Appendix B for details.

2. **Press Ctrl + End to move the insertion point to the end of the document.**

3. **Click Paste from the Edit menu.**

The image copied from the *Star* file appears in the document. Notice the frame surrounding the image and the square handles at each corner and midpoint of the frame. These features indicate that this image is an embedded object.

4. **Click to the right of the graphics frame.**

Your document should look similar to Figure 8.4. The handles disappear and the insertion point appears to the right of the image.

Figure 8.4
The embedded object in a WordPad document

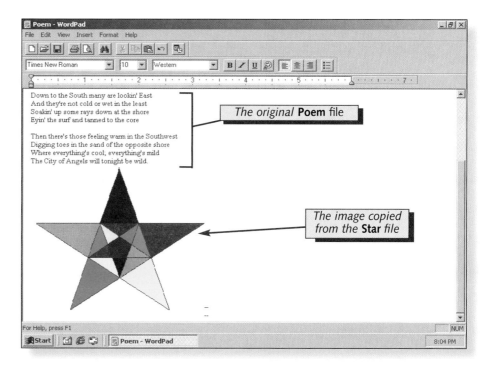

Windows
BASICS

Using Object Linking and Embedding

1. Create an object in the server application.

2. Select the object and save it or copy it to the Clipboard.

3. Open the destination document in the client application.

4. Click Insert New Object from the Insert menu if embedding a saved object, or click Paste if embedding from the Clipboard.

5. Double-click the object to edit it using the server application's tools.

Figure 8.5
The embedded object in a WordPad document with Paint tools

Editing an Embedded Object

Once you have an object embedded in your document, you can edit the document using the server's tools.

1. **Open the *Poem* document in WordPad, if necessary, and ensure that the star object is embedded from the previous exercise.**

2. **Click the star.**

Its frame and handles reappear to indicate that you selected the object. The document does not display an insertion point.

3. **Double-click inside the frame and wait while the Paint tools appear, as shown in Figure 8.5.**

Notice that the title bar still says "WordPad" and that the taskbar does not contain a Paint button. Paint is now open strictly inside of WordPad.

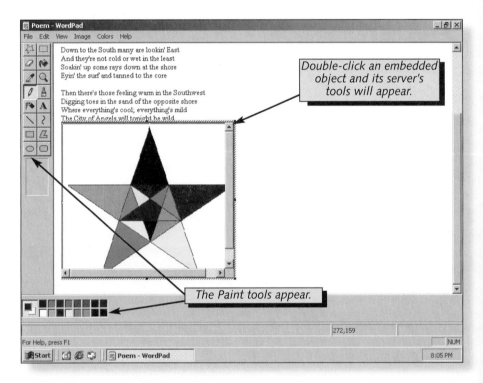

4. **Click the Fill with Color tool, click a light gray from the palette, and fill the background, as shown in Figure 8.6.**

5. **Click to the right of the graphics frame two times.**

The frame and the Paint tools vanish. The edited star appears in the WordPad document, with WordPad tools available.

6. **Replace your Student Data Disk with your Working Copy Disk.**

7. **Click Save As on the File menu.**

Figure 8.6 ◄
Editing the embedded object

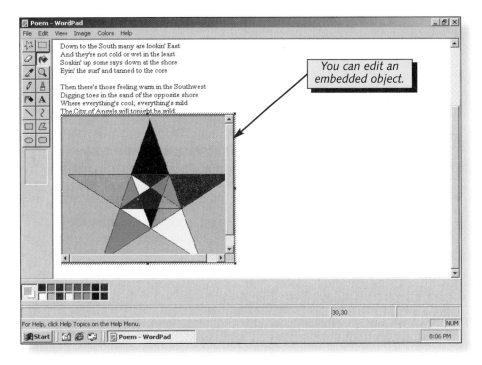

8. Change the Save in box to the *Documents* folder on your Working Copy Disk.

9. Type Winstar **as the file name and click** **Save**.

The document, containing the text from **Poem** and the image from **Star**, is saved in the new **Winstar** file on your Working Copy Disk.

10. **Click the** **Print button** 🖨.

The document is sent to the printer and begins printing.

11. **Close WordPad.**

12. **Remove the** **Working Copy Disk** **from the floppy drive.**

Note *You may explore Sharing Data Using E-mail by continuing with the On the Web section that follows, or you may proceed directly to the exercises for this lesson. If you are finished with your computer session, log off the computer you are using.*

Warning *Follow the "log off" procedures for your lab or school environment.*

ON*the*WEB

SHARING DATA USING E-MAIL

You can exchange information with other users over a network or on the Internet using electronic mail. All e-mail programs let you create a message using the same kinds of tools as Notepad. Like Notepad, the formatting features in these programs are very limited. If you want more sophisticated formatting, you can create your message in a program such as WordPad, save it, and attach the document to your e-mail message.

Composing an E-mail Message

In this activity, you will launch your e-mail program and write a short message.

1. Click the Launch Outlook Express taskbar button 🖳.

The icon launches your default e-mail program. If you are using a program other than Outlook Express, your screens and steps will be different, although the concepts are the same.

2. Click Cancel if you are prompted to select a connection.

Since you will not be sending your e-mail message in this activity, you do not need to go online. You will see your Outlook Express program as shown in Figure 8.7. Outlook Express is an applet that is installed with Internet Explorer. It lets you send, receive, and manage electronic mail messages.

Figure 8.7 ◀
The Outlook Express window

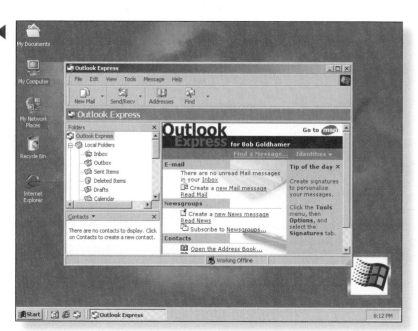

3. Maximize the Outlook Express window.

4. Click the **New Mail button** ⬚ on the toolbar.

Note ✎ *Click View, Layout, and click the toolbar check box if the toolbar is not visible.*

5. Click **Cancel**, if you are prompted to import either an address book or messages.

You will see the New Message window, as shown in Figure 8.8. In this window, you write your message, choose who to send it to, and attach any documents you want to share. Your insertion point should be in the To: text box, into which you enter the address of the recipient. E-mail addresses are in a specific format: a name and the at sign (@) and the name of the company or organization. Since you are not really sending the message, you will enter a fictitious e-mail address.

Figure 8.8 ◄
The New Message window

6. Maximize the New Message window.

7. Type bruce@acme.com **in the To: text box.**

You can maintain e-mail addresses and other information on people you frequently contact using the address book. If you have added a name to the address book, you can click the card icon to select the recipient.

8. Type Revised Budget **in the Subject: text box.**

When the recipient reads his or her mail, the sender, the date, and the subject are listed. Properly identifying an important message ensures that the message will receive the attention it deserves.

9. Type the following in the message text box :

Attached you will find the budget changes approved by the board.
Get back to me with your revised budget worksheet ASAP.
(your name)

Attaching a File to an E-mail Message

To send an extended message, you can either add more text in the message text box or attach a document you have already written and saved. In this activity, you will attach a document from your Student Data Disk.

1. Make sure the Revised Budget (New Message) window is on the screen from the previous activity.

2. Click the Attach File button on the toolbar.

The Insert Attachment dialog box appears, requesting the location and name of the file you want to attach.

3. Insert your Student Data Disk in the disk drive.

4. Change the Look in box to the *Word Processing* **folder of your Student Data Disk.**

5. Select the *Buford Proposal* **file.**

6. Click the Attach button.

An icon of the document, with its name and size, appears in the Attach text box, as shown in Figure 8.9. If you were ready to send the message, you would click the Send button ⊟. Since this is a fictitious message to a fictitious recipient, you will now cancel the message.

Figure 8.9 ◀
A message with
an attached file

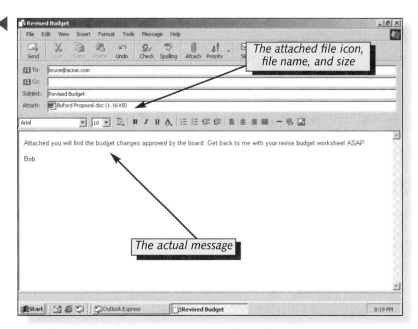

7. Click the **Close button** ☒ of the Revised Budget (New Message) window.

8. Click **No** when prompted to save the message.

9. Click the **Close button** ☒ of the Outlook Express window.

10. Remove your **Student Data Disk** from the disk drive.

11. Disconnect from the Internet, if necessary.

12. You may proceed directly to the exercises for this lesson. If, however, you are finished with your computer session, log off the computer you are using.

Warning

Follow the "log off" procedures for your lab or school environment.

Lesson Summary & Exercises

SUMMARY

After you complete this lesson, you should know how to do the following:

Sharing Data

- You may run more than one program at a time, using background processing techniques such as print spooling.

Using Application-Centric Sharing Methods

- Recognize importing/exporting, converting, linking, and integrated software packages as application-centric sharing methods.

Using Document-Centric Methods

- To move an object, select the object and drag it from one location to another.
- To copy an object, hold Ctrl while dragging and dropping.
- Click Start and then Run, type clipbrd, and click OK to run the ClipBook Viewer to see copied or cut data.
- Click Copy and Paste buttons to copy data; click Cut and Paste buttons to move data.

Using Object Linking and Embedding

- Embed an object using the Insert menu or Paste command.
- Double-click an embedded object to edit it using the server application's tools.

On the Web: Sharing Data Using E-mail

- To create an e-mail message, click the New Mail button while in Outlook Express.
- To attach a file to an e-mail message, click the Attach File button and enter the location and name of the file to be attached.

NEW TERMS TO REMEMBER

After you complete this lesson, you should know the meaning of these terms:

application-centric approach	document-centric approach	multitasking
background	Dynamic Data Exchange	Object Linking and
client	(DDE)	Embedding (OLE)
Clipboard	embedding	paste
ClipBook	exporting	server
copy	importing	
cut	linking	

Lesson Summary & Exercises

MATCHING EXERCISE

Match each of the terms with the definitions on the right:

Terms

1. client

2. document-centric

3. Dynamic Data Exchange (DDE)

4. embedding

5. export

6. import

7. linking

8. Object Linking and Embedding (OLE)

9. background

10. server

Definitions

a. Establishing a relationship between an object and the application originally used to create the object

b. To save data in a format that is compatible with the type of data used by another application

c. Rapidly evolving standard for application integration in which an object's server application tools become available when working with the object within the client application

d. Data-sharing component for an application that contains an embedded object

e. Linking technique for applications that allows you to move data from one application to another and in which changes made in one application are reflected automatically in the other

f. To insert data saved in a compatible format that was originally generated in another application

g. Concept of working with computer data that is based on the document and not the applications used to create it

h. Data-sharing component for the application used originally to create an object

i. Inserting data generated within one application into a document generated by another application, thereby establishing a link

j. Computer processing "behind the scenes" or other than in the active window

COMPLETION EXERCISE

Fill in the missing word or phrase for each of the following:

1. To the user, the concept of document-centric means focusing more on developing and editing _____, with less emphasis on the applications used to create them.

2. When you share data from one application to another, you are _____ the data.

3. A data link refers to a relationship between a(n) _____ and the _____ used to create it.

Lesson Summary & Exercises

4. Using the mouse to physically move or copy data from an application in one window to an application in another is accomplished through the _____ technique.

5. The Windows 2000 _____ is a special area set aside within the computer's main memory to temporarily store data that is to be copied or moved.

6. Click the _____ command if you wish to duplicate a selection to memory without removing the original from its current location.

7. The client application contains an embedded object that was created in the _____ application.

8. When you double-click an OLE 2.0 embedded object, the available menus and tools become those of the _____ application.

9. Inserting a table from a spreadsheet that was saved in text format into a document within a word processor is an example of _____ data.

10. One benefit of a(n) _____ operating system, such as Windows 2000, is the ability to establish dynamic links between multiple applications.

SHORT-ANSWER QUESTIONS

Write a brief answer to each of the following questions:

1. Distinguish between exporting and importing data.

2. List and describe briefly two methods in which you can move or copy data between two different applications within the Windows 2000 environment.

3. Describe briefly the main difference between Dynamic Data Exchange (DDE) and Object Linking and Embedding (OLE), in terms of the user's ability to link data.

4. List three specific examples of how you might create a compound document using the Object Linking and Embedding (OLE) technology.

5. Identify one advantage and one disadvantage of using integrated software packages.

6. Distinguish between the Edit menu's Cut and Copy commands. Which one would you use to move a folder from one disk to another and why?

7. What is the purpose of the Clipboard, how do you see its contents, and what are some of its restrictions?

8. What is multitasking? List three ways that multitasking might speed up your personal computing work.

9. Describe the process of embedding part of a Paint document into a text file. Use the terms *client* and *server* in your explanation.

10. Why does data sometimes fail to convert from one program to another?

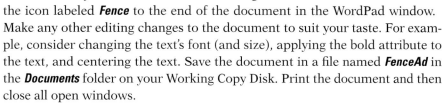

APPLICATION PROJECTS

Insert your Working Copy Disk or your Student Data Disk (as requested) into the disk drive. Perform the following actions to complete these projects:

1. Start WordPad. In a new document, list and define the methods of data sharing discussed in this lesson. Save the document in a new file named **DataShare** in the **Documents** folder on your Working Copy Disk, and then print the document. Close all open windows.

2. Open a new WordPad document and type the following text:

Gill's Fencing

Repairs and New Installations

All Work Guaranteed

Reasonable Rates

(505) 555-6942

Next, open the My Computer or Explorer window and select the device icon for the drive that contains your Student Data Disk. Drag the icon labeled **Fence** to the end of the document in the WordPad window. Make any other editing changes to the document to suit your taste. For example, consider changing the text's font (and size), applying the bold attribute to the text, and centering the text. Save the document in a file named **FenceAd** in the **Documents** folder on your Working Copy Disk. Print the document and then close all open windows.

3. Start Paint. Use the Paint tools to design a graphics image about 4 inches wide and 1 inch high that you can use to create personal stationery. Save the document as the 16 Color Bitmap type and name the file **My Logo1** on your Working Copy Disk. Copy only the design part of the document and close the Paint window. Open a new WordPad document and paste the design at the top of the page. Click to the right of the graphics frame, press Enter⏎ to start a new line, type your name, press Enter⏎, and then type your address. Save this file as **My Stationery** in the **Documents** folder on your Working Copy Disk. Print the document. Close all open windows.

4. Open **My Stationery** on your Working Copy Disk and save it as **Letter to My Instructor** on your Working Copy Disk. In the **Letter to My Instructor** file, write a letter to your instructor explaining what you do and do not like about your class. Save the document again and print your letter. Close all open windows.

5. *If you completed Application Project 1 in Lesson 5, skip this project.* With your Student Data Disk inserted, open the Explorer window and activate the icon of the appropriate floppy disk. Make two folders called **Graphics** and **Word Processing**. Use Cut and Paste to move appropriate files from the root directory of the Student Data Disk into these folders. Close all open windows.

6. You must be able to connect to a mail program to complete this On the Web project. Write an e-mail message, attaching the map you drew in a supplemental activity in Lesson 6. (If you did not complete this activity, attach any other graphics file you created.) If you have the e-mail address of a friend or relative, send the message. Make sure you tell the recipient of your message, and that you are just testing your e-mail skills.

APPENDICES

CONTENTS

COMMAND	DESCRIPTION	ICON
Start Button Shortcut Menu		
Open	Opens a Start Menu window	
Explore	Opens the Windows 2000 Explorer program	
Search	Opens the Search pane of the Explorer window to locate files or folders	
Taskbar Shortcut Menu		
Adjust Date/Time	Opens a dialog box for changing the system's time zone, date, and time settings (appears only when the mouse pointer is over the clock indicator)	
Cascade Windows	Arranges all open windows on the desktop so that they appear equally sized and stacked so that a small part of each inactive window is visible behind the active window	
Tile Windows Horizontally	Arranges all open windows on the desktop so that they appear equally sized and occupy an equal horizontal portion of the desktop	
Tile Windows Vertically	Arranges all open windows on the desktop so that they appear equally sized and occupy an equal vertical portion of the desktop	
Minimize All Windows	Reduces all open windows to buttons on the taskbar	
(Undo Minimize All)	Restores all windows minimized with the Minimize All Windows command	
Properties	Opens the Taskbar Properties dialog box for changing taskbar options	
Desktop Shortcut Menu		
Arrange Icons	Displays another pop-up menu of options for arranging desktop icons by name, type, size, date, or automatically	
Line Up Icons	Aligns desktop icons vertically from the left side of the desktop to the right	
New	Displays another pop-up menu of options for creating new desktop shortcut icons, folders, or other document icons corresponding to specific applications	
Properties	Opens the Display Properties dialog box	

COMMAND SUMMARY

COMMAND	DESCRIPTION	ICON

Device Icon Shortcut Menu
This menu may contain additional items, depending on the device type.

Open	Opens the selected icon's window	
Explore	Opens the Explorer window	
Search	Opens the Search pane of the Explorer window to locate files or folders	
Create Shortcut	Creates a shortcut icon for the selected object	
Properties	Displays the Properties dialog box for changing a variety of settings for the device	

Start Menu

Programs	Displays a submenu of group folders and Windows 2000 programs	
Documents	Displays a list of the most recently used documents	
Settings	Displays a submenu of group folders for changing your system's configuration	
Search	Displays a submenu of options to locate files or folders	
Help	Displays the Windows 2000 Help dialog box for looking up Help information	
Run	Displays the Run dialog box for entering a line command to open a folder or program	
Shut Down	Initiates the process for shutting down or rebooting the operating system or logging on as a different user	
Windows Update	Links to the Microsoft Web site and checks for potential updates to the operating system	

COMMAND	DESCRIPTION	ICON

Programs Menu
This menu may contain additional submenus or commands, depending on your system's configuration.

Accessories	Displays submenu of accessory program names	
Internet Explorer	Displays submenu of programs related to using the Internet	
Outlook Express	Lets you send, receive, and compose e-mail messages	

Accessories Menu

Accessibility	Lets you run the Accessibility Wizard, Magnifier, Narrator, or On-Screen Keyboard	
Command Prompt	Displays the Command Prompt window, which provides the MS-DOS command-line interface	
Communications	Displays submenu of programs that let you connect to other computers	
Entertainment	Displays submenu of programs for playing sound, animation, or video on computers equipped with CD-ROM drives and sound cards	
System Tools	Displays submenu of programs that provide advanced system management and maintenance features	
Windows Explorer	Opens the Explorer window, which provides disk and file management features	

Settings Menu

Control Panel	Opens the Control Panel window, which provides access to a variety of system management programs	
Printers	Opens the Printers window, which provides access to print queue windows for installed printers and a program for installing a printer	
Taskbar & Start Menu	Opens the Taskbar Properties dialog box for controlling taskbar options	

Control Panel Window
This window may have additional icons, depending on your system's configuration.

Accessibility Options	Changes accessibility options for your system	

COMMAND SUMMARY

COMMAND	DESCRIPTION	ICON
Add/Remove Hardware	Opens wizard for installing new hardware devices	
Add/Remove Programs	Opens wizard for installing or uninstalling programs	
Date/Time	Opens the Date/Time Properties dialog box	
Display	Opens the Display Properties dialog box	
Folder Options	Controls the way windows appear when you view them in Windows Explorer	
Fonts	Opens the Fonts (folder) window	
Keyboard	Opens the Keyboard Properties dialog box	
Mouse	Opens the Mouse Properties dialog box	
Phone and Modem Options	Opens a dialog box for changing modem settings	
Printers	Opens the Printers window	
Sounds and Multimedia	Opens a dialog box for changing sound board and video settings	
System	Opens the System Properties dialog box	

Search Menu

For Files or Folders	Opens the Search pane of the Explorer window with options to locate files or folders	

Optional Accessories Menu Commands
This menu may contain additional items, depending on your system's configuration.

Calculator	Opens a program that provides a standard or scientific calculator	
Notepad	Opens a program window for creating and editing unformatted text documents	
Paint	Opens a program window that provides tools for creating graphics objects	
WordPad	Opens a program window for creating, editing, formatting, and printing text documents	

COMMAND	DESCRIPTION	ICON
System Tools Menu Commands *This menu may contain different items, depending on your system's configuration.*		
Backup	Runs a utility that makes copies of important files and restores those files if they are needed later	
Disk Cleanup	Runs a utility that removes unneeded files from the hard disk drive	
Disk Defragmenter	Runs a utility that improves the performance of hard disk drives by moving file fragments to contiguous clusters	
Drive Converter	Runs a utility that changes the file system on your hard disk drive to NTFS	
Scheduled Task Wizard	Runs a utility that schedules disk maintenance utilities so they run automatically on a regular basis	
Scheduled Tasks	Opens a window that displays regularly scheduled maintenance tasks	
System Information	Opens a window that displays hardware and software data on the computer as well as menu options to run tools such as System File Checker	
Quick Launch Bar		
Launch Internet Explorer Browser	Runs the Internet Explorer	
Launch Outlook Express	Runs Outlook Express	
Show Desktop	Minimizes all windows	

COMMAND SUMMARY

COMMAND	DESCRIPTION	ICON

DEVICE WINDOWS

This menu may contain additional items, depending on the device type.

File Menu

Create Shortcut	Creates a shortcut icon for the selected object	
Delete	Deletes the selected object and places it in the Recycle Bin	
Rename	Highlights the selected object's name so that it can be edited	
Properties	Displays the Properties dialog box for changing a variety of settings for the device	
Close	Closes the active device window	

Edit Menu

Undo	Undoes (reverses) the last operation	
Cut	Cuts (removes) the selected object to the Clipboard	
Copy	Copies (duplicates) the selected object, placing the copy in the Clipboard	
Copy To	Opens a browser window to select a destination folder for an object to be duplicated	
Move To	Opens a browser window to select a destination folder for an object to be relocated	
Paste	Pastes (places) a previously cut or copied object from the Clipboard into the selected location	
Paste Shortcut	Pastes (places) a previously cut or copied object from the Clipboard into the selected location as a shortcut icon	
Select All	Selects (highlights) all objects in the active window	
Invert Selection	Selects (highlights) unselected objects and deselects (removes highlighting from) selected objects	

COMMAND	DESCRIPTION	ICON
View Menu		
Toolbar	Displays a submenu of toolbars	
Status Bar	Toggles the display of the window's status bar	
Large Icons	Changes the display of the window's objects to large icons	
Small Icons	Changes the display of the window's objects to small icons	
List	Changes the display of the window's objects to small icons, which are listed line by line	
Thumbnails	Displays small graphical images of certain file types	
Details	Changes the display of the window's objects to small icons, and a columnar list of the files' names, types, sizes, and creation dates and times	
Arrange Icons	Displays a pop-up menu that arranges the window's objects by name, date, type, size, or automatically when the window is sized	
Line up Icons	Aligns a window's objects vertically from left to right	
Refresh	Updates the information displayed in the window to reflect the most current changes	
Help Menu		
Help Topics	Opens Windows 2000 Help dialog box for displaying help information	
About Windows 2000	Displays information about who the system's version of Windows 2000 is licensed to and the current status of system resources	
EXPLORER WINDOW MENU BAR		
File Menu		
New	Creates a new folder object in the selected folder or storage device	
Create Shortcut	Creates a shortcut icon for a selected program or object	
Delete	Deletes (removes) selected objects to the Recycle Bin	

COMMAND SUMMARY

COMMAND	DESCRIPTION	ICON
Rename	Highlights the selected object's name so that it can be edited	
Properties	Opens a Properties dialog box for the selected object	
Close	Closes the Explorer window	X
Edit Menu		
Undo	Reverses the last operation performed with Windows Explorer	
Cut	Cuts (removes) a selected object to the Clipboard	
Copy	Copies (duplicates) a selected object and places the copy in the Clipboard	
Paste	Pastes (places) a previously cut or copied object from the Clipboard into a new location	
Paste Shortcut	Creates a shortcut icon for a selected object	
Select All	Selects (highlights) all objects in the active folder	
Invert Selection	Selects (highlights) unselected objects and deselects (removes highlighting from) selected objects	
View Menu		
Toolbars	Lets you choose which of the Explorer window's toolbars to display	
Status Bar	Toggles the display of the Explorer window's status bar	
Explorer Bar	Lets you choose what to display in the left pane of the Explorer window	
Large Icons	Changes the display of objects in the Contents pane to large icons	
Small Icons	Changes the display of objects in the Contents pane to small icons	
List	Changes the display of objects in the Contents pane to small icons and lists them line by line	
Details	Changes the display of objects in the Contents pane to small icons and lists them, line by line, with their type, size, and creation date and time information	

COMMAND	DESCRIPTION	ICON
Thumbnails	Displays small graphical images of certain file types	
Arrange Icons	Arranges objects by name, type, size, date, or automatically as the Explorer window is sized	
Line up Icons	Aligns objects vertically from left to right in the Contents pane	
Refresh	Updates the display of the Explorer window to reflect the most recent changes	
Go To Submenu		
Back	Returns to the display of the previous folder	⇐ Back ▾
Forward	Goes to the display of the next folder (if you have gone back to a previous folder)	⇒ ▾
Up One Level	Goes to the parent folder of the current folder	⊡
Favorites Menu		
Add to Favorites	Adds links to your favorite Web sites to the Favorites menu	
Organize Favorites	Allows you to create folders and organize your current favorite links	
Tools Menu		
Folder Options	Opens a dialog box in which you determine how files and folders display and perform	
Help Menu		
Help Topics	Opens the Windows 2000 Help dialog box for displaying help information	
About Windows 2000	Displays information about who the system's version of Windows 2000 is licensed to and the current status of system resources	

CALCULATOR ACCESSORY PROGRAM MENU BAR

Edit Menu

Copy	Copies the current value on the calculator's display to the Clipboard	
Paste	Pastes (inserts) a value from the Clipboard into the calculator's display	

COMMAND SUMMARY

COMMAND	DESCRIPTION	ICON
View Menu		
Standard	Reduces the calculator's appearance to display standard calculator features	
Scientific	Expands the calculator's appearance to provide scientific functions	
Help Menu		
Help Topics	Opens the Calculator Help dialog box for displaying help information	
About Calculator	Displays information about who the system's version of Windows 2000 is licensed to and the current status of system resources	

PAINT ACCESSORY PROGRAM MENU BAR

File Menu

New	Opens a new, blank, and untitled image area	
Open	Opens an existing image file for editing	
Save	Stores the current changes to the active image file or displays the Save As dialog box on a first-time save	
Save As	Displays the Save As dialog box so that a previously unsaved image can be named and saved or an existing file can be saved under a different name	
Print Preview	Opens a print preview window that displays a facsimile of how the image will appear when printed	
Page Setup	Opens a dialog box for changing page settings for the active image file	
Print	Opens a dialog box for selecting options and sending the active image data to the default printer	
Set As Wallpaper (Tiled)	Tiles this bitmap as the Desktop wallpaper	
Set As Wallpaper (Centered)	Centers this bitmap as the Desktop wallpaper	
Exit	Closes the Paint window (program)	

Edit Menu

Undo	Reverses the last editing operation	
Repeat	Repeats the last editing operation	

COMMAND	DESCRIPTION	ICON
Cut	Cuts a selected portion of the image to the Clipboard	
Copy	Copies a selected portion of the image to the Clipboard	
Paste	Pastes the contents of the Clipboard into the image	
Clear Selection	Removes the selection marker from a selected portion of the image	
Select All	Selects all objects or elements in the image	
Copy To	Copies a selected portion of the image to another file	
Paste From	Imports an object from another file into the active image file	
View Menu		
Tool Box	Toggles the display of the tool box	
Color Box	Toggles the display of the color box	
Status Bar	Toggles the display of the status bar	
Text Toolbar	Toggles the display of a toolbar for text editing	
Zoom	Modifies the display size of the image	
View Bitmap	Displays the active image temporarily in full-screen size	
Image Menu		
Flip/Rotate	Displays a dialog box for flipping or rotating a selected portion of an image vertically, horizontally, or by varying degrees about an axis	
Stretch/Skew	Displays a dialog box for stretching or skewing a selected portion of an image by varying degrees vertically or horizontally	
Invert Colors	Changes the current colors for a selected portion of an image	
Attributes	Displays a dialog box for changing size attributes for the current image	
Clear Image	Clears the image editing area	
Draw Opaque	Toggles between making the selection transparent or opaque	

COMMAND SUMMARY

COMMAND	DESCRIPTION	ICON
Colors Menu		
Edit Colors	Displays a dialog box for modifying existing colors or creating new colors	
Help Menu		
Help Topics	Opens the Paint Help dialog box for displaying help information	
About Paint	Displays the Paint icon, name, version number, and other information	
WORDPAD ACCESSORY PROGRAM MENU BAR		
File Menu		
New	Opens a new, blank, and untitled document	
Open	Opens an existing document file for editing	
Save	Stores the current changes to the active document file or displays the Save As dialog box on a first-time save	
Save As	Displays the Save As dialog box so that a previously unsaved document can be named and saved, or an existing file can be saved under a different name	
Print	Opens a dialog box for selecting options and sending the active document's data to the default printer	
Print Preview	Opens a print preview window that displays a facsimile of how the document will appear when printed	
Page Setup	Opens a dialog box for changing page settings for the active document file	
Exit	Closes the WordPad window (program)	
Edit Menu		
Undo	Reverses the last editing operation	
Cut	Cuts selected text to the Clipboard	
Copy	Copies selected text to the Clipboard	
Paste	Pastes the contents of the Clipboard into the document	

COMMAND	DESCRIPTION	ICON
Paste Special	Inserts the contents of the Clipboard with options	
Clear	Erases (deletes) selected text	
Select All	Selects (highlights) all the text in the document	
Find	Displays a dialog box for finding a specific text string in a document	
Find Next	Repeats the last Find operation	
Replace	Finds all or selected occurrences of a specified text string and replaces it with a specified text string	
Links	Provides for editing of linked objects	
Object Properties	Provides for changing the properties of a linked object	
Object	Activates a linked object for editing	
View Menu		
Toolbar	Toggles the display of the WordPad window's Standard toolbar	
Format Bar	Toggles the display of the WordPad window's format bar	
Ruler	Toggles the display of the WordPad window's ruler	
Status Bar	Toggles the display of the WordPad window's status bar	
Options	Displays the Options dialog box for setting WordPad window view options	
Insert Menu		
Date and Time	Inserts the current date and/or time into a document	
Object	Inserts a new embedded object in the active document	

COMMAND SUMMARY

COMMAND	DESCRIPTION	ICON
Format Menu		
Font	Displays a dialog box for changing selected text's font settings	
Bullet Style	Formats selected paragraphs with hanging indents and bullet characters	
Paragraph	Provides for changing selected paragraph's indentation and alignment	
Tabs	Provides for changing selected paragraph's tab stop settings	
Help Menu		
Help Topics	Opens the WordPad Help dialog box for displaying help information	
About WordPad	Displays the WordPad icon, name, and other information	
OUTLOOK EXPRESS		
New Mail	Creates a new e-mail message	
Attach File	Attaches a file to an e-mail message	
Send	Sends a completed e-mail message	
Read News	Displays a window containing newsgroups to which the user is subscribed	
INTERNET EXPLORER		
File Menu		
Open	Opens a Web page	
Save As	Copies the Web page so it can be viewed later or used as wallpaper	
Favorites	Contains links to frequently visited Web sites	

APPENDIX B

Windows 2000 includes a number of accessories to make Windows easier to use. Many of the accessories have particular significance for users with special needs or specific impairments. Appendix B provides an overview of several of the accessibility features. Throughout the tutorial, accessibility notes appear in the margin.

 Warning ***Always*** *secure permission from your instructor, computer lab assistant, or network administrator* ***before*** *you change any computer settings.*

THE ACCESSIBILITY WIZARD

When you run the Accessibility Wizard (Programs, Accessories, Accessibility, Accessibility Wizard), you will be asked a series of questions which allow you to customize Windows 2000 for your particular vision, hearing, and mobility needs.

MAGNIFIER

The Microsoft Magnifier (Programs, Accessories, Accessibility, Magnifier) splits your screen horizontally. The bottom portion of your screen appears as it did before. The upper portion of the screen enlarges the area in which your mouse pointer is located. You can control various options of the Magnifier including the amount of enlargement.

NARRATOR

The Narrator is an accessibility option that *reads* aloud the contents of the screen. Voice options let you choose the type, speed, volume, and pitch of the voice. Reading options determine the types of characters that will be read. The Event Notification settings let you choose whether or not to announce new windows and menus. The Mouse Pointer button forces the pointer to move to the active item on the screen.

ON-SCREEN KEYBOARD

The On-Screen Keyboard option displays a window containing one of several types of keyboards. You click the mouse on the desired key to have the corresponding character entered into the document area of the active application. ⇧Shift, Alt, and Ctrl keys work with the next key you click. For example, to enter the Ctrl + c combination, you click the Ctrl button, and then click *c*. Settings options let you hover over the key rather than click or use an alternate input device.

UTILITY MANAGER

The Utility Manager lets you start or stop any of the accessibility programs. You should use the individual programs or the Accessibility Wizard to choose the settings for the programs—the Utility Manager is used to temporarily turn accessibility programs on or off.

ACCESSIBILITY FEATURES OF WINDOWS 2000

ACCESSIBILITY PROPERTIES

You can set individual accessibility options through the Accessibility Options folder located in the Control Panel (Settings, Control Panel, Accessibility Options). In the Accessibility Properties dialog box, five tabs offer various settings. These tabs are described in Table B.1.

Table B.1	The Accessibility Properties dialog box
Keyboard	
StickyKeys	Lets you use ⇧ Shift , Ctrl , or Alt by pressing one key at a time.
FilterKeys	Windows will ignore brief or repeated keystrokes or slow the repeat rate.
ToggleKeys	Plays tones when pressing Caps Lock , Num Lock , or Scroll Lock .
Extra Keyboard Help	Displays text telling you how to complete tasks without using the mouse.
Sound	
SoundSentry	Displays visual warnings when your system makes a sound.
ShowSounds	Applications will display captions for the speech and sounds they make.
Display	
High Contrast	Changes to colors and fonts designed for easy reading.
Mouse	
MouseKeys	Lets you move the mouse pointer and click buttons with keys on the numeric keypad.
General	
Automatic Reset	Turns off accessibility features when they have not been used for a specified period of time.
Notification	Gives visual and/or sound warnings when turning an accessibility feature on or off.
SerialKey Devices	Lets you connect an alternative input device to replace the keyboard and/or mouse.

ADJUSTING THE MOUSE

Windows 2000 has many adjustable settings for your mouse. You can change some of these settings with the Accessibility Wizard. Double-clicking the Mouse icon in the Control Panel opens the Mouse Properties window. The exact keystrokes and clicks to adjust the mouse, however, depend on the mouse driver and mouse software installed on your computer system.

LEFT-HANDED MOUSE USERS

Any mouse can be set up so a user can keep the mouse to the left of the keyboard and reverse the roles of the buttons. In other words, the right mouse button becomes the button for selecting, dragging, and clicking. The left mouse button is then used to display shortcut menus and for special dragging. To adjust the mouse in most instances, click the Buttons tab in the Mouse Properties window and select the option button for a right- or left-handed configuration.

OTHER MOUSE PROPERTIES

You can customize other mouse properties in the Mouse Properties window, as shown in Table B.2.

Table B.2	The Mouse Properties window
Double-click Speed	Adjusting this control lets you set the time between clicks for double-clicking.
Pointers	Lets you choose different shapes or sizes for mouse pointers.
Pointer Speed	Changes the rate at which the pointer moves across the screen.
Pointer Trail	Attaches a trail to the pointer making its movement easier to track. A control lets you change the length of the trail.

THIRD PARTY HARDWARE AND SOFTWARE

Although not part of the operating system, Windows 2000 supports many hardware devices and programs designed to make the computer easier to use. While not complete, Table B.3 identifies some of the kinds of products that are available.

Table B.3	Third Party Hardware and Software

Input Devices

- Alternate keyboards, such as programmable, miniature, and chording.

- Switches for entering text or commands when using the keyboard or mouse is not feasible.

- Electronic pointing devices that allow the user to operate the pointer on the screen using ultra sound or an infrared beam.

- Pointing and typing aids let users strike keys on the keyboard without using their hands.

- Touch screens allow users to make selections by touching the screen.

- Joysticks, trackballs, and arm and wrist supports also help the user input data.

ACCESSIBILITY FEATURES OF WINDOWS 2000

Table B.3	Third Party Hardware and Software—cont.

Output Devices

- Braille embossers and translators transfer computer-generated text into tactile output.

- Refreshable Braille displays provide tactile output on the screen.

- Speech synthesizers read screen text out loud.

- Monitor additions help to enlarge text, reduce glare, and adjust the monitor's position.

Software

- Programs that accept voice commands to replace keystrokes and/or mouse clicks.

- Programs that allow you to "type" text by speaking into a microphone.

- Programs specially designed for Web navigation for visually or hearing-impaired users.

- Access utilities let users modify operation of input devices.

- Optical Character Recognition software works with scanners to convert printed data into editable electronic files.

- Talking and large-print word processors make it easier for visually or hearing-impaired users to work with text.

- Menu management programs provide simplified access to menus through the mouse or keyboard.

THE INTERNET SETUP WIZARD

Before you can access the Internet, you must verify that your computer is connected to the Internet. For most users, you must either be a part of a computer network that is connected to the Internet or be tied to the Internet via an Internet service provider (ISP) or an online service, a modem, and a telephone line. In either case, the Internet Connection Wizard runs when you install Windows 2000 or when you try to connect to the Internet for the first time. The Wizard screen asks how you want to connect to the Internet:

1. You can sign up for a new Internet account. Selecting this option connects you to the Microsoft Referral Service. Dialing a toll-free number lists ISPs from which you can choose—some with a free trial period.

2. You can set up your computer to use an existing Internet account through an ISP or an online service (such as The Microsoft Network or America Online). This option brings you to a screen that lists available accounts. If your account is not listed, you will have to contact the ISP or online service for technical support.

3. The final option allows you to inform Windows 2000 that you want to configure your connection manually, or that you connect via a local area network (LAN).

Glossary

A

accessory A small program built into the Windows 2000 operating system.

access privileges The rules governing use of the data available to networked computers.

Active Desktop A Windows 2000 interface option that sets your screen up to work like a Web page and to receive and display information from Internet content providers. Compare with *classic style desktop* and *Web style desktop*.

Active Directory The directory service introduced by Microsoft in Windows 2000 Server. See *directory service*.

active window The window ready to accept input from the mouse or keyboard, indicated by a colored title bar; only one open window is active.

add-on A program that works within a Web browser to act upon specific file types.

applets Operating system programs or third-party software that supplement Windows 2000 with application features, such as editing, drawing, and communications. Also called *accessories*.

application Specialized software program for accomplishing a specific task, such as creating text, manipulating financial information, or keeping track of records.

application-centric approach A theoretical view of using computers that emphasizes proficiency with a program's interface. Compare with *document-centric approach*.

application-oriented structure A file management system in which you use subfolders within an application's folder to store data files created with the application. Compare with *project-oriented structure*.

application window A rectangle on the desktop containing the menus and document(s) for an application.

archive (attribute) A property which Windows 2000 automatically assigns to objects that have never been backed up or have been modified since they were last backed up. See *back up*.

attribute (1) Enhancement or stylistic characteristic applied to text characters in a font; for example, bold, italic, and underlining. (2) A file or folder property that controls its use.

B

backbone Computers that make up the Internet.

background (1) The process of running a program while it is not on the screen. (2) The appearance of the screen behind the icons and open windows; see also *patterns* and *wallpaper*.

background color In the Paint program, the color that you can use to fill in shapes or the color that appears behind objects.

backup (n.) A copied and/or compressed set of data from which you can restore damaged or lost original data.

back up (v.) To copy (and/or compress) data for storage elsewhere in case you need to restore damaged or lost original data.

backup cycle A regular procedure and schedule for saving copies of data for purposes of safekeeping.

backup priority Categorization of data according to how damaging its loss would be and, therefore, how important saving a copy is.

backup set In Microsoft Backup, the collection of files included in a single backup operation.

backup set file In Microsoft Backup, a large file containing compressed copies of all files included in a backup operation.

bitmap files A representation of an image as a series of dots on a coordinate system.

bit-mapped font (or nonscalable font) A typeface in which each character is composed of a dot pattern that dictates the shape and size of the font.

booting the system (system boot) Another expression for starting up, which the computer often accomplishes by loading a small program, which then reads a larger program into memory.

browser A software package that lets the user access the major components of the Internet, such as the World Wide Web, e-mail, and so on. Also called *Web browser*.

buffer A memory area reserved to temporarily hold video or audio data waiting to be played.

bullet paragraphs Paragraphs which begin with a filled-in circle (the bullet) and in which each line is indented one-quarter inch from the left margin.

buttons Boxes labeled with words or pictures that you can click to select a setting or put a command into effect.

C

cache files   Files created by the Web browser to quickly load previously viewed Web pages.

cascade   A technique for arranging open windows in equal size and stacked so that only the top window is fully visible, and the upper-left corners and the title bars of the other windows appear behind it.

center alignment   Justification in which each line of text is centered between the left and right margins.

character formatting   The settings that affect how text characters appear within a document, including their font, size, and stylistic enhancements.

check box   A square box in a dialog box that contains a ✓ when an option is selected, or appears empty when the option is not selected.

classic style desktop   The Windows 2000 default desktop setting that gives the user interface the same look and feel as Windows 98. Compare with *Active Desktop* and *Web style desktop*.

clicking   The technique of quickly pressing and releasing the left button on a mouse or trackball.

client   In OLE technology, a program that receives an embedded object which was produced in another program. See *Object Linking and Embedding*.

client/server computing   A network in which workstations share the storage and processing load with a server.

Clipboard   A portion of random access memory (RAM) used to temporarily store one piece of information that you have cut or copied, so you can paste it in a new location.

ClipBook   Memory feature of Windows 2000 that allows many pieces of information to be cut or copied, stored, and shared with other users who are on a network. Compare with *Clipboard*.

close   To remove a window from the screen or desktop.

clusters   Units of disk storage; a file is saved in one or more clusters, which may be located next to each other or separated.

collapsed   A state of an item in which details or subordinate items are hidden from view. A plus sign (+) in the box to the left of the item indicates the item is collapsed. Compare with *expanded*.

color box (or palette)   A device at the bottom of the Paint window that contains a set of colors displayed in small squares that you can select to change a shape's color.

color matrix   A box for selecting a color, in which colors are arranged horizontally by hue and vertically by saturation.

command prompt   A series of characters, such as C:\>, in the Command Prompt window that indicates the computer is ready to accept DOS commands.

commands   Instructions that you issue to the computer, usually by choosing from a menu, clicking a button, or pressing a combination of keys on the keyboard.

compress   A method of increasing the storage capacity of an NTFS disk by combining files and folders into a single large file.

Contents tab   One of the four tabs in the Help window; this option provides a list of Help topics.

control menu icon   In Windows, a small control, typically on the left side of the title bar, that when clicked displays a menu to manipulate the window.

Control Panel   A dialog box that lets you change settings on your computer.

copy   (1) An operation that temporarily stores a duplicate of any selected object, such as text, image, file, or folder, in the computer's memory; (2) the name of the command that performs this operation; (3) any object that duplicates an original and, in the case of files or folders, may or may not have the same name as the original, depending on the copy's location.

copy backup   A Microsoft Backup option in which selected files and folders are backed up, without resetting the archive attribute, thus not affecting other backup operations.

cross-linked   Describes files identified by the error-checking program as sharing the same cluster location on a disk.

cursor   The blinking horizontal line that appears immediately after the command prompt, marking the place where typed DOS commands appear.

cut   An operation which removes any selected object, such as text, image, file, or folder, from its original location and stores it temporarily in the computer's memory; also the name of the command which performs this operation.

Glossary

D

daily backup   A Microsoft Backup option in which all files created or modified during the day are backed up without resetting the archive attribute, thus not affecting other backup operations.

dedicated file server   A computer whose sole function is to store the data and software shared by networked computers and regulate the flow of information.

default   A value or setting that software uses automatically unless you specify a different value or setting.

delete   An operation that removes any selected item, such as text, image, file, or folder, from a disk; in Windows 2000 the deleted item is sent to the Recycle Bin, which holds it until the user either restores it to its original location or removes it permanently.

deselect   To return an object to its original color or turn off an option, indicating that an item will not be affected by the next action you take or that an option will no longer be in effect.

desktop   The working area of the screen that displays many Windows 2000 tools and is the background for your computer work.

desktop accessory (or accessory)   A small program built into the Windows 2000 operating system.

device   A piece of equipment (hardware), such as a printer or disk drive, that is part of your computer system.

device driver   Software that manages computer resources for hardware such as the mouse, keyboard, monitor, disk drives, or modem.

device icon   A small image that represents a hardware device, such as a printer or disk drive, installed on the computer system.

dialog box   A rectangle containing a set of options that appears when Windows 2000 needs more information from the user to perform a requested operation.

differential backup   Copying only those files that have been added or changed since the last normal backup. Contrast with *normal backup* and *incremental backup*.

directory   An earlier term for *folder*.

directory server   A computer that maintains a list of logged-on users. NetMeeting uses the list to find IP addresses.

directory service   A tool that manages the users, computers, information, and security on a network.

disk structure   The organizational structure or relationship of folders to subfolders on a disk.

document-centric approach   A theoretical view of using computers that focuses on the document or product rather than the application(s) used to create it, and emphasizes tools that adapt to users' needs. Compare with *application-centric approach*.

document files   Files that store the work you have created with the computer.

document window   A rectangle within an application window for viewing and working on a document.

DOS-based applications   Software originally designed to be used by computers running the MS-DOS operating system.

DOS commands   Special instructions, such as DIR and VER, that you issue to the MS-DOS operating system by typing them at the command prompt.

double-click   The technique of rapidly pressing and releasing the left button on a mouse or trackball twice when the mouse pointer on screen is pointing to an object.

downloading   Process of copying a file from another computer to your computer.

dpi   dots per inch. See *resolution*.

draft   Lowest resolution print quality setting, typically used for printing rough drafts rapidly.

drag and drop (or dragging)   The technique of moving an object on screen by pointing to the object, pressing and holding the left mouse button, moving the mouse to the new location, and then releasing the button.

drive icon   A small icon or image that represents a storage device.

drop-down list   A list of options displayed when you click a triangle button.

Dynamic Data Exchange (DDE)   A data-sharing characteristic in which data modified in one application is also modified automatically in the application that shares the data.

E

e-mail   Another name for electronic mail, information that is exchanged between two computers via telephone lines or network connections.

embedding   A data-sharing method that involves integrating an object from one application into another.

Energy Star-compliant   Meeting an established standard for lower energy consumption.

erase   In the Paint program, to remove an undesired portion of an image and replace it with the background color.

expanded   A state of an item in which details or subordinate items are visible. A minus sign (-) in the box to the left of the item indicates the item is expanded. Compare with *collapsed*.

exporting   To share data from an application by converting it to a format that another application can read.

extension   A one- to three-character file name component that an operating system uses to identify the type of data stored in the file.

F

Favorites   Start menu option or button that contains shortcuts to frequently accessed documents, especially Web pages.

Favorites tab   A Help screen that lets you bookmark particularly useful Help pages for later reference.

file   A named, ordered collection of information stored on a disk.

File Allocation Table (FAT)   A file system used by Windows 95, 98, and DOS to control the reading and writing of data to disks. Used by all Windows operating systems when accessing diskettes. Compare with *NTFS*.

file icon   A small image that represents a specific type of named data on screen.

file management   The process of organizing and caring for your disks and files.

file name   The characters used to identify a file, limited to 255 characters in versions of Windows since Windows 95, and 8 characters in MS-DOS and older versions of Windows.

file-naming conventions   The rules governing the length and character requirements for file names created within a specific operating system.

file server   A computer responsible for storing and retrieving the files used by a group of computers that are joined in a network.

file system   The method the operating system uses to control access to a disk.

find   An operation that attempts to locate specific content within a document by selecting and displaying it.

first line indent   A paragraph setting that determines the distance from the left margin at which the first line of text starts.

folder   A named icon that contains files and other folders.

font   A set of characters that appears with a specific typeface, one or more attributes, and a specific size.

foreground color   In the Paint program, the color in which a line or shape you draw appears.

format bar   A row of buttons within a window, just below the toolbar, containing shortcuts for common formatting commands.

formatted file   A document containing elements that enhance the appearance of text, paragraphs, and other objects, in order to make the document more attractive and understandable. Compare with *text file*.

formatting   (1) An operating system process which removes all existing data from a disk and prepares the disk to receive new data; (2) enhancements applied within a document to make the document more readable and attractive.

fragments   A part of a file that may or may not be physically located close to other fragments of the file.

free-form line   A line drawn with no determined shape or direction.

full system backup   A copy of all the files on a disk to protect a computer from major stress, such as a hard drive crash or replacement, or the installation of a new operating system.

G

glossary term   In Windows 2000 Help windows, an underlined word or phrase that you can click to display a definition.

graphical user interface (GUI)   An operating environment in which controls and data are visible on screen so you can select items with a pointing device.

graphics accelerator card   A circuit board inside the system unit that lets the monitor display images more rapidly, at higher resolution, and with more varied colors.

graphics adapter card   A circuit board inside the system unit that regulates communication between the processor and monitor, allowing the computer to display images.

H

hanging indent   Arrangement in which the first line of a paragraph is to the left of the subsequent lines in the paragraph.

Glossary

hard copy   Information that has been printed from its electronic, or "soft," form of storage on a computer onto paper.

hard return   The character which marks the end of a paragraph of text, created by one press of the Enter key.

hardware   The parts of a computer system that you can see and touch.

hidden (attribute)   A setting that makes an object, such as a file or folder, not visible in the listing of a drive's contents.

highlight   To change the color of an object to one that contrasts with its usual appearance.

high-priority backup files   Files whose loss would be relatively catastrophic and for which saving a copy is of relatively high importance.

home page   The main page of a World Wide Web site which usually includes links to other pages at that site.

horizontal scroll bar   A rectangular bar that appears along the bottom side of a window that is too narrow to display all its contents; clicking or dragging in the scroll bar brings additional contents into view.

hot key   See *shortcut key*.

hue   Any specific color in the spectrum that results when white light passes through a prism (similar to a rainbow).

I

icons   Small images that represent devices, programs, files, or folders.

importing   To share data created in another application by converting it to a format that you can display and modify in the current application.

inactive window   Any window that will not accept mouse or keyboard input until it is made active; inactive windows have clear or gray title bars.

incremental backup   Copying only those files that have been added or changed since the last normal or differential backup. Contrast with *normal backup* and *differential backup*.

indent   To align text in a paragraph a set distance from the left or right margin.

indent markers   Markers on the horizontal ruler used to set paragraph indentations. Drag the markers (first-line indent, left indent, hanging indent, and right indent) to change the indentations in the paragraph that contains the insertion point.

Index tab   One of the four tabs in the Help window; this option provides an alphabetical listing of Help topics.

insertion point   A small blinking vertical line that indicates where the next character typed will appear on screen.

Internet   A worldwide system of interconnected computer networks, allowing users to exchange digital information in the form of text, graphics, and other media.

Internet service providers (ISPs)   Companies that provide Internet access to users for a monthly or an annual fee.

IP address   A series of numbers that identifies your computer to other computers on the Internet.

J

joystick   An input device used to control the on-screen pointer; a small joystick is often found in the middle of keyboards on laptop computers.

justification   General term for the way text is aligned in a paragraph; see also *left alignment*, *center alignment*, and *right alignment*.

K

keyword   Word or phrase used to define or narrow a search.

L

landscape orientation   A page layout option in which text and graphics are printed across the longer dimension of a page.

large icon   An icon displayed at full size.

left alignment   Justification in which each line of text begins flush at the left margin.

left indent   A paragraph setting which determines the distance from the left margin from which each line of text starts.

legacy hardware   Older hardware devices that may require additional software or manual settings by the user during installation with the Windows 2000 system. See also *Plug and Play*.

letter quality   Highest resolution print quality setting, typically used for printing final drafts.

link   Location on a Web page that you click to jump to other locations or parts of the Internet.

linking   Establishing a relationship between an object and the program that created it.

local area network (LAN)   A network in which nodes are located in close proximity.

log on   A procedure in which a user types in a user name and a password when starting up the computer.

lost file fragments   Data on a disk that does not seem to belong to any file which is on the disk.

low-priority backup files   Files whose loss would be a relatively minor inconvenience and for which saving a copy is of relatively low importance.

luminosity   The brightness of a color as determined by how much black or white the color contains.

M

main folder   The top level of a disk icon, which contains files and folders that are not nested within any other folder; also referred to as the *root directory*.

mapping   A method for assigning a drive letter to a shared drive or folder on another computer in a network.

maximize   A Windows sizing feature in which an open window is enlarged to fill the screen; also, the name of the button which performs this function.

menu   A list of items on the screen from which you can choose; menu usually refers to a list of commands or options.

menu bar   An area below the title bar of all application windows containing the names of menus which, when clicked, displays a list of commands.

minimize   A Windows sizing feature which reduces an open window to a button on the taskbar; also, the name of the button which performs this function.

modem   A device that lets your computer communicate with other computers over public telephone lines.

mouse   An input device operated by rolling it on a flat surface; used to control the on-screen pointer by pointing, clicking, or dragging objects on the screen.

mouse pointer   See *pointer*.

move   An operation that removes a selected folder and all its contents (or other object) from its original location and places it in a new location.

multimedia   Documents or software which combine sound, text, graphics, animation, and/or video.

multitasking   The ability of an operating system to carry out multiple operations at the same time; for example, running more than one program.

N

negative indent   In the WordPad Paragraph dialog box, enter a negative number in the First line indent box to move the first line to the left of the other lines in that paragraph. Produces the same effect as a *hanging indent*.

network   A system in which computers are connected to each other so that they can share information and resources.

network drive   A storage device you can access although it is connected to another computer on the network.

nonscalable font   See *bit-mapped font*.

normal backup   Copying all marked files, regardless of whether they have ever been backed up or not. Contrast with *differential backup* and *incremental backup*.

NTFS (NT File System)   A file system used by Windows 2000 and its Windows NT predecessors. NTFS is designed for network access and security. Compare with *File Allocation Table (FAT)*.

O

Object Linking and Embedding (OLE)   A data-sharing technology in which data created in one application is integrated into another application, and editing tools are available regardless of which application contains the embedded object.

online services   Companies that include Internet access as a part of their own proprietary offerings.

on-screen Help   A window that opens to provide contextual assistance and other learning aids.

opaque   Characteristic of a text box that completely hides any image behind it; contrast with *transparent*.

open   To access the contents of an icon in a window.

OpenType fonts   A category of scalable fonts. An improved version of TrueType fonts. Compare with *TrueType fonts*.

operating system software (operating system)   A collection of programs that allows you to work with a computer by managing the flow of data between input devices, the computer's memory, storage devices, and output devices.

Glossary

option button   A small circle which is filled with a solid dot when the button is selected; only one in a set of option buttons can be selected at one time. Also called *radio button*.

P

page formatting   The settings that affect the appearance of all pages in a document, including margins, paper size, and page orientation.

palette   See *color box*.

pane (window pane)   A bordered area within a window. Also called *window pane*.

paragraph   A block of text that ends with a hard return.

paragraph formatting   The settings that affect the appearance of all the lines of text in a paragraph; for example, line spacing, alignment, and the location of indents and tabs.

parent folder   A folder that contains one or more folders (or *subfolders*).

partition   A division of a disk drive which is assigned its own drive letter.

password   A string of characters known only to the user, which the user must enter before the system can be assessed.

password protection   A feature that prevents unauthorized use of a computer system.

paste   An operation which inserts an object temporarily stored in the computer's memory (the contents of the Clipboard) at the currently active location; also the name of the command which performs this operation.

path   The sequence of disk, folder, and subfolders that lead from the disk drive to the location of a particular file.

patterns   Geometric designs that appear on the desktop around the wallpaper to the edges of the screen.

peer-to-peer networks   A network in which each computer is an equal partner and shares responsibility for managing communication.

pixel   Short for picture element; the smallest dot you can draw on the screen and the smallest unit that images on the screen consist of.

Plug and Play   A standard for hardware devices that enables devices to configure themselves, so that users can install and use them without having to solve time-consuming installation problems.

point   (1) The action of pointing; (2) a unit of measurement equal to $1/72$ inch used to describe the height of type and other elements on a printed page.

pointer (or mouse pointer)   An arrow or other on-screen image that moves in relation to the movement of a mouse or trackball.

pointing   Moving the mouse pointer to position it over an on-screen object.

portrait orientation   A page layout option in which text and graphics are printed across the shorter dimension of a page.

Power On Self Test (POST)   A program that checks a computer system's memory, keyboard, display, and disk drives.

printer driver   A program that controls the operation of a specific printer model and is represented by a device icon.

Print Preview   A feature that lets users view a likeness of a printed document on screen.

print queue   Temporary storage area in memory or on disk for data sent to a printer; in Windows 2000, the name for a window showing active print jobs.

print spooling   Process of sending print jobs to a print queue so that printing can take place while you are using the computer for other tasks.

program files   The application software that lets you perform tasks on the computer.

project-oriented structure   A file management system in which you organize data files and folders according to the specific projects. Compare with *application-oriented structure*.

purging   Canceling all jobs in a print queue.

R

radio button   See *option button*.

read-only (attribute)   A setting that lets users view and use an object, such as a file, but not modify or delete it.

rename   To change the name of a file, a folder, or an icon.

repeat key   A key that continues to insert characters while it is held down; most keys on the computer keyboard are repeat keys.

Replace   The name of the command that lets users search for and replace occurrences of text within a document.

resolution   A measurement of image quality usually applied to printers and computer monitors; printer resolution is typically expressed in dots per inch (dpi).

restore   (1) To return a maximized window to its previous size; also the name of the button that performs this function; (2) To return a deleted item to its original location, generally from the Recycle Bin. (3) To replace damaged or deleted items with undamaged copies saved on another disk.

right alignment   Justification in which each line of text ends flush at the right margin.

right-click   The technique of quickly pressing and releasing the right button on a mouse or trackball.

right indent   A paragraph setting which determines the distance from the right margin at which each line of text ends.

root directory   An earlier name for the *main folder* in a disk.

ruler   A display of buttons and numbered tick marks beneath the WordPad format bar, which indicates measurements across the width of the document and is used to format paragraphs of text.

S

sans serif typeface   A typeface whose characters lack extra lines at the ends of the strokes; sans serif typefaces are generally used for headings or display text.

saturation   A value indicating how much intensity of hue a color has.

scalable font   Typeface that you can print in a range of sizes.

scheme   The overall appearance of desktop screen elements including colors, fonts, sizes, and spacing between icons.

screen savers   Animated images that appear when the computer is not used for a specified time.

scroll arrows   Buttons in a scroll bar that let you scroll information in a window in small increments—for example, scrolling text line by line.

scroll bar   A rectangular bar that appears along the right or bottom side of a window when not all the contents of the window are visible and which is used to bring the contents into view.

scroll box   A rectangle in a scroll bar that you can drag to display information; its location represents the location of the visible information in relation to the entire contents of the window.

search engine   Software that lists Web sites. The user may enter a keyword or choose a category and the search engine lists sites that most nearly match the keyword or relate to the category.

Search tab   One of the four tabs in the Help window; this option allows you to type words to search for in the Help system.

select   To designate (typically by clicking an item with the mouse) where the next action will take place, which command will be executed next, or which option will be put into effect.

separator line   A line dividing two panes in a window, which you can drag to make one pane larger and the other smaller.

serif   An extra line at the end of a text character stroke that is part of the character design.

serif typeface   A typeface whose characters have extra lines at the ends of the strokes which make text more readable; serif typefaces are generally used for paragraph text.

server   The application responsible for creating or editing an object shared by two or more applications.

shared drive   A storage device that other users of the computer or on the network can access.

shared folder   A folder that other users of the computer or on the network can access.

shared printer   A printer that other users of the computer or on the network can access.

share-level security   A technique of sharing data on a network that requires users to enter a password in order to access a particular file or folder.

sharing   Allowing others to use your computer's resources, such as files and printers.

shortcut   A command represented by an icon that provides access to a file, folder, or device.

shortcut icon   A picture representing a quick path to a program or task.

shortcut key (hot key)   A keystroke combination that you can use to run a program.

shortcut menu   A list of an item's most frequently used commands.

size   To change the dimensions of a window so that its contents remain visible, but the window occupies only a portion of the desktop.

slider control   An indicator that you drag along a vertical or horizontal line. Dragging the indicator increases or decreases the value shown on the line.

small icon   An icon displayed at quarter size.

Glossary

software   A collective term for programs, or instructions that are stored in electronic form and tell the computer what to do.

spinner buttons   A pair of controls used to change a numerical setting, consisting of an up arrow above a down arrow. Clicking the up arrow increases the setting; clicking the down arrow decreases it.

status bar   A bar at the bottom of a window that explains selected objects or menu commands.

streaming   A process by which video or audio data is played while more data is being received.

subdirectory   An earlier term for a *subfolder*.

subfolder   A folder nested within another folder.

subscribe   The act of signing up to a service that will send information to your desktop on a regular basis.

surfing the Web   Moving from one Web site to another.

system files   The files that operate the computer.

system icons   Pictures that represent operating system files.

system properties   Settings that affect the overall operation of your computer and the devices connected to it.

T

tab   (1) A control at the top of some dialog boxes that displays different screens within the dialog box. (2) A paragraph setting that lets users insert a specific amount of space in a line of text by pressing the Tab key.

taskbar   An area on the Windows 2000 Desktop that displays a button for the Start menu, icons for commonly used Windows 2000 features, an icon for any applications that are currently running, and a button for the Clock.

temp files   See *temporary files*.

template files   Files which contain the generic elements and text for each type of frequently used document and which users modify to create specific documents.

temporary files (temp files)   Files created by the operating system to store information while the computer is running.

text box   A rectangular control that displays the name or value of a current setting and in which you can type a different name or value to change the setting.

text editor   A program that creates unformatted text files.

text file (or unformatted file)   A data file containing text characters (letters, numbers, symbols, punctuation, spaces, and paragraph returns) without line, paragraph, or page formatting or typeface enhancements. Compare with *formatted file*.

tile   A technique for arranging open windows side-by-side either horizontally or vertically and equally sized so that all are visible.

title bar   An area at the top of a window that displays the name of the application, document, or device that the window represents.

toggle   A command or an option that you can turn on and off by repeatedly clicking the command or option.

toolbars   Rows of icons representing frequently used commands.

toolbox   An area in the Paint accessory window containing icons representing the tools you can use to create an image.

tool tip   Text which appears when you point to a tool and which provides information about the tool.

touch-sensitive pad   An input device used to control the on-screen pointer by pressing a flat surface with your finger; usually found on laptop computers.

trackball   An input device that functions like an upside-down mouse, containing a ball that is rolled by the thumb or fingers to move the on-screen pointer.

transparent   Characteristic of a text box in which those portions of any other image that are behind empty areas of the box are revealed; contrast with *opaque*.

tree   A branching, structured list that looks like the spreading branches or roots of a tree and whose branches display and hide the devices connected to a computer system.

triangle button   A button in the shape of a small downward-pointing triangle, which displays a menu of options when clicked.

TrueType font   Fonts designed for a graphical user interface. TrueType fonts are scalable and appear on the screen just as they print.

truncated   An object that is cut off, for example, by a border, so that part of the object is not displayed.

type (of icon/file)   The category of information or application to which an icon or a file belongs.

typeface   A family for type or characters that is determined by particular design or style characteristics; all the characters are similar in appearance.

U

unformatted file See *text file*.

Uniform Resource Locator (URL) Address of a Web site.

user interface The rules and methods by which a computer and the users communicate.

user-level security A technique of sharing data on a network that specifies the names or groups of people authorized to use the data.

user name A name by which you are identified on the computer. You enter a user name as part of the log on procedure.

user-oriented structure A file management system in which you organize data files and folders according to the individual users who share a computer or network server.

V

vertical scroll bar A rectangular bar that appears along the right side of a window that is too short to display all its contents; clicking or dragging in the scroll bar brings additional contents into view.

video conferencing Exchanging audio and video conversations electronically.

virtual memory Hard disk space used by the operating system as if it were additional main memory.

W

wallpaper Images that appear as background of the desktop.

Web browser See *browser*.

Web pages Screens that display information on the Web. Many Web pages contain text, graphics, animation, sound, and video.

Web site Specific location of pages on the World Wide Web. A Web site has an address, or URL.

Web style desktop A Windows 2000 desktop setting that gives the user the same look and feel as when on the Internet. Compare with *Active Desktop* and *classic style desktop*.

weight An attribute applied to on-screen text or printed characters that influences the thickness of the characters and the spacing between them.

wheel On a mouse, a button between the left and right buttons in the shape of a wheel; use this button to view text above or below the information on the screen.

wide area network (WAN) A network in which two or more LANs are connected together.

Win16 applications Software designed to be used by computers running pre-Windows 95 operating systems.

Win32 applications Software designed to be used by computers running Windows 95 and later operating systems.

window A rectangular area that displays information, such as the content of a document or the controls of an application; you can open, close, move, size, maximize, and minimize a window.

window pane See *pane*.

wizard An automated process that guides you through an operation by presenting a series of options from which you can select.

word processor A software application designed for writing, editing, and enhancing the appearance of text.

word wrap A word processing feature that automatically breaks lines at the right margin or right side of a window as you type.

workgroup A collection of workstations sharing common needs and resources.

workstations (or nodes) Individual computers in a network.

World Wide Web (the Web or **WWW**) An Internet service that allows users to view documents containing jumps to other documents anywhere on the Internet. The graphical documents are controlled by companies, organizations, and individuals with a special interest to share.

WYSIWYG An acronym for *What You See Is What You Get*, a GUI characteristic in which documents appear on screen much as they will appear on a printed page.

Index

Index

High-priority backup file, *def.*, 246
Home page, *def.*, 172, 246
Horizontal scroll bar, *def.*, 50, 246
Hot key, *def.*, 246
Hue, *def.*, 246
Hyperterminal, 151

I

Icons, *def.*, 8, 246
    arranging, 47–50
    changing size of, 50
    large, *def.*, 50
    small, *def.*, 50
Image, creating and editing, in
    Paint, 165–168
Imaging, 150
Importing, *def.*, 204, 246
Inactive window, *def.*, 36, 246
Incremental backup, *def.*, 246
Indent, *def.*, 246
Indent markers, *def.*, 246
Index tab, of Help window, *def.*, 53,
    246
    using Help, 55–56
Inkjet printer, 188, 187
Input device, 240
Insertion point, *def.*, 246
    moving, 133
Installation, device, 76
Integrated software package, 204
Internet, 139, *def.*, 246
    accessing, 172–173
    introducing, 26–27
    searching on, 140–141
Internet access, 4
Internet Connection Wizard, 151
Internet Explorer, 237
    switching between Windows
        Explorer and, 110–111
Internet service providers (ISPs),
    def., 172, 246

J

Joystick, *def.*, 9, 246
Justification, *def.*, 246

K

Keyboard, opening a window from
    the, 40–41
Keyword, *def.*, 140, 246

L

Landscape orientation, *def.*, 188,
    246, *illus.*, 189

Large icon, *def.*, 50, 246
Laser printer, 191
Left alignment, *def.*, 246
Left indent, *def.*, 246
Legacy hardware, *def.*, 76, 246
Letter quality, *def.*, 191, 246
Line tool, 164
Link, *def.*, 247
Linking, *def.*, 204, 247
    object, 210–213
Local area network (LAN), *def.*, 247
Local Help, 57
Log on, *def.*, 5, 247
Log off, 24–25, 139
Lost file fragments, *def.*, 247
Low-priority backup file, *def.*, 247
Luminosity, *def.*, 247

M

Magnetic fields, and disks, 67
Magnifier, 238
Main folder, *def.*, 89, 247
Mapping, *def.*, 247
Managing files, 118
Mathematical operations, 153, 154
Maximize, *def.*, 36, 247
Memory, calculator, 154–155
Menu(s), 224–237, *def.*, 14, 247
    clearing, 17
    start. *See* Start menu.
Menu bar, *def.*, 37, 247
Minimize, *def.*, 36, 247
Minimizing open windows, 46–47
Modem, *def.*, 76, 247
Mouse, *def.*, 9, 247
    adjusting, 239–240
    practicing, 12–14
    using the, 9–17
Mouse pointer, *def.*, 10, 247
Mouse properties, 240
Move, *def.*, 106, 247
    drawing, 168–169
    files, 127–129
    window, 38–39
MS-DOS file name, 118–119
Multimedia, *def.*, 151, 247
Multiple file
    copying, 126–127
    deleting, 130
Multiple objects, selecting, 126–127
Multitasking, *def.*, 204, 247
My Computer window, 118, *illus.*,
    13, 66
    using, 66–71

N

Name, file, 118
Narrator, 238
Negative indent, *def.*, 247
NetMeeting, 151
Network, *def.*, 4, 247
Network connection, 151
Network drive, *def.*, 67, 247
Network tab, system properties, 77
New file, creating, in WordPad,
    156–158
Nonscalable fonts, *def.*, 185, 247
Normal backup, *def.*, 247
Notepad, 150
Notepad window, *illus.*, 120
NTFS, *def.*, 99, 247
Numbers, entering, 153

O

Object(s)
    copying, 210–211
    editing embedded, 212–213
    embedding, 211
    selecting multiple, 126
Object linking and embedding
    (OLE), 210–213, *def.*, 247
Online Help, getting, 58–59
Online services, *def.*, 172, 247
On-screen Help, *def.*, 52, 247
    getting, 52–57
On-Screen Keyboard, 238
Opaque, *def.*, 247
Open, *def.*, 247
OpenType fonts, *def.*, 185, 247
Operating system software, 4, 247
Operations, mathematical, 153,
    154
Option buttons, *def.*, 21, 247
Orientation, selecting print,
    188–190
Outlook Express, 151, 237, *illus.*,
    214
Output device, 240

P

Page characteristics, selecting,
    187–189
Page formatting, *def.*, 248
Page orientation, restoring,
    190–191
Paint, 150, *illus.*, 165–168
    using, 163–170
Paint menu bar, 233–235
Palette, *def.*, 164, 248
Pane(s). *See* Window pane.

Index